Hellenic Studies 40

PINDAR'S VERBAL ART

Recent Titles in the
Hellenic Studies Series

Archilochos Heros: The Cult of Poets in the Greek Polis
Master of the Game: Competition and Performance in Greek Poetry
Yearning for the Infinite: Desire and Possession in Three Platonic Dialogues
Black Doves Speak: Herodotus and the Languages of Barbarians
Amphoteroglōssia: A Poetics of the Twelfth-Century Medieval Greek Novel
Victim of the Muses: Poet as Scapegoat, Warrior and Hero
Pointing at the Past: From Formula to Performance in Homeric Poetics
The Life and Miracles of Thekla: A Literary Study
Homeric Conversation
The Culture of Kitharoidia
The Power of Thetis and Selected Essays
Comparative Anthropology of Ancient Greece
Poetic and Performative Memory in Ancient Greece
Weaving Truth: Essays on Language and the Female in Greek Thought
Ritual and Performativity: The Chorus in Old Comedy
The Epic City: Urbanism, Utopia, and the Garden in Ancient Greece and Rome
Plato's Symposium: Issues in Interpretation and Reception
Paradise Earned: The Bacchic-Orphic Gold Lamellae of Crete
Concordia Discors: Eros and Dialogue in Classical Athenian Literature
King of Sacrifice: Ritual and Royal Authority in the Iliad
The Feast of Poetry: Sacrifice and Performance in Aristophanic Comedy
C. P. Cavafy, *The Canon: The Original One Hundred and Fifty-Four Poems*
Sappho in the Making: The Early Reception
The Oral Palimpsest: Exploring Intertextuality in the Homeric Epics
Practitioners of the Divine: Greek Priests and Religious Officials from Homer to Heliodorus
Zeus in the Odyssey
The Politics of Ethnicity and the Crisis of the Peloponnesian League
Genos Dikanikon: Amateur and Professional Speech in the Courtrooms of Classical Athens
Fragments of Sappho: A Commentary
Recapturing a Homeric Legacy: Images and Insights from the Venetus A Manuscript of the Iliad
Homer the Classic
Hippota Nestor
The New Sappho on Old Age: Textual And Philosophical Issues

PINDAR'S VERBAL ART

An Ethnographic Study of Epinician Style

James Bradley Wells

Center for Hellenic Studies
Trustees for Harvard University
Washington, DC
Distributed by Harvard University Press
Cambridge, Massachusetts, and London, England
2009

Pindar's Verbal Art: An Epigraphic Study of Epinician Style
by James Bradley Wells

Published by Center for Hellenic Studies, Trustees for Harvard University, Washington, D.C.
Distributed by Harvard University Press, Cambridge, Massachusetts and London, England

LIBRARY OF CONGRESS CATALOGING-IN-PUBLICATION DATA
Wells, James Bradley.
Pindar's verbal art : an ethnographic study of epinician style / by James Bradley Wells.
p. cm. — (Hellenic studies ; 40)
Includes bibliographical references and index.
ISBN 978-0-674-03627-7
1. Pindar—Technique. 2. Laudatory poetry, Greek—History and criticism. 3. Rhetoric, Ancient. I. Title. II. Series.

PA4276.W46 2009
884'.01—dc22 2009047742

Contents

Acknowledgments

I first arrived at Pindar via Gerard Manley Hopkins, and it was undoubtedly due to my anxiety over lyric influence that I one day read *Olympian* 1 in Greek when I should have been doing coursework at the University of Missouri, where the Department of Classical Studies had taken the risk of admitting me to its graduate program on the strength of my only-just-self-taught knowledge of ancient Greek. To my teachers there—Cathy Callaway, Victor Estevez (*in memoriam*), John Miles Foley, whose influence is ampler than documentation and bibliography make known, Dan Hooley, Gene Lane (*in memoriam*), Susan Langdon, Lawrence Okamura, Charles Saylor, David Schenker, and Barbara Wallach—I extend my deepest gratitude.

It might be a thrill—I would not know about this—to write a book that shoots across the sky from the perimeter of the universe, but given the epistemological ramifications of dialogue and situated practice (ontology as emergent), this project is the product of more mappable and, for that reason, more meaningful influences and support. I selected my book's title in homage to Richard Bauman's *Verbal Art as Performance*. My study of epinician speech and performance really began in graduate seminars that I took with him at Indiana University, and he has remained an advocate for my philology of Pindaric vernacular. When others expressed concern about my emerging research interest in a "too theoretical" approach to a "fringe" author, William Hansen, my dissertation adviser at Indiana University, encouraged the work that has culminated in the publication of this book. Richard Martin has given generously of his time to answer questions, to read drafts, and to advise, in addition to being a model of the kind of classical philology that I have attempted to pursue.

I would like to thank Mike Smith of Bloomington, Indiana, and friends of the Smith family, who have helped me in more than documentable ways: Jeff Ehman, Jon Fitch, W. Harvey Hegarty, James McNamara, Scott Owens, and Ken Pattillo.

More debts of gratitude. When I was on the fence about the fitness and timing of pursuing this book, the encouragement of Diane Rayor and Sarah Ferrario got me to the tipping point. My colleagues at Hamilton College, Barbara Gold, Amy Gowans, Shelley Haley, Chaise LaDousa, Nancy Rabinowitz, and Carl Rubino, steadied my sense of purpose through the course of completing this project. Others who have helped me in various ways, at various times include David Branscome, William Caraher, Noelle Zeiner Carmichael, Edwin Cole, Georgia Duerst-Lahti, Rebecca Edwards, Chris Giroux, Don Giroux, Colman Grabert, Carol King, Julie Langford, William Levitan, Ben Lockerd, James McDonough, Nigel Nicholson, Elizabeth Richey, Brett Robbins, Yvette Rollins, and John Allen Wyatt (*in memoriam*).

A special thanks is due to the Center for Hellenic Studies. It has been a pleasure to work with Casey Dué, Leonard Muellner, Jill Curry Robbins, and Noel Spencer. Their guidance and collaboration have effected my manuscript's metamorphosis into a book. I alone am responsible for any stylistic infelicities and other deficiencies that might remain in the final product, but credit goes to Jill Curry Robbins and Noel Spencer for what does work. I would also like to thank everyone else, though unknown to me, who had some role to play in this project, including the anonymous reader of my manuscript. And although his influence is ubiquitously evident throughout my book, I would here like to acknowledge the prodigious service and scholarship of Gregory Nagy, Director of the Center of Hellenic Studies.

Stacey Giroux Wells read sections of my manuscript at various stages, including a very careful reading of the final version of the entire manuscript, and, to the extent that my prose has developed more awareness of the existence of an audience of English-readers than it did before her intervention, she is responsible for the upgrade. Add to this that she is a medical anthropologist, and classicists who know just how much more onerous than Pindar Pindar scholarship can be will appreciate that hers is help far exceeding any call to duty. But more important is that the time during which I have been writing about Pindar happens to coincide with the best sweet-spot of my life, when we have partnered our way through Ph.D. ambitions, the academic vagabondage of five consecutive annual summer moves, more unpublished manuscripts than published, and, among many other things, the adoption of one stray cat that, magically it almost seemed, turned into the adoption of three.

PINDAR'S VERBAL ART

Introduction

Philology as Perspective on the Interaction of Language and Social Life[1]

Proverbially difficult[2] and commissioned by the elite, Pindar's victory songs have the reputation of being "high art." Epinician song, however, served the interests of the elite rulers and families whom it commemorated, not solely by becoming symbols of exclusive power and prestige, but by making itself and the *laudandus*'s achievement a popular possession through the inclusive appeal of entertainment, folk wisdom, and even laughter.[3] Accordingly, *Pindar's Verbal Art* lays the philological foundations for approaching Pindar's *epinikion* as a form of popular entertainment. My subtitle, "An Ethnographic Study of Epinician Style," aligns my approach to Pindar's stylistics with that of scholars in the overlapping fields of linguistic anthropology, folklore, and oral tradition studies. As this allegiance may suggest, speech and performance are the fundamental descriptive and interpretive foci of *Pindar's Verbal Art*. Since the central findings of this book—Pindar is an oral poet; the epinician

1 I programmatically adapt the title to my introduction from the title of Hymes 1972.

2 On Pindar's perceived obscurity see Most 1985:11–25 and Hamilton 2003. Pfeijffer's treatment of Pindar's style hinges upon attributing the poet's obscurity to the qualities of "implicitness," an absence of explicit cues about how the variety of features in epinician song work together (1999a:23–34), and the "fiction" of extempore composition (1999a:34–41). I discuss Pindaric *poikilia* 'stylistic variation' in Chapter 5 and in Chapter 1 critically evaluate the claim that internal evidence for the extempore composition of epinician song is a fiction.

3 With choral performance of Pindar's *epinikia* in mind, it is interesting to note that, as Burnett 2005:6n20 observes, Plato (*Laws* 654a) etymologically derives the word *khoros* 'chorus' from *khara* 'joy'. A caution is in order: for Pindar laughter can be derisive, even annihilating, as at *Isthmian* 1.68. What I mean by "laughter" is suggested by Plato's juxtaposition of *khoros* and *khara*, by Bundy's description of *euphrosuna* 'delight' (1962:2), and by Pindar *Pythian* 8.85 (the absence of laughter implies here a regrettable absence of joy). Newman and Newman 1984:38–50 conceive of Pindar's style as carnivalesque, tapping into the resonance between *kômos* 'revel' and *kômôdia* 'comedy' or '*kômos* song' (cf. Nicholson 2001). Dickie's study of *hêsukhia* gives a more tempered, even genteel, characterization of *euphrosunê* (1984). Robbins's perception of an absence of festive mood in *Pythian* 3 supports his argument (1990) that the song is not a true *epinikion*.

text records a speech (not text) event; *epinikion* is a centrifugal, stylistically diverse form of traditional art—hinge upon a rigorous, ethnographic description of Pindar's language, this Introduction addresses questions of philological methodology—where we have been in the study of epinician performance and where this study will go. In other words, what makes *Pindar's Verbal Art* a new and necessary contribution to scholarship on Archaic Greek poetry and poetics?[4] I will address this question, first, in terms of linguistics and, second, by comparing my ethnographic approach to Pindar's style to current studies of epinician performance.

Existing scholarship describes epinician language primarily in terms of grammar (e.g. Des Places 1947, Hummel 1993) or content (e.g. Bischoff 1938, Lefkowitz 1963, Bowra 1964, and Boeke 2007) or some combination of the two (e.g. Forssman 1966, Hamilton 1974, Race 1990, and Mackie 2003). From the point of view of linguistics, Pindarists' focus on grammatical form and textual content privileges the referential function of epinician language over its poetic function. This characterization draws upon Roman Jakobson's model of communication (1960), which linguistic anthropologist Dell Hymes (1974:10) incorporates into the Ethnography of Speaking.[5] Jakobson identifies the following "constitutive factors in any speech event, in any act of verbal communication": addresser, message, addressee, "a context referred to," a code, and contact, "a physical channel and psychological connection between the addresser and the addressee, enabling both of them to enter and stay in communication" (1960:353). Jakobson associates each of the constituent factors of a speech event with a particular function, respectively: emotive, poetic, conative, referential, metalingual, and phatic (1960:354–357; cf. Hymes 1974:146). To summarize the relationships between

4 Young 1970 is the benchmark study of the history of Pindaric scholarship. Most 1985:11–41 offers a fine critical survey. See also Lloyd-Jones 1973, Kopff 1981, and Heath 1986. Morrison 2007:5–7 reviews literature on epinician performance, concluding that upon closer inspection existing studies prove in his view to focus upon audience more than performance itself, and focus specifically on the audience to an original performance. Morrison's project sustains this audience-centered trend, but expands the conception of audience to include "overlapping audiences," which "have heard another Pindaric ode when they hear a given ode," "secondary audiences," "the audiences of reperformances of Pindar's odes" (19) and "tertiary audiences," which "include all later audiences of the odes, including readers and, ultimately, us modern Pindarists" (21). As my methodological statements below make clear, I see performance and audience as integrated, not "separable," as Morrison maintains. I address the reperformance of Pindar's *epinikia* in Chapter 5.

5 See Hanks 1996a:104 for the context of Jakobson's model of language in the history of linguistics. Martin 1989:14–15 applies Jakobson's model of a speech event to his study of Homeric speech acts.

a constitutive factor of a speech event (in CAPS) and its function (lower case):

CONTEXT/referential
MESSAGE/poetic
ADDRESSER/emotive
ADDRESSEE/conative
PHATIC/contact
CODE/metalingual

In contrast to the referential function of language, Jakobson defines the poetic function as "[t]he set (*Einstellung*) toward the message as such, focus on the message for its own sake" (1960:356; cf. Jakobson 1956:84–85 and Waugh 1980:58).[6] Linguistic anthropologists Richard Bauman and Charles Briggs explain that "the poetic function manipulates the formal features of the discourse to call attention to the formal structures by which the discourse is organized" (Bauman and Briggs 1990:73). Since "[t]he verbal structure of a message depends primarily on the predominant function" (Jakobson 1960:353) and since Pindar's songs are forms of verbal art, we should expect that, in terms of Jakobson's model, the poetic function is dominantly constitutive of *epinikion*.[7] Since, as Bauman and Briggs go on to say, performance is "the enactment of the poetic function," the appropriate focus for a study of epinician style, which embraces performance and speech, is the poetic function of language (Bauman and Briggs 1990:73).[8] In *Pindar's Verbal Art* the referential function of language, which existing studies of epinician language privilege, is subordinate to the poetic function of language. Such methodological appropriateness inheres in the ethnographic thrust of *Pindar's Verbal Art*.

I can further qualify how *Pindar's Verbal Art* differs from the existing studies of epinician language in terms of the three subfields of linguistics:

6 Jakobson's famous, more qualified definition of the poetic function is: "The poetic function projects the principle of equivalence from the axis of selection into the axis of combination" (1960:358).

7 To observe Jakobson's important stress upon the relationality of components of speech events and their corresponding functions, I am in more accurate terms striving for a correspondence between the dominantly constitutive language function and the dominant mode of analysis. Thus Jakobson: "Poetic function is not the sole function of verbal art but only its dominant, determining function, whereas in other verbal activities it acts as a subsidiary, accessory constituent" (1956:85). For the concept of the dominant, see Jakobson 1935, and cf. Waugh: "Dominance presumes a hierarchization of functions, not an absolutization of functional differences" (1980:58).

8 Cf. Bauman's observation that "performance may be understood as the enactment of the poetic function" (1986a:3).

(1) *syntactics* is the study of the relationships among signifiers; (2) *semantics* is the study of the relationships between signifiers and signifieds; and (3) *pragmatics* is the study of the relationships among signifiers and the people who use them.[9] Whereas approaches to Pindar's language that depend upon grammatical form methodologically foreground syntactics and those that depend upon message content foreground semantics, the ethnographic stylistics of *Pindar's Verbal Art* is firmly committed to the perspective of linguistic pragmatics.[10] Although such a stylistics necessarily cannot be purely ethnographic in the sense that it involves participant-observation field research or *in situ* documentation of communicative practices, linguistic pragmatics offers a set of descriptive and interpretative resources that enable us to penetrate the silence of the text-artifact and adopt the perspective of the community members who participated in epinician performances.

The difference that foregrounding the poetic function of language and rigorously applying the methods of linguistic pragmatics makes for our understanding of Pindar's art will become clear as this study progresses. For the moment, I hope that this Introduction so far provides a theoretical foothold for understanding what I mean when I claim that I explore epinician performance from an ethnographic perspective, whose descriptive and interpretive charter embraces the methodological criteria of inductive analysis, culture-specificity, and the application of analytical controls that ensure, to the degree possible, an agent-centered approach to analysis of the epinician text. To locate such an ethnographic perspective vis-à-vis existing scholarship, I will briefly review the three most important developments in recent studies of epinician performance: (1) a series of articles that I refer to as the choral-monody debate (Lefkowitz 1963, 1988, 1991, and 1995; Heath 1988; Burnett 1989; Carey 1989 and 1991; Heath and Lefkowitz 1991; and Morgan 1993); (2) Hilary Mackie's book *Graceful Errors: Pindar and the Performance of Praise* (2003); and (3) New Historical studies of Pindar and *epinikion* (Kurke 1991, Dougherty

9 I have adapted this delineation of subfields of linguistics from Hanks (1996a:57, emphasis in original): "The relation between the sign form and its designatum/denotatum is the focus of *semantics*. The relation between the sign form and the interpretant is the focus of *pragmatics*. The study of the relations among sign forms is *syntactics*." Hanks 1996a:54–64 contextualizes Charles Morris's theory of semiotics (1938), upon which he draws in the quoted passage. For the sake of simplicity I have recast the characterization of these relations in terms of signifier, signified, and sign-users.

10 Anna Bonifazi (2000, 2001, 2004a, 2004b, and 2004c) and Egbert Bakker (1997 and 2005) admirably model the application of linguistic pragmatics to ancient Greek poetics. Essays collected in Felson 2004a apply deixis to the study of Archaic Greek poetry, with significant focus on Pindar.

1993, and Nicholson 2005). The common denominator of these various studies of epinician performance is methodological, to approach the context of epinician performance in an outside-in, deductive fashion: after defining context, Pindarists interpret *epinikion* in terms of how context so conceived influences epinician performance. By contrast, *Pindar's Verbal Art* promises to present an inside-out, inductive description of epinician speech and performance that will embrace Pindar's entire epinician corpus.

In the choral-monody debate there are two recurrent analytical movements: first, to reconstruct a hypothetical contextual backdrop of historical events and circumstances putatively associated with the composition of an individual victory song; second, to interpret individual passages or songs on the basis of such a reconstructed contextual backdrop. These two analytical movements constitute *literal exegesis* as defined by Tzvetan Todorov in *Introduction to Poetics*: literal exegesis is a method of literary study that "consists in elucidating the meaning of such and such an incomprehensible word, in supplying the references for such and such an allusion, in explicating such and such a syntactical construction" (1981:xxii). Todorov identifies two branches of literal exegesis, "one linguistic and the other historical" (1981:xxix). Linguistic analysis "distinguishes the true from the false," and "[t]he same is true of historical analysis" (1981:xxix–xxx).[11] Scholars participating in the choral-monody debate apply these branches of literal exegesis to the word *kômos* 'revel'.[12] Burnett (1989) and Carey (1989 and 1991), who argue in favor of a choral epinician performance, maintain the view handed down by ancient commentators, that *kômos* refers to a group of performers and, so, to

11 Note that Todorov's characterization corresponds closely with Saussure's criticism of grammar which "aims solely at providing the rules which distinguish between correct and incorrect forms," as distinguished from the study of linguistic structure (1983:1). Saussure's criticism of grammar is a particular criticism embedded in his general critique of philology (1983:1): because "[p]hilology seeks primarily to establish, interpret and comment upon texts" the philological method is "too slavishly subservient to the written language, and so neglects the living language." The juxtaposition of Todorov's characterization of exegesis and Saussure's criticism of grammar is relevant because, from a historical point of view, literal exegesis in Pindar scholarship entails interpretive methods that predate and motivate Saussure's counterstatement to grammar, which in turn motivates the counterstatement to structural linguistics that is represented by linguistic anthropologists who adopt an ethnographic approach to linguistics (see Gumperz and Hymes 1972 and Hymes 1974). In other words, the choral-monody debate employs descriptive and interpretative methods that predate major intellectual advances in the study of language, texts, and literature during the twentieth century.

12 Lefkowitz 1963 and Davies 1988 raise issues that inform the choral-monody debate, in which Heath 1988, Burnett 1989, Carey 1989 and 1991, and Heath and Lefkowitz 1991 engage. *Kômos* occurs fifteen times in Pindar's *epinikia*: *Olympian* 4.9, 6.18, 6.98, 8.10, 14.16; *Pythian* 3.73, 5.22, 5.100, 8.20, 8.70; *Nemean* 3.5, 9.50; *Isthmian* 2.31, 6.58, 8.4 (cf. Slater 1969b:296–297).

a chorus.[13] Heath and Lefkowitz, who advocate for the possibility of a monodic mode of performance, claim that *kômos* identifies not specifically epinician performers or performance but the celebration of the athlete's victory in general, one component of which would have been the performance of the victory ode (1991:176). If we sever the long-assumed connection between *kômos* and a chorus, then, according to scholars in the monody camp, a solo performance of *epinikion* is possible. For both sides of the debate, the analytical process involves an outside-in approach to context: first, historical analysis in the form of reconstructing a conjectured sequence of events in order to define *kômos* (see especially Heath 1988); second, linguistic analysis in the form of interpreting individual passages of *epinikia* on the basis of that reconstructed context.[14]

To turn to more recent scholarship, Hilary Mackie's *Graceful Errors* is the first book-length study of epinician song as oral performance (2003). Although Mackie does not methodologically define "the perspective of oral performance" (2003:2) that she adopts, it is possible to glean what her perspective is on the basis of her treatment of social interaction between composer and audience. Mackie approaches genre and convention from an outside-in perspective, from which the relationship between Pindar and his audience is a matter of fulfilling prefabricated roles: "I interpret the persona constructed and projected by the epinician poet as a convention specific to the genre and its function. I read the concerns the narrator expresses (both directly and indirectly) about the responses of his audience the same way" (2003:3). By formulating the performer-audience relationship in such terms, Mackie seems to conceive of human interaction, much like break-offs (9–37) and wishes and

13 Cf. Morgan 1993 and Mackie 2003:1n2. Burnett more recently differentiates *khoros* and *kômos*, contrasting the choral performance of a victory song with spontaneous celebration by "[i]nformal bands of *kômos*-singers" on the same night of an athlete's victory at the victory site (2005:6).

14 Of the phrase *tonde kômos* 'this revel' (*Olympian* 4.9, 8.10, 14.16; *Pythian* 5.22), Bonifazi writes, "this deictic utterance provides little objective information about either the inclusion of the comiasts among the performers (thus a choral hypothesis) or their exclusion (thus a soloist hypothesis)" (2004a:398). Cole captures both the *kômos*' exuberant recklessness and the threat it poses, "not simply 'epic exhilaration' and excitement, but the confused mixture of triumph and let-down, apprehension and expectation to be found in a band of revelers that might have included, not simply members of a king or victor's immediate circle, but invited guests, admirers from afar, foreign visitors, and possibly even rivals and enemies" (1992:11–32). Nagy 1994–1995:24 identifies the *kômos* as the prototypical occasion for the genre of *epinikion*. In his study of antecedents for the animal choruses of Greek comedy, Rothwell assembles literary and plastic testimonia for *kômos* practices (2007:6–35). Reflecting Rothwell's findings about the relationship between the *kômos* of Archaic Greece and comic choruses, Lowe 2007:168–169 traces the meaning of *enkômion* from its original synonymity with comedy to its fourth-century BCE application to any form of eulogy.

prayers for the future (77–106), as a category of formal convention rather than an intersubjective and emergent process.[15] Interpretation, then, is a matter of identifying how passages or songs reflect Mackie's analytical template. What proves to be missing in Mackie's study is Pindar's point of view, which surfaces when we apply linguistic pragmatics and, more generally, ethnographic methods to the study of epinician speech and performance.

New Historicist Leslie Kurke has revolutionized how students of *epinikion* understand the contextual backdrop for the art form, and the work of Carol Dougherty and Nigel Nicholson further proves how productive New Historicism can be for our understanding of the social functions of Pindar's victory songs. In her important book *The Traffic in Praise* Kurke demonstrates that "[t]o understand the social dimension of Pindar's odes we must make sense of their economics, for he composed at a time when the economy was largely embedded in various social, political, and religious structures and institutions" (1991:7). To illustrate how Kurke's study informs our understanding of the context for epinician performance, she draws a cultural map for an athlete's departure and return that spatially delineates a loop whose starting and end point is the athlete's house, or *oikos* (1991:15–82). Participation in athletic competitions that figure in Panhellenic religious festivals implicate, not only the athlete's *oikos*, but also his *polis* and social class, institutional and ideological domains that the athlete's loop of departure from and return to his *oikos* embrace. Kurke's cultural map also charts how the athlete's return creates a temporal loop that recycles the past *kleos* 'renown', which distinguishes his *oikos*, as well as augmenting the social capital of *kleos* in the present and for the future. The athlete's return involves reintegration, a process of simultaneously welcoming the athlete to his hometown and actualizing the trade in social capital.[16] Since the traffic in praise embraces the domains of the *polis* and the aristocracy, the returning athlete must be reintegrated into

15 Corroborating this characterization of Mackie's view is her qualification of what she means by referring to "the poet": "I am speaking of the constructed, fictional narrator of the odes—I do not mean to imply anything about the real live poet Pindar" (2003:3n8). In line with Mackie, for Kurke the performed quality of lyric poetry gives rise to "role-playing" in which the performer adopts "a more or less fictive position from which to speak" (2007:143). While I share the concern to avoid conjecture about the life and times of the historical Pindar, I disagree with the idea of treating Pindar's agency as a constructed fiction; from an agent-centered point of view, Pindar as a traditional artist *is* "the real live poet Pindar." As Bonifazi rightly explains, "from the pragmatic [i.e. linguistic pragmatics] point of view, the 'I' is never fictive" (2004a:398). See also Nagy 1994–1995:20 on the limitations of a "fictional" first person, instead of which he proposes the concept of a "generic I."

16 Dougherty expresses the same view: "the victory song both celebrates the victor as he is welcomed home and orchestrates his reintegration" (1993:103). Cf. Crotty 1982:121, to whom Kurke 1991:6 directly responds.

his *oikos*, his *polis*, and his social class. This process of reintegration provides a contextual backdrop for identifying the social function of epinician performance: "it is the task of Pindar's poem in performance to accomplish this reintegration."[17] In an outside-in manner, Kurke's elegant analysis locates *epinikion* as a coordinate on a cultural map and explains how the economics of aristocratic gift-exchange conditions the traffic in praise.[18]

Carol Dougherty's important study of colonial discourse, *The Poetics of Colonization* (1993), has provided another view of the contextual surround for the composition and performance of *epinikion*. Colonial discourse is characterized by a pattern of colonial narrative, whose elements include crisis, Delphic consultation, colonial foundation, and resolution (1993:15–30), and by the cultural metaphors of purification (31–44), riddling (45–60), and marriage (61–80). Given this definition of colonial discourse, Dougherty explores "the extent to which the narrative pattern, cult, and metaphors of archaic colonization participate in the rhetoric of drama and the epinician ode" (10). For Dougherty, then, the performance of epinician song provides a public forum for transmitting colonial discourse, and "[t]he poet's role is that of teacher; his poetry transmits a society's ethical value system, and the community participates in this civic education both as audience and insofar as it is represented in the composition of the chorus itself" (95–96). On the basis of this outside-in approach to epinician performance, Dougherty's discovery of strategies for representing the ideological armature of colonization provides a context for understanding *epinikion* as a medium of colonial discourse.

Nigel Nicholson's book *Aristocracy and Athletics in Archaic and Classical Greece* (2005) is a trenchant, interdisciplinary study of how victory memo-

17 Kurke 1991:6. On the athlete's return see also Crotty 1982:104–138, Slater 1984, and Kurke 1993:139–140. Dougherty describes how "the victorious athlete was met outside his city and led as part of a magnificent procession through the main streets and into the center of the city, the agora" (1993:88). See also Dougherty's description (1993:96) of epinician performance during the ceremony commemorating the victorious athlete's return as a "ritual occasion." Nicholson relates that "[t]he odes were performed mainly in the victor's city of residence, although other locations, including the site of victory were possible" (2005:11). Fränkel earlier suggested such a scenario: "A suitable occasion for the public performance of epinician odes was the return of the winner to his city. The successful athlete entered in a joyous procession, and the chorus of friends and compatriots that escorted him sang the epinician to welcome him and sing his praises during the procession" (1973:429).

18 I note here that in a recent study of the ritual context for the performance of choral song, Kurke signals a shift in her thinking about context by addressing the "critical pitfall" of "the assumption that the context of 'religion' or 'ritual' is real, preexistent, and inert, while the literary text in relation to it becomes a mere secondary reflection thereof; or in other terms, that a literary text can be entirely explained by reference to a preexistent historical or ritual context" (2005:82).

rials come to represent aristocratic ideology. Nicholson confronts the fact that, "although these victory memorials could speak of the victors at length, they were almost entirely silent concerning the drivers, jockeys, and athletic trainers who helped them win" (2005:1). The practice of commemorating athletic victories with a memorial provided a medium for representing those achievements "in ways that made them accord with aristocratic ideology" (2005:3).[19] Against the backdrop of ideology and exchange systems, victory memorials, like Pindar's epinician songs, "proved an excellent tool for fixing the meaning of victory to [competitors'] advantage" (2005:11). Nicholson's study, then, enables us to interpret epinician performance from the outside-in as one medium among several for memorializing athletic victories.[20]

As David Young has written, "we usually search history to explain Pindar, not vice versa" (1968:113). New Historical approaches to the study of epinician performance give us insight into what Bauman describes in his *Verbal Art as Performance* as the "context of performance as a generalized cultural system in a community" (1977:37). Indeed, Kurke's description of *epinikion* as a "communal drama" is the premier example of approaching *epinikion* at this level of context (1991:257–262).[21] To draw from Pierre Bourdieu's distinction between structured structures and structuring structures, however, the innovative scholarship of Kurke, Dougherty, and Nicholson describes how epinician performance is structured by the cultural schemas entailed in ancient Greek athletics and

19 Burnett 2005:51 is skeptical of the view that Pindar's alleged categorical alignment with aristocratic ideology would have been an incentive to suppress the role of trainers in athletic victories.

20 Cf. Steiner 1998 and Smith 2007, who compare plastic and literary media for victory commemoration. Thomas 2007:152–163 describes the historical development of *epinikion* in the context of the broader development of victory monuments.

21 While outside-in approaches to Pindar are the norm, I have focused on those most compelling (the New Historicists) and most relevant to this study of epinician speech and performance. Krummen's highly regarded book is also exemplary of this norm; she describes her study in the following way: "Ein erster Teil der Untersuchung [31–151] beschäftigt sich mit der Rekonstruktion dieses kultisch-festlichen Erwartungshorizontes... In einem zweiten Teil [153–266] wird diese rezeptionsorientierte Fragestellung auf die Eingrenzung der mythisch-kulturellen 'Erwartung' des Publikums erweitert; dies drängt sich bei den hier zur Diskussion stehenden Gedichten (*Olympie* 1 und 3) besonders auf, da ihre mythischen Erzählungen als 'Neuschöpfungen' Pindars gelten" (1990:9). Burnett prefaces a detailed study of each of Pindar's Aiginetan odes (2005:55–238) with an admirably detailed presentation of the documented and mythological history of Aigina (13–28), discussion of the Aphaia Temple sculpture and practices associated with the monument (29–44), and Aiginetan patterns for participation in the crown games (45–54)—dimensions of context that inform her interpretation of individual songs in an outside-in manner. For other studies that opt for an outside-in view of epinician performance, see also Bernardini 1983:9, 76–77, and 80, Slater 1984, Clay 1999, Pfeijffer 1999a:2–21 (with critical discussion of secondary literature on the context of epinician performance), Currie 2005, Carey 2007, and Morrison 2007.

their commemoration in the victory song, but does not explore the communicative strategies that structure the event of epinician performance itself.[22] In terms of Jakobson's model of a speech event, by treating the epinician text as a discursive realization or ramification of its contextual surround, outside-in approaches to the study of epinician performance implicitly assume the dominance of the referential function of language in the constitution of the speech event that the epinician text records. As Bauman goes on to say, "one wants to be able to appreciate the individuality of each [performance], as well as the community-wide patterning of the overall domain" (1977:37). My approach to the context of epinician performance looks at this more local level of "the emergent quality of performance" (Bauman 1977:37–45), where the focus is upon the verbal means used to produce a unique work of verbal art in the situated context of interaction among participants in the event of performance.

An inside-out understanding of epinician performance depends upon a method of philology that collaborates with a text artifact in order to describe and interpret the cultural practices that the artifact records.[23] Through a performance-centered, ethnographic approach to our textual artifacts of epinician song, fortified by linguistic pragmatics, it is possible to discover how Pindar's art represents its ambient cultural world and the persons who populate it. To pursue this ideal, I adopt the overarching principle of dialogue as a methodological premise. In the first instance, epinician art entails dialogical relationships among participants in the event of epinician performance. This site of communicative practices is the ultimate object of my analysis. Second, I approach the various analyses constituting the whole of my study as vantage points comprising dialogically a composite picture of Pindar's art; each dimension of analysis depends upon and informs others. Finally, by making explicit

22 As an illustration of Bourdieu's ideas here, I cite the following: "The structures constitutive of a particular type of environment (e.g. the material conditions of existence characteristic of a class condition) produce *habitus*, systems of durable, transposable *dispositions*, structured structures predisposed to function as structuring structures, that is, as principles of the generation and structuring practices and representations which can be objectively 'regulated' and 'regular' without in any way being the product of obedience to rules, objectively adapted to their goals without presupposing a conscious aiming at ends or an express mastery of the operations necessary to attain them and, being all this, collectively orchestrated without being the product of the orchestrating action of a conductor" (1977:73, emphasis in original).

23 Russian Formalism (Èjxenbaum 1927, Tynjanov 1927, Brik 1923, and Jakobson 1935) and the Prague School of Linguistics (Bogatyrev and Jakobson 1929, Bogatyrev 1936, Havránek 1932, Bühler 1934, and Mukařovský 1940) are important points of reference for my understanding of the problem of meaning in artistic language and of how to conceive of a philological method equipped to take up the challenges of confronting that problem. Newman and Newman 1984:32–38 integrate Russian Formalism and Pindar criticism.

my methodological predispositions, I hope to enable a dialogue of shared inquiry. Such explicitness often takes the form of substituting methodological statements for the more conventional review of secondary literature on specific Pindaric questions. As mentioned, the strategy that I adopt to achieve these ends is to develop an ethnographic description and analysis of epinician song. In Hymes's terms, I conceive of authentic understanding of Pindar's art as a matter of "intersubjective objectivity": "[e]thnographic objectivity is intersubjective objectivity, but in the first instance, the intersubjective objectivity in question is that of the participants in the culture" (1974:11).[24] The methodological ideal of intersubjective objectivity captures my analytical focus upon approaching context from the inside, adopting an "agent-centered line of analysis" (Bauman 1992:142) and pursuing a philological description of communicative resources that shape "the emergent quality of performance" (Bauman 1977:37–45).

Pindar's Verbal Art is principally a study of epinician style. In his essay "Ways of Speaking" Hymes demonstrates that culture-specific patterns among the sociolinguistic features of speaking—for example, participants, linguistic code, rules for appropriate speaking, and social functions of speech—constitute ways of speaking, or styles, understood in terms of sociolinguistics: "one can characterize whatever [sociolinguistic] features go together to identify a style of speech in terms of rules of co-occurrence among them" (1989:434).[25] This conception of style has a crucially ethnographic orientation in that it refers to "a way or mode of doing something" (Hymes 1989:434); speech styles are ways of doing social life, and the study of style, conceived of from an ethnographic point of view, is concomitantly the study of human social practice. Thus I do not conceive of *Pindar's Verbal Art* as a(nother) recapitulation of the long-standing quarrel between formalist (or just literary-critical) and historicist approaches to Pindar, so that I would be giving voice to the formalist cause.[26] First, I conceive of this project as more radical, as an attempt to reformulate fundamentally how we think about Pindar's language and his entextualized records of epinician performance. Second, my method is radically integra-

24 Cf. Hymes: "The ethnographer is likely to look at communication from the standpoint and interests of a community itself, and to see its members as sources of shared knowledge and insight" (1974:8).

25 Cf. Bakhtin's discussion of "particular social dialects" (1981:293) and his reference to "*different languages*, even from the point of view of abstract socio-dialectological markers" (1981:295–296, emphasis in original).

26 For a historical perspective on this quarrel within Pindaric studies, see Young 1970. Recently Currie 2005:11–15, Hornblower and Morgan 2007, and Nicholson 2007:208 indicate that this quarrel is alive and well, with the historicists in the ascendancy.

tive: since registers are "major speech styles associated with recurrent types of situations" (Hymes 1989:440), when we approach Pindar's language as a way of speaking or register, a speech style dedicated for use in a particular context for speech practices, then we undertake the kind of linguistic analysis that is firmly grounded in practice and, so, history.[27]

Hymes's ethnographic conception of stylistics informs the performance approach to the study of entextualized records of verbal art. In his seminal work *Verbal Art as Performance* (1977), Bauman imports the Ethnography of Speaking into a philological method for the description and analysis of artistic texts, highlighting the relationship between ways of speaking, or registers, and performance as a matter of descriptive method:

> Performance, as we conceive of it...is a unifying thread tying together the marked, segregated esthetic genres and other spheres of verbal behavior into a unified conception of verbal art as a way of speaking. Verbal art may comprehend both myth narration and the speech expected of certain members of society whenever they open their mouths, and it is performance that brings them together in culture-specific and variable ways, ways that are to be discovered ethnographically within each culture and community.[28]

Since Pindar's victory songs survive as an entextualized record of the epinician register, that text also bears information about the speech event of epinician performance, the context to which the use of the epinician register is dedicated.[29] A crucial sociological dimension of the use of the epinician register is its artistic style of communication with culture-specific patterns of participant interaction. By treating Pindar's language as a register, a sociological

27 Cf. Hymes: "We can understand the perspective [of speech styles] as applying to any and all organization of linguistic features, of verbal means, in relation to a social context" (1974:59). My approach to style, then, has a more inclusive scope than that of Race, for whom style involves "the poet's selection and placement of words" (1990:1–2).

28 Bauman 1977:5. On the relationship between style and performance in Homer's *Iliad*, see Martin 1989:160–161.

29 Given that linguistic registers are situated and that conventional speech situations are genred—and approaching genre with Bourdieu 1977 as fields of social practice (as Hanks 1987 does)—my observations here are highly resonant with Kurke: "we must correlate genre with performance: if we define genre as the set of audience expectations which shapes and constrains each individual composition, we must take into account the nature of the audience *and* the occasion that informed their expectations" (1991:1, emphasis in original). Fearn 2007:220n168 has recently challenged Kurke's conception of genre as "too limiting," but as his discussion of genre in general (219–225) and his description of generic features of Bakkhulides' poetry in particular (224) make clear, a static conception of tradition hamstrings his own approach to genre.

conception of style, the epinician text turns out to be a record of interaction among the participants in performance, so that it is possible to move analytically from entextualized words to historically embodied voices.

In broad strokes, I describe Pindar's art in terms of what Hymes identifies as the "fundamental notions" of the Ethnography of Speaking: "ways of speaking, fluent speaker, speech situation, speech event, speech act, components of speech events and acts, rules (relations) of speaking, and functions of speech" (1974:45). Along the way I apply a new approach to the most salient problems in the study of Pindar and his art: genre, epinician performance, the relationship between *epinikion* and Archaic Greek poetic tradition, and the unity of the victory ode. Whereas "Ways of Speaking" is the dominant analytical perspective in the Ethnography of Speaking, "speech community" designates the fundamental object of analysis. Hymes stresses the speech community as a "necessary, primary concept" because "it postulates the unit of description as a social, rather than linguistic, entity" (1974:47).[30] In the intellectual-historical context of his book *Foundations in Sociolinguistics*, Hymes here formulates a counterstatement to structural linguistics. In an analogous vein, my ethnographic approach to epinician performance is intended as a counterbalance to outside-in approaches to the study of the context of epinician performance. Just as structuralism in the study of language runs the risk of generating theories and descriptions of language that do not account for what actually happens in social practice, literal exegesis and New Historicism depend upon structural rules that can over-determine how we interpret ancient texts.[31] Central to my study of epinician style and performance is to step back and reconsider: What is the primary field of cultural description in the study of Pindar's art? Accordingly, in Chapter One, "Text and Sign," I demonstrate that Pindar represents his art as a spoken form of communication. The communication rules that obtain in Pindar's *epinikia* are specifically rules for speaking. My further description of the epinician way of speaking depends upon establishing conclusively that Pindar's art represents itself as an orally transmitted and aurally received mode of communication. Analogous to the place of the analytical category of speech community in Hymes's *Foundations in Sociolinguistics*, the first tier of my ethnographic study of *epinikion*, then, is to demonstrate that *speech* practices recorded in the epinician

30 In her study of the performance of Archaic Greek poetry, Stehle defines "community" as "a collection of families organized under a system of governance, laying claim to a demarcated territory, worshipping common cults, and recognizing one another as fellow members" (1997:18).

31 Here I call attention to Martin's (2003:158–159) balanced critique of structuralist approaches to the analysis of myth.

text are the primary object of philological analysis in the study of epinician performance.

In Chapter Two, "*Epinikion* as Event," I move from the speech community stratum of analysis to that of speech situation and speech event. Hymes applies the concept of speech event specifically "to activities, or aspects of activities, that are directly governed by rules or norms for the use of speech" (1974:52). Speech situations, however, "may comprise both verbal and nonverbal events, and the verbal events may be of more than one type" (1974:52). The empirical record for *epinikion* is fuzzy here. We possess the text-artifact of epinician performance, which records the poetry, but so much more is missing: information about music, dance, the locations of epinician performances, and the events (e.g. procession or feast) associated with such performances. Due to the status of the evidence, I have decided to define the speech situation, the context of situation in which epinician performance occurs, in a circumspect way as the typical *frame* of epinician performance. Relative to such a frame, the individual epinician song is a *framework*, an actual speech event. Here I am applying linguistic anthropologist William F. Hanks's working definition of frame and framework: "frames are relatively static resources defined at the level of schematic structure, whereas frameworks are dynamic productions defined at the level of local usage" (1993:128).[32] These definitions of frame and framework will apply at various points in *Pindar's Verbal Art*. In Chapter Two I also explore the strategies by which *epinikion* delineates itself as a conventional speech situation through the use of certain performance keys.[33] I describe performance keys at the schematic level to show how the epinician way of speaking typically marks out the frame for epinician performance. On the basis of our understanding of the typical keys to epinician performance, it is possible to identify how they function in an individual epinician song to key the framework of a particular performance, a level of analysis where we are dealing with a speech event, a "level of local usage" of the epinician way of speaking, as Hanks defines framework.

In Chapters Three and Four, "Ways of Epinician Speaking I" and "Ways of Epinician Speaking II," I describe the most stable and recurrent stylistic patterns occurring in Pindar's *epinikia*—that is, the styles associated with, for example, prayers, mythological narrative, and the gnomic statement. Each of these stylistic patterns is a speech genre, in Mikhail Bakhtin's terms, and I draw upon his essay "The Problem of Speech Genres" (1986:60–102) as a principal theoretical and methodological point of departure for my analysis of

32 See also Hanks 1990:78–80.

33 On performance keys see Bauman 1977:15–24 and Foley 2002:85–93.

the *ways* of epinician speaking that constitute the epinician *way* of speaking. This tier of analysis provides a partial practical (versus syntactic, semantic, or referential) taxonomy of speech acts, components of speech events and acts, and functions of speech, to refer again to Hymes's fundamental notions of the Ethnography of Speaking.[34] Such a taxonomy enables us, first, to develop a participant-centered analysis of *epinikion* and, second, to demonstrate that the epinician *way* of speaking is a composite of speech styles, the *ways* of epinician speaking.

What emerges from this description of the ways of epinician speaking is that epinician art, like Bakhtin's characterization of the novel, is "a phenomenon multiform in style and variform in speech and voice. In it the investigator is confronted with several heterogeneous stylistic unities, often located on different linguistic levels and subject to different stylistic controls" (Bakhtin 1981:261). In Chapter Five, "Novelistic Features of Epinician Style," I advance the thesis that, based upon the fact that the epinician way of speaking is a complex blend of registers, *epinikion* is novelistic discourse. Perhaps it is just a statement of the obvious to stress that this is not to say that *epinikion* belongs to the genre of the novel. Rather, I am identifying Pindar's art as a novelistic form of discourse in order to challenge the more conventional perception that Pindar's art is strictly a "high genre" possessed of "hierarchical distance" projecting "the events, victors and heroes of 'high' contemporary reality" into a "heroic past and tradition."[35] Rather than being a high form of art charac-

34 See Hymes 1974:52–65 for a discussion of each of these notions of the Ethnography of Speaking.

35 Here I am quoting from Bakhtin's description of epic specifically in contrast to the novel: "The three characteristics of the epic posited by us above are, to a greater or lesser extent, also fundamental to the other high genres of classical antiquity and the Middle Ages. At the heart of all these already completed high genres lie the same evaluation of time, the same role for tradition, and a similar hierarchical distance. Contemporary reality as such does not figure in as an available object of representation in any of these high genres. Contemporary reality may enter into the high genres only in its hierarchically highest levels, already distanced in its relationship to reality itself. But the events, victors and heroes of 'high' contemporary reality are, as it were, appropriated by the past as they enter into these high genres (*for example, Pindar's odes or the works of Simonides*); they are woven by various intermediate links and connective tissue into the unified fabric of their heroic past and tradition. These events and heroes receive their value and grandeur precisely through this association with the past, the source of all authentic reality and value. They withdraw themselves, so to speak, from the present day with all its inclusiveness, its indecisions, its openness, its potential for re-thinking and re-evaluating. They are raised to the valorized plane of the past, and assume there a finished quality" (1981:18, my emphasis). To illustrate the prevalence of such a view of Pindar's poetry among scholars, consider the following: "Given Pindar's intellectual archaism in which the past is insistently viewed as a collective and generalized model for the particular events of the present, each epinician ode necessarily moves back and forth between the two modes

terized by distance from its own present, Pindar's art form exhibits the basic characteristics that Bakhtin identifies with the novel (1981:11):

> (1) its stylistic three-dimensionality, which is linked with the multi-languaged consciousness realized in the novel; (2) the radical change it effects in the temporal coordinates of the literary image; (3) the new zone opened by the novel for structuring literary images, namely the zone of maximal contact with the present (with contemporary reality) in all its openendedness.

In Chapter Five I will explore each of these stylistic dynamics in the course of a sociolinguistic analysis of Pindar's *Olympian* 1.

Although *Pindar's Verbal Art* ventures a new approach to the study of Pindar and *epinikion*, my work does not proceed in isolation from existing Pindaric scholarship. Elroy Bundy's *Studia Pindarica* exhibits the methodological tenets of an ethnographic approach to the study of texts. Bundy urges the importance of understanding "the conventional aspects of choral *communication*," indicating that he regards the epinician text as a record of practices organized by social rules for communication (1962:2, my emphasis). His observation that "a community of poets working within well-recognized rules of form and order" produced epinician art and, in general, his both praised and maligned emphasis upon genre, show that for Bundy *epinikion* is to be understood as a special way of communicating between a performer subject to critical assessment by an audience that was fluent in those "rules of form and order" (1962:3 and passim). Two of Bundy's often-cited sources, Franz Dornseiff and Wolfgang Schadewaldt, greatly influenced the sociological dimension of *Studia Pindarica*. In the preface to his *Pindars Stil* Dornseiff stresses what Hymes would come to call "ways of speaking": "Es gibt für veile griechische Dichter Arbeiten *de genere dicendi*, Programme über einzelne Tropen und Figuren" (1921:iii). Schadewaldt defines the scope of his work on the structure of *epinikion* as having stylistic-formal, objective-historical, and subjective-personal standpoints, but asserts that the stylistic-formal stand-

of description" (Greengard 1980:48). In a similar vein, Mackie writes that "in spite of [an] apparent emphasis on the present and its importance, most epinician odes set out to understand the significance of the present victory by setting it against the backdrop of the heroic past" (2003:40), and Athanassaki that "[a]lmost all extant epinicians display a common pattern: they commemorate a specific historical victory in light of memorable heroic and divine deeds in the remote past" (2004:317). As I will show in Chapter 5, the past-present relationship alone does not account for other and more dynamic temporal trajectories operating in epinician performance.

point is the dominant consideration (1928:263).[36] Christian Gottlob Heyne, who produced a 1798 edition of Pindar, is the source for the earliest attested use of the expression "ways of speaking."[37] Heyne observes, anticipating Hymes's ethnographic conception of style, that ways of speaking, or registers, are defined by the events with which they are conventionally associated: "Hence follow all the precepts for the interpretation of mythic narrations—or the words, and sentences, and expressions of mythical usage. First, 1): we know that in very ancient mythic or symbolic *ways of speaking*, the senses and thoughts were communally uttered..."[38]

Beyond these traces of intellectual heritage shared by classical philology and linguistic anthropology, Bundy's philological method corresponds in important ways to the performance method of approaching a verbal art form as a way of speaking. His innovation in the study of Pindar is to describe epinician language from the standpoint of literary genre. Genre and style are inextricably related in communicative practices. Accordingly, Bundy asserts the importance of pursuing "a thorough study of conventional themes, motives, and sequences in choral poetry—in short, a grammar of choral style that will tell us what systems of shared symbols enabled the poet and his audience to view the odes as unified artistic wholes" (1962:32). Whereas Bundy adopts a formalist approach to establish that *epinikion* has a functional unity comprised of conventional elements, I adopt a practice-centered description of epinician language. This difference can be seen as integrative: *Pindar's Verbal Art* resumes Bundy's project of developing a grammar of choral style.

Following Young's advice that "we must learn the language" of *epinikion*, the notion of fluency perhaps best captures what I hope will be the ultimate outcome of my study (1968:107). In a dialogical fashion, fluency cuts both ways: as we develop our understanding of what makes for fluency from the point of view of participants in the event of epinician performance, we simultaneously become a more fluent audience to epinician art (cf. Bonifazi 2004a:392). I further maintain that the description of and fluency in the communicative means used by participants in epinician performance and recorded in the text-artifact methodologically precedes the study of the relationship between Pindar's art and the cultural contexts in which it is embedded. For a practice-centered, ethnographically grounded philology, meaning is not a tautological function of the relationship between words on a page and their lexicographic

36 Cf. Schadewaldt 1928:265, where he describes his work as *Stilforschung*. See Hamilton 1974:4–6 for an assessment of Schadewaldt 1928.

37 Richard Bauman *per litteras*.

38 Cited in Feldman and Richardson 1972:222 (my emphasis).

essence; it emerges from the social actions—the deeds—that the speaking of those words entails. A corresponding mode of philology takes the description of communicative practices as its point of departure and acknowledges that meaning is socially situated and a product of human interaction. By adopting a practice-centered philology that looks to the event of social interaction, namely performance, between Pindar, the composer-performer of *epinikion*, and his audience, and by employing an empirical analysis grounded in linguistic pragmatics, we can discover the historical actualities implicated in the art form of *epinikion*, beginning crucially with its poetics understood as a special way of communicating that is associated with a particular event by ancient Greek cultural conventions. While the historical circumstances determining the current status of the evidence for epinician performance present obstacles to understanding the social practices entailed in that community event, a practice-based, participant-centered approach to the study of epinician language nevertheless enables us to discover how people interacted in the event of performance through the ways of speaking that they used. And when we can identify the actual social moves employed through the use of the epinician way of speaking by participants in the event of epinician performance, a description of epinician art as performance becomes also a historiographic project.

1

Text and Sign

Following the Ethnography of Speaking, whose descriptive focus is the socially conventional ground rules for a community's speech practices, this first chapter of *Pindar's Verbal Art* explores a question fundamental to the study of epinician style: in what context of situation did people use epinician language?[1] In other words, the point of departure for an ethnographic analysis of epinician performance is to discover the communicative context of which Pindar's text is a record from the point of view of *epinikion* itself. My analysis in this chapter takes its cue from the strong precedent in the history of Pindar scholarship for treating the opening lines of *Pythian* 1 as a passage indicative of the context of epinician performance:[2]

> Χρυσέα φόρμιγξ, Ἀπόλλωνος καὶ ἰοπλοκάμων
> σύνδικον Μοισᾶν κτέανον· τᾶς ἀκούει μὲν βάσις ἀγλαΐας ἀρχά,
> πείθονται δ' ἀοιδοὶ σάμασιν
> ἁγησιχόρων ὁπόταν προοιμίων ἀμβολὰς τεύχῃς ἐλελιζομένα.
>
> *Pythian* 1.1–4
>
> Golden lyre, Apollo's and the violet-haired Muses'
> rightful possession: a footstep [*basis*], the beginning of celebra-
> tion, hears it,
> but singers [*aoidoi*] heed the signs [*sâmata*]
> whenever with your vibrating strings you strike up the *prooimia*
> that guide the dancing.

1 I take the concept "context of situation" from Malinowski 1923:306. Because of its emphasis upon situated practice, "context of situation" became a theoretical and methodological rallying point for formulating an ethnographic approach to the study of texts, a concern that is central to *Pindar's Verbal Art*.

2 Except where noted, I use Snell and Maehler 1997 for Pindar's text. All translations are my own.

This passage has provoked much discussion about the performance of epinician song, but there is a remarkably stable consensus in the interpretation of what the lines describe and virtually no variation in the *method* of interpretation applied by critics. Of the two branches of literal exegesis, linguistic and historical (Todorov 1981:xxix), commentators' interpretations of *Pythian* 1.1–4 privilege historical description, an interpretive methodology that, when applied to the study of epinician performance, involves producing a reconstructed scenario for performance context; such a scenario, in turn, becomes the critical touchstone for interpreting a particular passage or song. On the basis of this passage, ancient commentators reconstruct choreographic and musical arrangements, blocking out a performance scenario whose sequence of events includes a musical ante-prelude (*prooimia*), followed by a prelude of dance (*basis* 'footstep'), succeeded by the song (thus, *aoidoi* 'singers'). Modern commentaries largely take their exegetical cue from the scholia.[3] I want to

3 This performance scenario is the consensus view in the scholia, but ancient commentators offer different interpretations of what the key words—*basis*, *aoidoi*, and *sâmata*—mean (Σ *Pythian* 1.1-4, Drachman 1910:8–9). For Heyne *basis* is "the step of the chorus to the rhythm, with which begins the dancing, the 'beginning of celebration,' of festivity, of festal happiness. Then too the song of those very dancers hangs on the music of the lyre; [Pindar] refers to 'singers' instead of 'song'" (1798:146–147). Dance and song obey the lyre, according to Boeckh, and *basis* refers to the entrance of dancers; *aoidoi* are simply the singers of the chorus (1821:226–227). Dissen 1830(II):163–164 endorses Boeckh's interpretation of the passage. Gildersleeve reproduces the scholiasts' understanding of the sequence of events—the lyre's music, the dancers' foot-step, followed by the chorus' song: "In the first part of the poem the lyre is the organ of harmony, in the second the organ of praise. In the first part everything is plain. Apollo and the Muses are to the Greek the authors of all harmony, artistic, political, social, spiritual... Everything that owes allegiance to Zeus obeys his son Apollo, obeys the quivering of the lyre's strings. So the foot-step of the dancer, the voice of the singer" (1890:240). According to Fennell, *aoidoi* refers to the chorus, but not to bards, presumably to distinguish between choral poetry and the solo Homeric *aoidos* 'singer' of tales (1893:145). Farnell gives an exceptionally imaginative reading of *ambalai* 'strikings up' (line 4) based, it seems, on vase-painting conventions: "The word was probably suggested by the singer flinging back his head to give full voice to his song" (1932:107). Burton writes: "The first illustration of the function of the lyre arises naturally from what the audience could see and hear: vv. 2–4 give in fact a vivid impression of the elements that constitute a performance of choral lyric. Βάσις [*basis*] is to be taken literally and signifies the actual steps of the dancers as they begin the spectacle" (1962:94). Kollmann reproduces the consensus view on *Pythian* 1.1–4: "Die Leir, die am Beginn des Prooimions angerufen wird (V. 1), beherrscht den Tanz und den Gesang (V. 2–4)" (1989:9). Gentili observes that choral performance is referred to in the passage and that it draws a parallel between divine celebration and the epinician celebration in honor of Hieron, the poem's *laudandus* (1995:12). For other applications of literal exegesis to *Pythian* 1.1–4, specifically in connection with the question of epinician performance, see Heath 1988:185, Burnett 1989:286, Heath and Lefkowitz 1991:180, Carey 1991:199–200, and Morrison 2007:68–69 (note that Morrison 2007:99–100 explores how the opening of *Pythian* 1 anticipates context(s) of reperformance). Hubbard 1985:90–92

bring into focus my approach to epinician performance, generally, and to Pindar's oral poetics, specifically, by thinking about the *sâmata* referred to at *Pythian* 1.3 in light of these methodological considerations. The scholiasts' literal exegesis of the word leads to the reasonable view that these signs are some sort of cue, but this view gives way to interpreting *sâmata* in terms of the reconstructed performance scenario: the 'signs' are the rhythm guiding music and dance or some other form of previously agreed upon guiding element, including, according to some, written instructions in the form of a performance script.[4] In this chapter I will apply descriptive and interpretive methods of linguistic anthropology to discover the features of epinician language and performance that these *sâmata* signal. From this methodological vantage point, we can interpret Pindar's *sâmata* as sociolinguistic and traditional conventions that cue the singers' performance of epinician song and, crucially, the audience's participation in that performance.

---

analyzes thematic oppositions of light/dark and harsh/delicate in the proem of *Pythian* 1. Herington 1985:181–183 assembles internal references to performance in Pindar's and Bakkhulides' songs.

4 For the scholiasts' interpretations of *sâmata* (*Pythian* 1.3), see Drachman 1910:9. Kirkwood 1982:131 follows the scholiasts. Schroeder 1922:5 speculates that the *sâmata* are marked out by the composer. Burton 1962:94 endorses Schroeder: "As for σάμασιν [*sâmasin* = dative plural of *sâmata*] Schroeder is probably right in referring it to the various directions given by the accompanying lyre player to the chorus, such directions being marked, together with musical notation, on the performance-copy of the text; and the natural Greek word for them is σάματα [*sâmata*], signs which give a cue to the singers." Kollmann 1989:54 cites Schroeder's interpretation of *sâmata*. Note that the historical evidence actually contradicts the hypothesis that the *sâmata* are written notations on the manuscript: we know, for example, that accent marks were an innovation of Hellenistic scholars. Herington writes: "We must emphasize once more that on our present evidence the archaic and classical poetic texts, however and wherever preserved, are most unlikely to have been anything more than mere rows of capital letters without word division, without line division (except, probably, where stichich meters were concerned), without accents, with no more than a minimum of punctuation, and without musical or choreographic indications in any form" (1985:46). As a further illustration, consider Nagy 1990:29 on the role of writing in rhapsodic reperformance of Homeric song: "There is no compelling reason to believe that the medium of writing had anything to do with the traditions of the rhapsodes. In fact there is positive evidence that their mnemonic techniques were independent of writing. The textual tradition of Homeric poetry as we have it stems from Hellenistic Alexandria, where the practice of accentual notation was invented. This textual tradition bears witness to certain archaic patterns of Homeric accentuation that were no longer current in the everyday Greek language—patterns that can now be verified through the application of Indo-European linguistics. This comparative evidence leads to the conclusion that these patterns were preserved through norms of recitation inherited by rhapsodes; the factor of writing seems to be ruled out, since a textual tradition for the notation of accents was evidently lacking before Alexandrian times."

Epinician Text: Status and Voicing

To address the question of whether Pindar's extant texts are records of spoken or written communication I begin by drawing from the work of linguistic anthropologist William Hanks (1989), who identifies two key issues in textual analysis: the status of the text and voicing in the text. The *status* of the text has to do with "how different approaches [to textual analysis] objectify different aspects of the total textual formation" (1989:102). The prevailing position is that written composition forms the epinician text. It is possible to discover whether or not this is actually the case from the point of view of Pindar's language by asking: what communicative functions does epinician language claim as its own?[5] Hanks refers to this kind of evidence as "functional regimentation" (1989:106–107). There is a dialogical dynamic involved here. On the one hand, a text delineates its functional domain by giving empirical clues about the context(s) and function(s) for which its author(s) composed it. On the other hand, our understanding of a text's functional domain regiments our description and interpretation of it, so that, in a dialogical way, textual analysis is responsive to the text's representation of its language. *Voicing* in the text "subsumes the relation between the textual artifact and the framework of production and participation from which it arises" (Hanks 1989:102). In Pindar's case voicing has everything to do with performance; *epinikion* is a performed verbal art form (the "framework of production") and, as such, entails at least three categories of participation: composer, chorus, and audience. I follow five steps to assemble empirical evidence for the status of and voicing in Pindar's texts:

(1) Identify Pindar's most common forms of metalanguage;
(2) Determine whether each instance of metalanguage refers to representing or represented communication;
(3) Identify indices for the status of the text;
(4) Identify indices for voicing in the text;
(5) Identify methodological controls applied in steps 3 and 4.

[5] For Goldhill, Pindar's reflexive language works together with *kleos*-building and Pindar's first-person to illuminate dimensions of the poet's voice in Greek poetry (1991:129). García 2002 applies an ethnographic analysis of reflexive language in his study of the role of ritual speech in Homeric performance.

Step 1: Metalanguage

"One particularly important instance of functional regimentation," as Hanks writes, "is *metalanguage*, which consists of textual elements that refer to, describe, or otherwise characterize text itself, including the very one of which they are a part" (1989:107, emphasis in original). By analyzing the most common forms of metalanguage, we can discover whether epinician language characterizes itself as spoken or written communication. The forms of Pindar's metalanguage that I analyze include: *epos* 'word', *eipein* 'to say', *en(n)epein* 'to tell', *erein* 'to say (future tense)', *humnos* 'song of praise', *humnein* 'to sing in praise of', *humnetos* 'praised in song', *logos* 'word', *logios* 'chronicler', and *legein* 'to say, to tell'.[6]

Step 2: Representing and Represented Communication

The presence of metalanguage used in representing communication that indicates the same status of and voicing in Pindar's texts as represented communication, and vice versa, will substantiate my analysis. Drawing from the method of frame analysis, I define representing communication and represented communication in terms of how they relate to each other.[7] For present purposes, the *frame* is the individual epinician song, a communicative event that embraces other communicative acts, the *frameworks*, that constitute the frame. The *frame* is representing communication—for example, in mythological narrative, the addresser's communicative stance characterized by the third-person voice. The *framework* is represented communication—for example, in a mythological narrative, indirect or direct discourse.

Pindar's texts evidence two types of representing communication. The first type is a singular or plural first-person utterance that describes an act or event of communication in terms of one of the forms of metalanguage that I analyze here. Consider the following passage:

> Τυνδαρίδαις τε φιλοξείνοις ἁδεῖν καλλιπλοκάμῳ θ' Ἑλένᾳ
> κλεινὰν Ἀκράγαντα γεραίρων εὔχομαι.
> Θήρωνος Ὀλυμπιονίκαν ὕμνον ὀρθώσαις ἀκαμαντοπόδων
> ἵππων ἄωτον. Μοῖσα δ'οὕτω ποι παρέστα μοι νεοσίγαλον εὑρόντι
> τρόπον
> Δωρίῳ φωνὰν ἐναρμόξαι πεδίλῳ

[6] I do not include *phâmi* 'I say', *phatis* 'speech', and *rêma* 'word' or 'saying' in this analysis because they self-evidently name speech, not writing, practices.

[7] On frame analysis see Goffman 1974 and Hanks 1993.

ἀγλαόκωμον· ἐπεὶ χαίταισι μὲν ζευχθέντες ἔπι στέφανοι
πράσσοντί με τοῦτο θεόδματον χρέος,
φόρμιγγά τε ποικιλόγαρυν καὶ βοὰν αὐλῶν ἐπέων τε θέσιν
Αἰνησιδάμου παιδὶ συμμεῖξαι πρεπόντως, ἅ τε Πίσα με γεγωνεῖν·
    τᾶς ἄπο
θεόμοροι νίσοντ᾽ ἐπ᾽ ἀνθρώπους ἀοιδαί.

Olympian 3.1–10

To please the descendents of Tyndareus, who are kind to friends,
    and to please Helen, whose hair is lovely,
I pray, as I honor famous Akragas,
now that I have erected an Olympian victor's *humnos* for Theron—
for horses with indefatigable feet, the best thing. The Muse so
    stood beside me when I found a bright new way
to harmonize the celebratory sound with the Dorian sandal,
since wreaths bound to hair
give me this divinely established duty: to fittingly blend together
    the multisonic lyre and the voice of pipes and a foundation of lyrics [*epea*]
for the son of Ainesidamos. And Pisa urges me to speak out;
from there the god-allotted songs reach humans.

In this passage there are two instances of metalanguage: *humnos* (3) and *epea* (8). I characterize this passage as representing communication because first-person singular forms (lines 2, 4, 7, and 9) signal that the words in the passage are the addresser's; the passage is an instance of representing communication that frames instances of represented communication in *Olympian* 3.[8]

The second type of representing communication in Pindar's texts is the gnomic statement, which often expresses norms about appropriate or effective communication from the point of view of *epinikion*. Whereas I designate *words* that refer to Pindar's language as forms of *metalanguage*, *statements* that describe Pindar's language I designate *metacommunication* (cf. Babcock 1977). Analyzing gnomic statements as forms of metacommunication in conjunction with specific instances of metalanguage makes it possible to discover what these gnomic statements tell us about the status of and voicing in Pindar's texts. The following passage is an example of the gnomic statement as representing communication:

8 E.g. Herakles' *logos* at line 16.

ἄλλοις δέ τις ἐτέλεσσεν ἄλλος ἀνήρ
εὐαχέα βασιλεῦσιν ὕμνον ἄποιν' ἀρετᾶς.

Pythian 2.13–14

Some men requite some
kings with a sonorous *humnos* as a reward for virtue.

This gnomic passage characterizes representing communication as orally generated and aurally received by virtue of the adjective *euakhês* 'sonorous', which modifies *humnos*. Since Pindar's gnomic statements regularly express norms about language use, the gnomic style of *Pythian* 2.13–14 makes such a characterization all the more characteristic.

Frequently recurring types of represented communication in Pindar's *epinikia* include indirect discourse, direct discourse, and what I call, for the sake of convenience, an "other" type of represented discourse. To explain this designation, I offer an example of reported communication that is neither direct nor indirect discourse:

Λάμπων δὲ μελέταν
ἔργοις ὀπάζων Ἡσιόδου μάλα τιμᾷ τοῦτ' ἔπος,
υἱοῖσί τε φράζων παραινεῖ.

Isthmian 6.66–68

Lampon,[9] by exerting effort
in his deeds, especially honors this saying [*epos*] of Hesiod's;
he relates it to his sons and advises them of it.

In this passage *epos* (line 67) names a form of represented communication that is not direct or indirect discourse, but an "other" type of represented discourse—in this case, Hesiod's saying, which is not "quoted" but referred to in the passage.[10]

To summarize Step 2, forms of Pindar's metalanguage occur in the following categories and subcategories:

I. Representing Communication
  A. First-Person Statements
  B. Gnomic Statements
II. Represented Communication
  A. Direct Discourse

9 Father of Phylakidas, the *laudandus* of *Isthmian* 6.

10 The saying is from Hesiod *Works and Days* 412 (cf. Farnell 1932:362 and Kurke 1990:89).

B. Indirect Discourse
C. "Other" Reported Discourse

Step 3: Status of the Epinician Text

I have recorded whether each instance of metalanguage occurs in conjunction with indications of oral production and aural reception of messages or of written communication.[11] *Olympian* 3.1–10, for example, contains metalanguage that indicates oral production and aural reception of messages: *phôna* 'sound' (5), *poikilogarus phorminx* 'multisonic lyre' (8); *boa aulôn* 'voice of *auloi*' (8); and *aoidai* 'songs' (10). On the basis of how Pindar himself describes his communicative medium, I interpret the occurrences of *humnos* (3) and *epos* (8) at *Olympian* 3.1–10, as instances of metalanguage that indicate the oral production and aural reception of messages, especially in light of the complete absence of any indication of written communication. I have followed the same criteria throughout my analysis of Pindar's metalanguage.

Step 4: Voicing in the Epinician Text

Here I simply record whether each instance of metalanguage occurs in a context characterized by face-to-face interaction or by reader-text interaction. In both representing and represented communication, oral production and aural reception of communication necessarily entail face-to-face interaction and do not at all indicate a reader-text interaction. In terms of the status of and voicing in the epinician text, both song and speech contrast with writing in terms of communication and context of situation: in antiquity, song and speech entail oral production and aural reception of communication and face-to-face interaction.[12]

Step 5: Methodological Controls

First, with respect to voicing in the epinician text, I interpret forms of metalanguage in represented communication as an index of speech only when the text explicitly represents reported speech as occurring in the context of face-to-face interaction. I do not assume that represented communication entails

[11] Cf. Aloni's view: "Melodia, ritmo, intonazione e dizione sono dunque altrettanti tratti e vincoli che sanciscono la separazione della lingua testuale da quella non testuale" (1998:23).

[12] Of Pindar's use of the verb *garuein* 'to sing of' at *Olympian* 1.3, Gerber notes that "the distinction between 'speech' and 'song' is much greater in English than in Greek" (1982:16). See Nagy 1990:17–51 for the most important discussion of the relationship between song and speech in Archaic Greek poetry, as well as Nagy 1994–1995:12.

(represented) oral production and aural reception of messages, but seek evidence for the text's voicing in the text itself. Take the following example:

> τὸν δὲ θαρσήσαις ἀγανοῖσι λόγοις
> ὧδ' ἀμείφθη· "Φαμὶ διδασκαλίαν Χίρωνος οἴσειν. ἀντρόθε γὰρ νέομαι
> πὰρ Χαρικλοῦς καὶ Φιλύρας, ἵνα Κενταύρου με κοῦραι θρέψαν ἁγναί.
> εἴκοσι δ' ἐκτελέσαις ἐνιαυτοὺς οὔτε ἔργον
> οὔτ' ἔπος ἐκτράπελον κείνοισιν εἰπὼν ἱκόμαν
> οἴκαδ', ἀρχαίαν κομίζων πατρὸς ἐμοῦ, βασιλευομέναν
> οὐ κατ' αἶσαν, τάν ποτε Ζεὺς ὤπασεν λαγέτᾳ
> Αἰόλῳ καὶ παισὶ τιμάν."
>
> *Pythian* 4.101–108

> Then taking courage, with mild words
> Jason answered him [Pelias] in this way: "I say that I will produce the teaching of Khiron; for, I come from a cave,
> from Khariklo and Philura, where the revered daughters of the Centaur raised me. After rounding out twenty years, and saying to those people neither a deed
> nor word out of place, I have come
> home, retrieving the ancient honor of my father, which is being ruled
> not according to destiny—the honor that Zeus once granted to the leader of the people, Aiolos, and to his sons."

This passage occurs in a context in which Jason responds to Pelias' direct questions before a group of onlookers and, so, is an example of how represented communication bears indices of face-to-face interaction. Quotation marks do not suffice to indicate the status of and voicing in the text; it is the context of situation depicted in represented communication that matters.

The second analytical control that I apply is to record only explicit indices of spoken or written communication and to consider closely whether these indices are consistent in both categories of communication, representing and represented. Consider, for example, the following passages:

> ἐγὼ δ' Ἡρακλέος ἀντέχομαι προφρόνως
> ἐν κορυφαῖς ἀρετᾶν μεγάλαις, ἀρχαῖον ὀτρύνων λόγον...
>
> *Nemean* 1.33–34

I willingly embrace Herakles
among the greatest heights of virtues, beginning with the old
story...

ἔλπομαι
μέγα εἰπὼν σκοποῦ ἄντα τυχεῖν
ὥτ' ἀπὸ τόξου ἱείς· εὔθυν' ἐπὶ τοῦτον, ἄγε, Μοῖσα,
οὖρον ἐπέων
εὐκλέα.

Nemean 6.26–29

I hope,
by saying something great, to hit the target straight on,
shooting, as it were, from my bow. Go, Muse, direct toward that
[home]
a wind of words,
a glorious wind.

In contrast to *Olympian* 3.1–10, quoted above, these two passages do not have explicit indices of the mode of communication involved. I do not interpret the occurrence of *logos* at *Nemean* 1.34 as an index for the status of or voicing in Pindar's texts because there is no evidence in the passage for the type of communication, oral or written, that this *logos* is. It can be argued on the basis of linguistic pragmatics that imperative forms at *Nemean* 6.28 suggest face-to-face interaction between a first-person addresser and second-person addressee. But again, the passage bears no explicit indication of the mode of communication. I apply these methodological controls throughout my analysis of Pindar's metalanguage.

Findings

Whenever Pindar's metalanguage in both representing and represented communication evidences indices of status and voicing of the epinician text, it regularly describes the mode of communication as speech and never describes it as a written mode of communication. For the status of the epinician text, the metalanguage in representing communication indicates that the performance of epinician song entails oral generation and aural reception of communication[13] and never indicates written communication. For voicing in

13 *Epos*: *Olympian* 3.8, 9.47, 13.98; *Pythian* 2.66, 3.2, 3.113; *Nemean* 7.16, 7.104, 9.3, 9.7. *Eipein*: *Isthmian* 1.46, 4.41. *En(n)epein*: *Nemean* 7.69. *Erein*: *Pythian* 5.108. *Humnos*: *Olympian* 1.8, 2.1, 9.48, 11.4;

the epinician text, the metalanguage in representing communication indicates face-to-face interaction[14] and never indicates text-reader interaction. So too in represented communication: Pindar's metalanguage evidences spoken communication for the status of the text[15] and face-to-face interaction for voicing in the text,[16] but never evidences written communication or a text-reader interaction. We can conclude, then, that Pindar's epinician texts have the status of being records of spoken communication and that the voicing in the epinician texts indicates that the intended context for reception is face-to-face interaction in the performance of epinician song. Again, functional regimentation is dialogical: just as the language recorded in the text is functionally regimented, that language also functionally regiments description and interpretation of the text. From this it follows that epinician language can appropriately be described in its own terms as an oral medium. I stress a final point: even if material texts and writing play a role in some phase in the process of composition and transmission of Pindar's *epinikia*, the speech event of performance—not a writing event—is *constitutive* of epinician language.[17]

Pythian 2.14, 3.64; *Nemean* 1.5, 3.65, 4.16, 7.81, 9.3; *Isthmian* 2.45, 7.20. *Logos*: *Olympian* 1.28, 2.92, 6.90, 7.21, 9.12, 9.35; *Pythian* 2.66, 6.16; *Nemean* 4.94, 6.30, 9.54; *Isthmian* 5.13. *Legein*: *Olympian* 13.12, 102; *Pythian* 5.108.

14 *Epos*: *Olympian* 13.25; *Pythian* 2.66; *Nemean* 9.3. *Eipein*: *Olympian* 6.92. *En(n)epein*: *Nemean* 7.69. *Humnos*: *Pythian* 1.60; *Nemean* 5.42, 7.81, 9.3; *Isthmian* 2.45, 4.3, 5.20, 7.20. *Logos*: *Olympian* 6.90, 9.12, 9.35; *Pythian* 2.66, 3.80, 5.48, 6.16; *Nemean* 7.51. *Legein*: *Isthmian* 5.39.

15 *Epos*: *Olympian* 1.86, 6.16; *Pythian* 4.9, 4.57, 4.138, 6.37; *Nemean* 2.2, 10.80; *Isthmian* 4.39, 6.42, 6.67. *Eipein*: *Olympian* 1.75, 6.16, 8.46, 13.71, 14.22; *Pythian* 3.40, 4.11, 4.86, 4.100, 4.156, 4.229, 8.43; *Isthmian* 6.51. *En(n)epein*: *Olympian* 1.86, 8.41; *Nemean* 1.69, 10.79; *Isthmian* 8.45. *Erein*: *Pythian* 9.51. *Humnos*: *Isthmian* 2.3, 8.60. *Humnein*: *Nemean* 5.25. *Logos*: *Olympian* 2.60, 11.5; *Pythian* 4.59, 9.43; *Nemean* 7.21, 9.6; *Isthmian* 5.27. *Legein*: *Pythian* 4.189.

16 *Epos*: *Olympian* 1.86; *Pythian* 4.9, 4.29, 4.57, 4.138, 4.299, 6.37; *Nemean* 10.80; *Isthmian* 6.42, 8.46. *Eipein*: *Olympian* 1.75, 4.23, 6.16, 8.46, 13.71, 14.22; *Pythian* 4.11, 4.86, 4.100, 4.105, 4.156, 4.229, 8.43, 9.66, 9.119; *Isthmian* 6.51, 6.55, 8.31. *En(n)epein*: *Olympian* 1.86, 8.41, 8.82; *Pythian* 4.242; *Nemean* 1.69, 10.79; *Isthmian* 8.45. *Erein*: *Pythian* 9.51. *Humnos*: *Isthmian* 2.3. *Humnein*: *Nemean* 5.25. *Logos*: *Pythian* 4.59, 4.101, 4.116, 4.128, 4.132, 4.240, 8.38, 9.43. *Legein*: *Pythian* 4.189.

17 This position is *contra* D'Alessio 2004, who argues that in performance Pindar's songs index an original written composition. Herington 1985:45–47 describes the functions of written texts—preservation of texts in temples and family archives and the use of texts in schools—but cites two Aristophanic passages (*Acharnians* 383–479 and *Thesmophoriazusai* 25–265) as the only pre-fourth-century BCE representations of the composition process, neither of which, tellingly, figures writing. Mackie writes: "Although the victory ode would have been composed and rehearsed in advance of the performance, the performance itself was oral and public. In other words, these poems were composed to be performed orally" (2003:1). Discussing Aristophanes' *Clouds* 1354–1357, where Strepsiades describes the inability of his son Pheidippides to sing a Simonidean song, Morrison 2007:21, following Nagy 1990:400–413, says that written texts would have been "the basis for the teaching and learning of the odes in schools." Cf. Irigoin 1952:11–20 and Currie 2004:52.

The "Oral Subterfuge" Hypothesis

Given that Pindar's art is choral song, which implies *per se* that the epinician text has the status of being a record of speech (singing) and the voicing indicative of a record of face-to-face interaction, to identify Pindar as an oral poet is perhaps only a statement of the obvious. But existing studies of epinician performance do not adequately account for the fact that epinician performance is a speech event, and, as I am about to show, they in fact attribute to Pindar's language characteristics that contradict well established views about the relationship between language and culture. To explore this problem, I introduce here the concept of markedness. Roman Jakobson's definition is the *locus classicus* for this concept (1957:47):

> [O]ne of two mutually opposite grammatical categories is "marked" while the other is "unmarked." The general meaning of the marked category states the presence of a certain (whether positive or negative) property A; the general meaning of the corresponding unmarked category states nothing about the presence of A, and is used chiefly, but not exclusively, to indicate the absence of A.[18]

As linguist Linda Waugh has written, "it would seem that in the context of the history of humanity as a whole, 'spoken' language is the unmarked term and 'written' language the marked term. 'Written' language is more specialized in many ways than 'spoken' language" (1982:308). We might expect the language of Pindar's performed works to reflect this cross-culturally observed pattern in human language use, but there is an entrenched consensus that his artistic medium is written.[19] To illustrate, and by way of further strengthening my thesis that Pindar is an oral poet, I consider in terms of markedness a serious attempt to reconcile a putatively literary Pindar with the performed quality of his *epinikia*, the "oral subterfuge" hypothesis.

Christopher Carey has described Pindar's "oral subterfuge" as an "illusion created by the poet and shared by the audience" whereby Pindar "deliberately creates and sustains the impression of informal, extempore composition" (1981:5). Carey elsewhere describes the "oral subterfuge" as a "fiction" or "pretense" whereby Pindar presents already completed composition as if it were being composed in performance (1989:551–553). Here I cite Carey more

18 See also Waugh 1982. For applications of the concept of markedness in the study of the speech of Archaic Greek poetry, see Martin 1989:29–30, Nagy 1990:5–8, and Aloni 1998:21–22.

19 Among many possibilities, see Irigoin 1952:5–9, Hubbard 1985:65–70, Segal 1986:153–164, Race 1990, and D'Alessio 2004.

fully: "This fiction is common in Pindar, who frequently speaks as though he were meditating on the contents or shape of his song prior to or during composition, whereas of course the ode is complete by the time of the performance" (1989:552). Especially since Carey describes Pindar's songs as "written in literary 'Doric'" (1989:562), his claim that the composition of the song would have been completed prior to performance seems to depend upon the assumption of a written mode of composition that took place prior to and apart from the context for which the composition was intended, namely performance.[20] In his study of Pindaric mimesis Andrew Miller (1993b:22) adopts Carey's thesis

> to draw attention to the central importance of Pindar's "oral subterfuge" as a compositional technique and at the same time to demonstrate the practical utility of maintaining throughout the interpretive process a clear-cut distinction between the fictional (or at least quasi-fictional) speaker whose spontaneous utterance the poem purports to be and the hard-working professional poet who actually crafted it with care and skill.[21]

Carey and Miller segment performance into two stages: written composition, which they valorize as the truly creative act, and production of the song, which approaches interpretation as a matter, in part, of understanding how a written composition acts like a spoken one; the reality is written composition, the fiction, speech.

In terms of markedness, the "oral subterfuge" hypothesis contradicts the cross-culturally observed relationship between speech and writing in human history, suggesting that in the case of Pindar's texts writing is unmarked and speech is marked. Existing scholarship on the question of how Pindar composed his songs generally reflects Gregory Nagy's observations about the impulse "to define *oral* in terms of *written*" in the study of oral poetry: "if something is *oral*, we tend to assume a conflict with the notion of *written*."[22]

20 Carey 1989 explicitly claims that Pindar composed his songs prior to performance, but is less explicit about his view of what mode of composition Pindar used.

21 Miller 1993a also advances the "oral subterfuge" hypothesis. See also Kurke on Pindar's "scripted spontaneity" (1991:113 and 113n13), Carey 1995:99–103, Pfeijffer 1999a:34–37 and passim on "fictional mimesis of ex tempore speech," Bonifazi 2000, and Burnett on the "familiar choral conceit by which well-rehearsed performers mime the spontaneity of a *kômos* as they begin to sing" (2005:109-110) and on "the fiction of spontaneity," one of "the tricks of inclusion and interaction that Pindar took from the sacred choruses," (241) exemplified in her discussion by Alkman 3 PMG.

22 Nagy 1990:8, emphasis in original.

Just so, current understandings of epinician composition and performance upend the testimony of linguistic and anthropological evidence, so that writing is the given (i.e. unmarked) and orality is predicated upon that given (i.e. marked).

Note again that by stressing the constitutive place of speech for epinician composition and performance, I do not rule out the possibility that material texts were involved in the transmission of Pindar's songs. It is possible to admit the hypothesis that a text form of libretto served as a mechanism for transmitting an epinician song from Pindar, say, to a production group, or for transmitting an epinician composition to contexts for reperformance, but only if it is understood that such a text entails not written art, but spoken art composed according to conventions for speaking and intended for actualization in a speech event, or, as Anna Bonifazi describes it, activation of the *hic et nunc* performance experience (Bonifazi 2000:82–83). From this point of view, the idea that the epinician libretto is brought to life in performance is not a fiction, but an immanent fact of the social reality upon which epinician performance bears.

Indeed, speech is so fundamentally constitutive of epinician style that, given a speech/writing opposition, we witness the plus-interpretation of speech in passages where Pindar characterizes his composition in terms of language associated with a material form of communication. To explain the designation "plus-interpretation," recall that, from the point of view of linguistics, given an opposition between speech and writing, speech is unmarked and writing is marked. Waugh demonstrates that it is possible to interpret the opposition between speech and writing in three ways: zero-interpretation, minus-interpretation, and plus-interpretation (1982:302–306). The zero-interpretation is "that interpretation where the presence or absence of the unit of information is for the most part irrelevant"; given the speech/writing opposition, where speech is unmarked and writing is marked, the zero-interpretation of the marked member is "speech" (without regard for the marked term, "writing"). The minus-interpretation "signals the absence of the unit of information associated with the marked term"; in terms of the speech/writing opposition, the minus-interpretation is "speech, not writing" (the absence of writing is specifically signaled). Given a speech/writing opposition, indices for the status of and voicing in the epinician text occur in passages that evidence just such a minus-interpretation of that opposition; metalanguage that occurs without such indices affords a zero-interpretation of the speech/writing opposition. The plus-interpretation signals the presence of the marked term; in terms of the speech/writing opposition, the plus-interpretation is "writing."

In my analysis of Pindar's metalanguage, the plus-interpretation of the marked term, writing, in the speech/writing opposition never occurs. Waugh points out, though, that the plus-interpretation of the *unmarked* term of an opposition can occur; again, in terms of the speech/writing opposition, the plus-interpretation of the unmarked term is "speech (as opposed to writing)." Bearing in mind Waugh's caution that the plus-interpretation of the unmarked term "has to be forced by very specific contexts," I will next demonstrate that passages in which Pindar metaphorically describes composition in terms of some material medium of communication provide just such specific contexts.

A crucial example of such a metaphorical representation of Pindar's language is the only passage in which he refers to a *skutala* 'message-stick':

> ματρομάτωρ ἐμὰ Στυμφαλίς, εὐανθὴς Μετώπα,
> πλάξιππον ἃ Θήβαν ἔτικτεν, τᾶς ἐρατεινὸν ὕδωρ
> πίομαι, ἀνδράσιν αἰχματαῖσι πλέκων
> ποικίλον ὕμνον. ὄτρυνον νῦν ἑταίρους,
> Αἰνέα, πρῶτον μὲν Ἥραν Παρθενίαν κελαδῆσαι,
> γνῶναί τ' ἔπειτ', ἀρχαῖον ὄνειδος ἀλαθέσιν
> λόγοις εἰ φεύγομεν, Βοιωτίαν ὗν. ἐσσὶ γὰρ ἄγγελος ὀρθός,
> ἠυκόμων σκυτάλα Μοισᾶν, γλυκὺς κρατὴρ ἀγαφθέγκτων ἀοιδᾶν·
> εἶπον δὲ μεμνᾶσθαι Συρακοσσᾶν τε καὶ Ὀρτυγίας·
> τὰν Ἱέρων καθαρῷ σκάπτῳ διέπων,
> ἄρτια μηδόμενος, φοινικόπεζαν
> ἀμφέπει Δάματρα λευκίππου τε θυγατρὸς ἑορτάν
> καὶ Ζηνὸς Αἰτναίου κράτος. ἁδύλογοι δέ νιν
> λύραι μολπαί τε γινώσκοντι.
>
> *Olympian* 6.84–97
>
> My mother's mother was Stymphalian, blooming Metopa,
> who bore horse-driving Thebes, whose lovely water
> I drink as I weave for warrior men
> an elaborate *humnos*. Now urge our companions,
> Aeneas, first to sing of Hera the Maiden
> and then to know whether we escape the old reproach, "Boiotian pig," with true
> words. You are an upright messenger,
> a message-stick [*skutala*] of the Muses, whose hair is lovely; you are a sweet drinking bowl of loudly uttered songs.
> Tell them to remember Syracuse and Ortygia,
> which Hieron oversees with an untainted scepter,

planning justly;
he is devoted to Demeter with her red foot, and to the festival for
her daughter, whose horses are white,
and to the power of Aetnan Zeus. Sweetly worded
lyres and songs know him.

Pindar addresses an Aeneas (line 88), whom the scholia identify as the chorus leader, and metaphorically calls him "a message-stick of the Muses" (line 91).[23] Ancient commentators describe the *skutalê* as a Spartan practice: the message-sender inscribed a message on a leather strip that was wrapped around a stick in such a way that the edges of the strip touched and formed a writing surface; when re-wound around a stick with the appropriate diameter, the notation could be decoded by the recipient of the message.[24] The message-stick is a device that entails a material mode of communication, potentially introducing at lines 84–87 the plus-interpretation of the marked member, writing, of the speech/writing opposition. But, as I now show, the passage actually obviates such a reading by evidencing the plus-interpretation of the unmarked member (speech) of the speech/writing opposition.

The chiastic structure of the passage articulates this interpretation, if we take into account the following: first, the last sentence of the passage (line 96–97) is a gnomic statement, making it an instance of representing communication that parallels the opening lines of the passage (line 84–87), an instance of first-person representing speech; second, the composer characterizes the addressee as an *angelos* (line 90) and in the next lines introduces elements of the conventional epinician *angelia*—mention of the victor's name and reference to his home *polis*.[25] With these considerations in mind, we can see that the passage has a chiastic structure that highlights song—witness *humnos* (line 87), "loudly uttered songs" (line 91), "sweetly worded lyres," and "songs" (line 96–97)—and, consequently, the oral production and aural reception of messages, in the outer terms of the chiasmus:

A: Representing communication, first-person speaker (lines 84–87)
B: Aeneas as *angelos* (lines 87–92)
b: *Angelia* for Hieron (lines 93–96)
a: Representing communication, gnomic statement (lines 96–97)

23 Nicholson 2005:90–91 interprets this passage as a representation of the victory song as a gift, as opposed to a commodity.

24 See West 1988:42 for an evaluation of ancient sources on the meaning of *skutalê*.

25 Note the parallel between Pindar's Aeneas as *angelos* and as *skutala* and Archilochus' use of *skutalê* in conjunction with the vocative form *Kêrukidê* (recalling *kêrux* 'herald') at Fr. 185, as discussed by West 1988:46–47.

Indices of spoken communication leak into the interior terms of this chiasmus as the result of a crucial parallel between the representing communication of the first-person addresser and the represented communication of the addressee: the first-person speaker characterizes himself as "weaving an elaborate *humnos*" (lines 86–87) and characterizes Aeneas as "a message-stick of the Muses" (line 91), pointing to the connection between the sung *humnos* and the model performance of the Muses, also song. Given that we must understand the first-person plural form *pheugomen* 'we escape' (90) as inclusive either of addresser and addressee or of addresser, the chorus, and addressee, the word's occurrence in the middle of the passage near the crux of the chiasmus is yet another stitch binding together representing and represented communication, articulating still more emphatically the predominance of song and, so, speech in the passage. For further evidence that *Olympian* 6.84–97 is a record of spoken communication, first-person (lines 84, 86, and 90) and second-person forms (lines 87, 90, and 92) are indices of face-to-face interaction. Here, then, we have a compelling example to demonstrate that, in a context in which Pindar uses the metaphor of a material mode of communication, he applies the plus-interpretation of the unmarked term in the speech/writing opposition—namely, speech—to signal unambiguously the constitutive role of speech for this composition.[26]

In Pindar's corpus there is another remarkable occurrence of the plus-interpretation of the unmarked term (speech) in the speech/writing opposition. It is well known that in the broader context of ancient Greece, *anagignôskein* 'to recognize' can refer to reading and *graphein* 'to make a mark' can refer to writing. Such forms of metalanguage occur extremely infrequently in Pindar,[27] especially in comparison to words that refer to song or music, such as *aoida* 'song',[28] *aoidos* 'singer',[29] *melos* 'song',[30] *melpesthai* 'to sing',[31] *molpa* 'song',[32] *humnos*,[33] and *humnein*.[34] The only Pindaric passage that contains occurrences of both *anagignôskein* and *graphein* bears indices of spoken communication:

26 Hubbard 2004:91 interprets *Olympian* 6.87–91 as evidence that Pindar viewed writing as crucial to the preservation of his songs. Cf. Descat 1985:69–70.

27 *Anaginôskein* (Pindar's variant for *anagignôskein*) occurs twice and *graphein*, three times.

28 Thirty-two occurrences in the *epinikia* (s.v. Slater 1969b).

29 Three occurrences in the *epinikia* (s.v. Slater 1969b).

30 Thirteen occurrences in the *epinikia* (s.v. Slater 1969b).

31 Three occurrences in the *epinikia* (s.v. Slater 1969b).

32 Three occurrences in the *epinikia* (s.v. Slater 1969b).

33 Forty-three occurrences in the *epinikia* (s.v. Slater 1969b).

34 Four occurrences in the *epinikia* (s.v Slater 1969b).

> Τὸν Ὀλυμπιονίκαν ἀνάγνωτέ μοι
> Ἀρχεστράτου παῖδα, πόθι φρενός
> ἐμᾶς γέγραπται· γλυκὺ γὰρ αὐτῷ μέλος ὀφείλων ἐπιλέλαθ'.
>
> *Olympian* 10.1–3
>
> Read out [*anagnôte*] to me the Olympian victor,
> the son of Arkhestratos,[35] where
> he has been inscribed in my heart; for I owe him a sweet song
> [*melos*] and have forgotten it.

The voicing in this passage indicates face-to-face interaction (not a text-reader interaction) by virtue of the second person plural imperative *anagnôte* 'read out' (line 1) and first-person singular forms (lines 1 and 3). The word *melos* 'song' (line 3) indicates the status of the text as a record of spoken, not written, communication. We can note as well that the passage is integrated as an instance of representing communication: the addresser represents the communication happening here as spoken (as always, taking song to mean also speech). As with *Olympian* 6.84–97, in the context of language that we might associate with a material mode of communication in *Olympian* 10.1–3, the plus-interpretation of the unmarked member (speech) of the speech/writing opposition surfaces, resolving any ambiguity about whether Pindar is representing his composition as spoken or as written.[36] Whereas the "oral subterfuge" hypothesis presents a theory of epinician composition predicated upon the putative given of written composition, *Pindar's* theory of epinician composition is predicated upon the constitutive role that speech plays in his art, as status of and voicing in his texts and the test of markedness show. This brings us back to *Pythian* 1.1–4: in light of the fact that, when subject to an ethnographic analysis of metalanguage and metacommunication, Pindar's texts represent themselves to us as records of speech, not writing, of what are the epinician *sâmata* signs?

[35] Father of Hagesidamos, the *laudandus* of *Olympian* 10.

[36] Nagy interprets *Olympian* 10.1–3, as follows: "Thus the image of reading out loud can even serve as the metaphor for the public performance of a composition, and the image of writing, as the metaphor for the composition itself" (1990:171). Segal 1986:10 interprets the few references to writing in Pindar's songs as an indication of the poet's awareness of writing; if so, the plus-interpretation of the unmarked term of the speech-writing opposition foregrounds speech over and against writing. Another passage where the plus-interpretation of the unmarked member of the speech-writing opposition, speech, surfaces, is *Nemean* 8.46–51.

Epinician *Sâmata* 'Signs'

In his essay "*Sêma* and *Noêsis*: Some Illustrations" Nagy (1983) demonstrates that in Archaic Greek poetic tradition a *sêma* 'sign' serves as a key to recognition and reception of a message, both for figures within a narrative and between the composer and audience. By looking closely at the "working relationship" between *sêma* and *noos* 'mind', the instrument of *noêsis* 'recognition', we can draw from Nagy's collection of comparative evidence within Archaic Greek poetic tradition to show that Pindar's use of the word *sâmata* at *Pythian* 1.3 refers to the epinician way of speaking.[37] I will ultimately argue that *Pythian* 1.1–4 records an act of composition, encoding Pindaric *sâmata*, that is expressed in terms of recognition, the decoding of *sâmata*, which turn out to be conventional rules for epinician speech and performance. The following analysis of patterns in Pindar's use of the words *noein* 'to recognize', *noos* 'mind', and *sâma* 'sign' supports this claim.

At *Olympian* 13.48 *noêsai* expresses Pindar's recognition of social conventions for appropriate speech.[38] Pindar claims that he is unable to enumerate the athletic achievements of Xenophon's (the *laudandus*'s) family, likening them to the number of pebbles in the sea. In the gnomic passage where the verb *noêsai* occurs, Pindar gives his rationale for passing over a detailed account of these achievements, then goes on to give a catalogue of the *laudandus*'s mythological ancestors, framing this as praise of Xenophon's *polis*, Corinth:

ἐν δ' ἀμφιάλοισι Ποτειδᾶνος τεθμοῖσιν
τοιοδώρῳ σὺν πατρὶ μακρότεραι
Τερψίᾳ θ' ἕψοντ' Ἐριτίμῳ τ' ἀοιδαί·
ὅσσα τ' ἐν Δελφοῖσιν ἀριστεύσατε
ἠδὲ χόρτοις ἐν λέοντος, δηρίομαι πολέσιν
περὶ πλήθει καλῶν· ὡς μὰν σαφές
οὐκ ἂν εἰδείην λέγειν ποντιᾶν ψάφων ἀριθμόν.
ἕπεται δ' ἐν ἑκάστῳ
μέτρον· νοῆσαι δὲ καιρὸς ἄριστος.
ἐγὼ δὲ ἴδιος ἐν κοινῷ σταλείς
μῆτίν τε γαρύων παλαιγόνων
πόλεμόν τ' ἐν ἡρωίαις ἀρεταῖσιν

[37] Nagy 1983:35. My discussion of epinician semiotics is heavily indebted to Foley 1999.

[38] There are in all four occurrences of *noein* 'to recognize' in Pindar's corpus (s.v. Slater 1969b). The occurrence of the verb at *Nemean* 10.86, where the verb's sense is 'to intend' rather than 'to recognize', is necessarily an exception to the pattern that I describe here.

οὐ ψεύσομ' ἀμφὶ Κορίνθῳ.

Olympian 13.40–52

In Poseidon's festival between the seas,
longer songs will follow his[39] father, Ptoiodoros,
and Terpsias[40] and Eritimos.[41]
As many achievements as you enjoyed at Delphi
and in the lion's fields,[42] I dispute with many
over the abundance of excellence.
I would not know how to count out accurately the number of sea pebbles.
In every matter
moderation matters. The best discretion is to recognize [*noêsai*] this.
As a private individual sent before the public
singing out about their ancestors' ingenuity
and warfare among their heroic successes,
I will not speak falsely about Corinth.

Pindar's (rhetorical) inability to list all of the achievements of Xenophon's family results from his recognition of propriety as expressed in the gnomic statement, "In every matter moderation matters" (line 47). In the context of Pindar's praise poetry *kairos* 'timing' can entail, as at *Olympian* 13.48, what Bundy (1962:73–76) has called the *siga* 'silence' motif, which is a conventional acknowledgement that excessive praise runs the risk of violating decorum or inciting jealousy. If, as Nagy demonstrates, the poetics of *noêsis* entails recognition, then at *Olympian* 13.48 Pindar represents the act of composition as recognition of social conventions concerning appropriate speech, as witnessed by his use of the verb *noêsai*.[43]

39 I.e. Xenophon's.

40 According to the scholia, Ptoiodoros' brother.

41 According to the scholia, Terpsias' son or grandson.

42 I.e. at Nemea.

43 The same concern for appropriate speech is involved in the occurrence of the verb *noein* at *Nemean* 5.16–18, where Pindar uses language of *noêsis* to express his selection of mythological topics according to the criterion of *alatheia* 'truth'. He declines to tell the story of how the heroes Peleus and Telamon killed Phokos, their half brother: "I will stop; every truth [*alatheia*] is not more advantageous when it starkly shows its face; to be silent is often the wisest thing for a person to recognize [*noêsai*]" (στάσομαι· οὔ τοι ἅπασα κερδίων / φαίνοισα πρόσωπον ἀλάθει' ἀτρεκές· / καὶ τὸ σιγᾶν πολλάκις ἐστὶ σοφώτατον ἀνθρώπῳ νοῆσαι). As at *Olympian* 13.47–48, we see at *Nemean* 5.16–18 that Pindar uses the *siga* motif to explain why he will not

This relationship between communication and social rules for appropriateness is crucial from the point of view of the Ethnography of Speaking. In order to discover how and why members of a community select, organize, evaluate, and participate in the speech acts and speech events that constitute a community's speech economy, it is necessary to understand the social rules for appropriateness that condition that selection, organization, evaluation, and participation. Bauman (1977:11) has described the relationship between performance and the social rules for appropriateness as follows: "Fundamentally, performance as a mode of spoken verbal communication consists in the assumption of responsibility to an audience for a display of communicative competence. This competence rests on the knowledge and ability to speak in socially appropriate ways."[44] Pindar's uses of the verb *noein* entail the display of such knowledge and ability. If, as Nagy writes, "a true recognition of the sign, a true *nóēsis* of the *sêma*, can be achieved only by recognizing the internally coherent system of signals" (1983:38–39), my analysis of the occurrences of *noein* in Pindar's *epinikia* recommends that we identify that system as a *social* semiotics, not semiotics in the strict sense of the relationship between a sign and its referent(s), but a pragmatic (social) semiotics of the relationships among signs and their users. As an "internally coherent system of signals" the epinician way of speaking comprises a host of appropriateness rules that regiment the composition of each victory song and the audience's participation in its performance. Pindar's social semiotics entails recognition of the ready-made social conventions for praise poetry, as well as the display of competence in creative adaptation of those conventions. If this observation bears out, we should expect that upon further analysis Pindar's sign language

---

relate mythic material whose content is inappropriate according to the criterion of *alatheia* and expresses his observance of social conventions for appropriate speech in the language of *noêsis*. In *Paean* 2 (= *Fragment* 52b), lines 54–55, Pindar uses the language of recognition to describe the process of composition by addressing a potential response of hearers of his song: "once it recognizes enmity, envy for those who have died long ago passes away" ([ὁ δ]' ἐχθρὰ νοήσαις / ἤδη φθόνος οἴχεται τῶν πάλαι προθανόντων). The potential for praise to provoke *phthonos* 'envy' is a recurrent concern in Pindar's songs. Here he abstractly represents *phthonos* itself as recognizing (*noêsais*, line 54) social conventions for praise, describing in the next line one such convention in the form of a gnomic statement: "It is necessary for a person to convey the profound glory due to ancestors" (χρὴ δ' ἄνδρα τοκεῦσι<ν> φέρειν βαθύδοξον αἶσαν, *Paean* 2.56). See Bulman 1992 for a detailed study of *phthonos* in Pindar's songs, as well as Kirkwood 1984 and Mackie 2003:9–37.

44 Cf. Hymes's critique (1974:94–95) of Noam Chomsky's conception of communicative competence on the basis of generative grammar's inability to account for appropriateness understood as "whether and to what extent something is in some context suitable, effective, or the like."

will continue to evidence recognition of, as Bundy (1962:11) describes it, the "propriety that determines the relationship between song and merit."

Occurrences of the word *noos* in Pindar's songs express just such recognition of this propriety. Consider the following example:

> ἔπεχε νῦν σκοπῷ τόξον, ἄγε θυμέ· τίνα βάλλομεν
> ἐκ μαλθακᾶς αὖτε φρενὸς εὐκλέας ὀιστοὺς ἱέντες; ἐπί τοι
> Ἀκράγαντι τανύσαις
> αὐδάσομαι ἐνόρκιον λόγον ἀλαθεῖ νόῳ,
> τεκεῖν μή τιν᾽ ἑκατόν γε ἐτέων πόλιν φίλοις ἄνδρα μᾶλλον
> εὐεργέταν πραπίσιν ἀφθονέστερόν τε χέρα
> Θήρωνος.
>
> *Olympian* 2.89–95

> Aim now the bow at its target—let's go, heart. Whom do we strike
> when we launch glorious arrows from our subtle mind?
> Taking aim at Akragas
> I will voice a claim pledged with a true mind [*noos*],
> that for one hundred years no city has produced a man who is for his friends a greater
> benefactor thanks to his thoughtfulness or more generous with his strength
> than Theron.

Pindar vouches for his *logos* with an *alathês noos*, where this 'true mind' serves as the faculty of recognition of the praiseworthy qualities (lines 93–95) of Theron, the song's *laudandus*. The representation of the composition in terms of an interior dialogue conditions Pindar's use of *noos* (line 92). In this connection, witness the self-address in the form of a prayer directed to the speaker's *thumos* (line 89) and the description of metaphorical arrows of song being launched from the speaker's *malthaka phrên* 'subtle mind' (line 90). In the absence of evidence indicating otherwise, it is methodologically appropriate to interpret inductively such an interior dialogue as representing composition as a process of recognition, a process that is in progress. From this point of view Pindar's exercise of *noos* to enact recognition can be interpreted as a live display of the composer-performer's competence in an original performance, as composition-in-performance. In *Olympian* 1 the same dynamic occurs in a prayer addressed to composer's *êtor* 'heart': "But take the Dorian lyre from its peg, if at all the grace of Pisa and Pherenikos put your mind [*noos*] under the influence of the sweetest thoughts" (ἀλλὰ Δωρίαν ἀπὸ φόρμιγγα πασσάλου / λάμβαν', εἴ τί τοι Πίσας τε καὶ Φερενίκου χάρις / νόον ὑπὸ γλυκυτάταις ἔθηκε φροντίσιν, lines 17–19). The mention of Pisa is a topographical reference to the site of the Olympic Games, where the *laudandus*, Hieron, enjoyed his victory; Pherenikos is the name of his horse; and these features of Hieron's athletic contest motivate recognition by the composer's *êtor*. This occurrence of *noos* is accordingly a display of "propriety that determines the relationship between song and merit." Like *Olympian* 2.89–95, *Olympian* 1.17–19 depicts the composition process by representing the composer as engaged in an internal dialogue, as evidenced by the word *noos* and the phrase ὑπὸ γλυκυτάταις...φροντίσιν 'under the influence of the sweetest thoughts' (line 19), about how to compose his song.[45]

In *Pythian* 1 Pindar describes Apollo's reception of a prayer addressed to him in the language of recognition: "I hope that you are willing to put these things in your *noos* and to make the land a place for noble people" (line 40). The context of the passage shows that the referent for "these things" is a passage celebrating Hieron's recently founded city of Aetna:

ναυσιφορήτοις δ' ἀνδράσι πρώτα χάρις
ἐς πλόον ἀρχομένοις πομπαῖον ἐλθεῖν οὖρον· ἐοικότα γάρ
καὶ τελευτᾷ φερτέρου νόστου τυχεῖν. ὁ δὲ λόγος
ταύταις ἐπὶ συντυχίαις δόξαν φέρει
λοιπὸν ἔσσεσθαι στεφάνοισί ν<ιν> ἵπποις τε κλυτάν
καὶ σὺν εὐφώνοις θαλίαις ὀνυμαστάν.
Λύκιε καὶ Δάλοι' ἀνάσσων Φοῖβε Παρνασσοῦ τε κράναν Κασταλίαν
φιλέων,
ἐθελήσαις ταῦτα νόῳ τιθέμεν εὔανδρόν τε χώραν.
ἐκ θεῶν γὰρ μαχαναὶ πᾶσαι βροτέαις ἀρεταῖς,
καὶ σοφοὶ καὶ χερσὶ βιαταὶ περίγλωσσοί τ' ἔφυν. ἄνδρα δ' ἐγὼ
κεῖνον
αἰνῆσαι μενοινῶν ἔλπομαι

45 Cf. Gerber 1982:45–46. Another occurrence of *noos* is analogous to Pindar's use of *noein* at *Nemean* 5.16–18, cited in note 42 above, where he similarly expresses recognition of the criterion of *alatheia*: "If any mortal stays the path of truth with his mind [*noos*], then it is necessary for him to fare well because he gets this from the blessed ones" (εἰ δὲ νόῳ τις ἔχει θνατῶν ἀλαθείας ὁδόν, χρὴ πρὸς μακάρων / τυγχάνοντ' εὖ πασχέμεν, *Pythian* 3.103–104). Other occurrences of *noos* that entail the use of the word as a faculty of recognition of a message include: *Olympian* 9.75, 10.87; *Pythian* 1.95, 2.89, 3.5, 3.29, 5.44, 5.110, 5.122, 6.46, 6.51, 8.67, 10.68; *Nemean* 3.42, 6.5, 7.88; *Isthmian* 1.40, 5.61; *Paean* 5.45; *Fragment* 43.2.

μὴ χαλκοπάραον ἄκονθ' ὡσείτ' ἀγῶνος βαλεῖν ἔξω παλάμᾳ
δονέων,
μακρὰ δὲ ῥίψαις ἀμεύσασθ' ἀντίους.

Pythian 1.33–45

The first gift for sea-traveling men
when they set out on a voyage is for a favorable wind to come;
then it is likely
that at the completion of their journey they have a secure return.
This statement,
given the present success, suggests
that in the future this city will be renowned for crowns and
horses
and famed for its lovely sounding celebrations.
Lycian, you who rule Delos; Phoibos, you who cherish Parnassus'
Kastalian spring,
I hope that you are willing to put these things in your mind [*noos*]
and to make the land a place for noble people;
for all devices for mortal virtues originate with the gods,
and the wise, the mighty, and those gifted at speech are born that
way. And that man [Hieron], I
want to praise him and hope that,
as if in a contest, brandishing in my hand the bronze-cheeked
spear, I do not throw it out of bounds,
but that by casting it far I surpass my opponents.

In this passage the application of *noos* and the criterion of *alatheia* again serve as a display of the composer's recognition of the "propriety that determines the relationship between song and merit." In the prayer addressed to Apollo, the zeugma[46] involving the infinitive *tithemen* 'to put' (line 40) effectively links the two requests uttered by the praise poet: first, to recognize the validity of the praise communicated in lines 35–37 and, second, to actualize the *doxa* 'glory' (line 36) of Hieron's city by making the land prosperous.

Pindar does not limit his language for representing the act of composition as a recognition of epinician social semiotics to words morphologi-

46 As I interpret the passage, taking *euandros* 'noble' as a predicate adjective modifying *khôra* 'land'. For discussion of the zeugma in this passage see Gildersleeve 1890:245, Gerber 1982:136–137, and Gentili 1995:342.

cally related to *noêsis*.[47] One salient example of another way in which Pindar expresses this recognition, as suggested by *Olympian* 1.17–19 discussed above, is to use the word *êtor* 'heart'. Of the nine occurrences of *êtor* 'heart' in the Pindaric corpus, four involve workaday applications of the word.[48] The rest of Pindar's uses of *êtor* operate like *noein* and *noos*: to represent the act of composition as an enactment of existing social rules for appropriate speech. In another passage of *Olympian* 1, for example, Pindar addresses his *êtor* in a form of representing communication that stages composition as an internal dialogue: "But if you wish to sing of victory prizes, my heart [*êtor*]..." (εἰ δ' ἄεθλα γαρύεν / ἔλδεαι, φίλον ἦτορ..., lines 3–4). In addition to contextualizing the use of *noos* at *Olympian* 1.19, discussed above, this passage explicitly reflects propriety concerning the relationship between song and athletic achievement.[49]

47 Pelliccia 1995:292–306 analyzes Pindar's use of the words *êtor* 'heart', *kear* 'heart', *thumos* 'impulse', *phrên*/*phrenes* 'mind', *psukhê* 'soul', and *noos* as physiological or psychological organs that motivate or enable speech.

48 In the direct discourse of Erginos at the end of *Olympian* 4, whose brief mythological narrative concerns the hero's victory in a race in armor, the hero's words are: "Such am I when it comes to speed; hands and heart [*êtor*] are alike" (οὗτος ἐγὼ ταχυτᾶτι· / χεῖρες δὲ καὶ ἦτορ ἴσον, lines 24–25). In *Pythian* 9 Apollo invites Kheiron to witness firsthand the qualities of Kyrene: "a young woman with heart [*êtor*] superior to toil" (μόχθου καθύπερθε νεᾶνις / ἦτορ ἔχοισα, lines 31–32). In *Nemean* 8 Pindar explains that even fortitude does not secure renown without song: "Any man who is inarticulate but brave in his heart [*êtor*] obscurity suppresses in ruinous quarrel" (ἦ τιν' ἄγλωσσον μέν, ἦτορ δ' ἄλκιμον, λάθα κατέχει / ἐν λυγρῷ νείκει, lines 24–25). In *Isthmian* 3, Pindar characterizes the song's *laudandus* in the following way: "what is due to Melissos for his twin prizes is to direct his heart [*êtor*] to sweet delight" (ἔστι δὲ καὶ διδύμων ἀέθλων Μελίσσῳ / μοῖρα πρὸς εὐφροσύναν τρέψαι γλυκεῖαν / ἦτορ, lines 9–11).

49 In *Olympian* 2 Pindar lists figures dwelling on the Isle of the Blessed, among whom, thanks to his mother's intercession, is Achilles: "And his mother brought Achilles, after she persuaded the heart [*êtor*] of Zeus with entreaties" (Ἀχιλλέα τ' ἔνεικ', ἐπεί Ζηνὸς ἦτορ / λιταῖς ἔπεισε, μάτηρ, lines 79–80). In this occurrence of *êtor* we witness the reflexive relationship between narrated events and the act of narration. In a passage of mythological narrative Pindar represents the persuasive power of Thetis' entreaties in terms of her ability to move Zeus' *êtor* (line 79). Here I would suggest that what moves Zeus' *êtor* is as much the effective performance of the speech act of entreaty (*litai* 'entreaties', line 80) on the part of Thetis and Zeus' accordingly positive evaluation of that performance as any emotional quality that may be implied in Thetis' unreported words. Just as Zeus recognizes Thetis' use of appropriate speech within the framework of narrated events, so in performance Pindar uses the term *êtor* to express his recognition of the social semiotics of *epinikion*. In *Nemean* 4 the composer represents himself as being moved to include another topic in his song: "I am drawn in my heart [*âtor*] by the influence of a love charm to touch upon the feast of the new moon" (ἴυγγι δ' ἕλκομαι ἦτορ νεομηνίᾳ θιγέμεν, line 35). Note that here Snell and Maehler 1997 give the Doric form *âtor* for *êtor*. Pindar attributes the identification of the topic of "the feast of the new moon" to the faculty of recognition as expressed by *âtor*. Note too that *êtor* can describe an instance of misrecognition, as at *Nemean* 7.20–27, where Pindar illustrates how a blind *êtor* is susceptible to uses of *êtor* that do not satisfy the criterion of *alatheia*. I discuss below the occurrence of *êtor* at *Paean* 6.12.

To illustrate another pattern in his sign language, Pindar regularly uses the verb *peithein* 'to persuade' or 'to obey' to describe responses to specific speech acts. This pattern suggests that *peithein* has a special application that entails recognition on the part of the addressee that an appropriate response is recommended according to the social conventions of the context in which a speech act is uttered. To consider occurrences of *peithein* in narrated events (i.e. represented communication), Pindar relates the story of how Herakles brought the olive tree to Olympia, where he founded a sanctuary for Zeus, "after he persuaded [*peisais*] with his speech the Hypoborean people, attendants of Apollo" (δᾶμον Ὑπερβορέων πείσαις Ἀπόλλωνος θεράποντα λόγῳ, *Olympian* 3.16). In another passage Pindar describes the confidence accorded to the hero Aiakos: "without a summons the leading heroes who dwelt nearby willingly wished to obey [*peithesthai*] his commands" (ἀβοατὶ γὰρ ἡρώων ἄωτοι περιναιεταόντων / ἤθελον κείνου γε πείθεσθ' ἀναξίαις ἑκόντες, *Nemean* 8.9–10). These examples of narrated events represent both the persuasive power of the speakers and the recognition on the part of the addressees of the propriety—i.e. effective performance—of the speech acts that the speakers utter.[50]

In *Pythian* 1 there is an especially remarkable occurrence of *peithein* in a passage of representing communication in which the first-person voice of the composer-performer addresses a prayer to the Muse using an imperative form of the verb: "Muse, obey [*pitheo*] me and for Deinomenes too sing a song of praise as a reward for the four-horse chariot" (Μοῖσα, καὶ πὰρ Δεινομένει κελαδῆσαι / πίθεό μοι ποινὰν τεθρίππων, lines 58–59). Here the middle voice of the verb *peithein* with a dative object has the meaning 'obey'. Rather than requesting the Muse's guidance in the composition of song, as we might expect, the composer entreats the Muse to heed him. Based upon the uses of *peithein* that involve the addressee's recognition of a successfully performed speech act, the composer's request implies that his addressee recognizes his competence as a speaker. One gauge of this competence, as we have seen, is that the passage is an exact expression of the "propriety that determines the relationship between song and merit," to refer again to Bundy's formulation, because it links song and merit, explicitly characterizing the song of praise as "a reward for the four-horse chariot" (*Pythian* 1.59).[51]

50 See also *Olympian* 2.79–80 (quoted in previous footnote) where persuasion is a consequence of Thetis' speech act identified as *litai* 'entreaties'.

51 Of twenty-one occurrences of forms of *peithein* in Pindar's corpus, I have so far analyzed four: *Olympians* 2.80, 3.16, *Pythian* 1.59, and *Nemean* 8.10. Below I consider another of Pindar's uses of *peithein* at *Paean* 6.12 and discuss two other occurrences of the verb in connection with Pindar's

At this point I return to a last example of Pindar's use of *êtor* to represent the process of composition as an act of recognition. In this passage *êtor* occurs as the object of the verb *peithein*:[52]

> ὕδατι γὰρ ἐπὶ χαλκοπύλῳ
> ψόφον ἀϊὼν Κασταλίας
> ὀρφανὸν ἀνδρῶν χορεύσιος ἦλθον
> ἔταις ἀμαχανίαν ἀ[λ]έξων
> τεοῖσιν ἐμαῖς τε τιμ[α]ῖς·
> ἤτορι δὲ φίλῳ παῖς ἅτε ματέρι κεδνᾷ
> πειθόμενος κατέβαν στεφάνων
> καὶ θαλιᾶν τροφὸν ἄλσος Ἀ-
> πόλλωνος.
>
> *Paean* 6.7–15

> At the water from the bronze gates
> I heard the sound of Kastalia
> bereft of men's dancing and came
> to ward off helplessness
> from your kinsmen and from my honors.
> Obeying [*peithomenos*] my heart like a child obeys his cherished mother
> I came
> to the nurse of crowns and festivities,
> the sanctuary of Apollo's.

If, like *noos*, *êtor* functions as the faculty of recognition and if *peithein* is a word that Pindar frequently uses to characterize the effect of a speech act upon an addressee, then at *Paean* 6.12–13 we have an especially outstanding case of composition represented as recognition. In some ways similar to Pindar's entreaty to the Muse at *Pythian* 1.58–59, the phrase *êtori de philô...peithomenos* 'obeying my heart' (*Paean* 6.12–13) describes the persuasive power of a speaker; in this passage the speaker represents his composition as an interior dialogue, as an act of recognition-as-reception that guides composition and performance.

---

use of the word *sâma* (*Pythian* 1.3 and *Pythian* 4.200). I do not claim, then, that Pindar's use of forms of *peithein* are characteristically linked with the poetics of *sêma* and *noêsis*; I only want to demonstrate that this connection exists in the examples that I have given. Cf. *Bakkhulides* 5.21, where the functionally analogous construction *pisunos* + dative occurs.

52 My reading then is *contra* Kurke 2005:106n77, who, following Radt 1958:117–118, writes that "it is impossible to understand these lines to mean that the speaker obeys his own heart as a child its mother; therefore we must supply Pytho as implied object of πειθόμενος [*peithomenos*]."

Now that we have seen some ways in which Pindar uses the language of recognition to describe composition, we can turn to a consideration of Pindar's applications for the word *sâma*, which occurs only five times in the *epinikia*.[53] Corresponding to Nagy's observation that "*sêma* bears not only the general meaning of 'sign' but also the specific meaning of 'tomb'" (1983:45), Pindar uses *sâma* in just those two ways: first, to name a tomb; second, to describe the recognition of 'signs'. In *Olympian* 10 Pindar selects the topic of his mythological narrative: "The proclamations of Zeus urged me to sing about the outstanding contest that Heracles founded with six altars beside the ancient funeral mound [*sâma*] of Pelops" (ἀγῶνα δ' ἐξαίρετον ἀεῖσαι θέμιτες ὦρσαν Διός, ὃν ἀρχαίῳ σάματι πὰρ Πέλοπος / †βωμῷ ἑξάριθμον ἐκτίσσατο, lines 24–25). A mythological narrative in *Pythian* 9 describes the burial of Iolaos: "After he [Iolaos] laid waste to Eurustheus' head with the edge of a sword, they buried him [i.e. Iolaos] below, under the earth, in the funeral mound [*sâma*] of the charioteer Amphitryon" (τὸν, Εὐρυσθῆος ἐπεὶ κεφαλάν / ἔπραθε φασγάνου ἀκμᾷ, κρύψαν ἔνερθ' ὑπὸ γᾶν / διφρηλάτα Ἀμφιτρύωνος σάματι, lines 80–82). A gnomic statement in *Nemean* 7 stresses the importance of moderation: "The wise learn of the wind to come on the third day and are not harmed by the influence of success. Rich and poor to death's funeral mound [*sâma*] go" (σοφοὶ δὲ μέλλοντα τριταῖον ἄνεμον / ἔμαθον, οὐδ' ὑπὸ κέρδει βλάβεν· / ἀφνεὸς {τε} πενιχρός τε θανάτου παρά / σᾶμα νέονται, lines 17–20).[54]

In the two occurrences of *sâma* that remain, the word refers to an act of communication in which the focus is upon the reception end of the communication process—to the process of decoding *sâmata*. The context for the first instance of the word that I will consider is a mythological narrative in *Pythian* 4. The crew has just embarked upon the Argo and the seer Mopsos is prophesying with birds and lots. Jason prays to Zeus, who answers favorably with lightning flashes.[55] The Argonauts acknowledge the signs of Zeus' thunderbolts, an omen that bears a message requiring recognition: "Heeding the signs [*sâmata*] of the god, the heroes took heart" (ἀμπνοὰν δ' ἥρωες ἔστασαν θεοῦ σάμασιν / πιθόμενοι, *Pythian* 4.199–200). The reaction of the Argonauts indicates that they interpret correctly Zeus' *sâmata*, which the narrative describes as "the propitious sound of a thunderbolt" (βροντᾶς αἴσιον φθέγμα, lines 197–198). The working relationship between *sêma* and *noêsis* that takes place in narrated acts of communication is a reflex of how it operates in actual performance, in the interaction between performer and audience (Nagy 1983:51).

53 *Olympian* 10.24; *Pythian* 1.3, 4.199, 9.82; *Nemean* 7.20.

54 On this passage see also Nagy 1983:49.

55 Nagy 1983:43 identifies lightning as "the most ubiquitous *sêma* of Zeus."

This crucially communicative process of encoding a message by way of a *sêma* happens, in a sense, both within poetry and without: between figures in mythological narrative within the boundaries of a given work; between composer and audience at the surface of those boundaries. This observation is another way of formulating the reflexive relationship between representing and represented communication. Just as the Argonauts must have the right interpretive framework to effect recognition of Zeus' *sâmata* in *Pythian* 4, the audience to epinician performance must be familiar with the social conventions for performance that are constitutive of epinician poetics and that enable composition and reception.

At the beginning of this chapter, I reviewed the strong precedent in existing scholarship for approaching *Pythian* 1.1–4 as an outstanding record for the performance of *epinikion*. Where I part company with those interpretations of the passage is to apply Nagy's discovery of the communicative and functional relationship between *sêma* 'sign' and *noêsis* 'recognition' in order to read the Pindaric *sâmata* at *Pythian* 1.3 as "signpost[s] for *nóos*" (Nagy 1983:50) that point the way toward the existence of a social semiotics, a set of social conventions for epinician speech and performance that are to be discovered ethnographically. In particular, I have shown that Pindar frequently uses *noos* to describe the poet's competence at observing propriety concerning the relationship between praise poetry and the athletic achievement that merits it. We have further observed that Pindar regularly displays such competence in the performance of praise as an act of reception in the form of recognition. In this connection I call attention to a common feature of Pindar's uses of *sâma* at *Pythian* 1.3 and *Pythian* 4.199. In both passages a form of the word *sâma* is the object of *peithein* in the sense of 'to obey', a word, as I have shown, that Pindar uses to describe recognition of an appropriately and effectively performed act of communication. Just as the heroes at *Pythian* 4.199–200 recognize Zeus' *sâmata*, so the singers of *Pythian* 1.1–4 recognize certain *sâmata*. What is remarkable about the occurrence of *sâmata* at *Pythian* 1.3 is that the act of composition is described in such language of reception.

My analysis of Pindar's sign language has focused upon how that language evidences the existence of a social semiotics, a system of conventions for speaking that Pindar and his audience share.[56] I have stressed one dimen-

[56] Referring specifically to deixis in Pindar's *epinikia*, Bonifazi captures well this process of producing situated meaning through the use of a shared code, what I am calling a social semiotics, writing that the victory song's "deictic system constitutes a linguistic sub-code of various shared contexts and of associated shared meanings, including the symbolic one" (2004a:413–414).

sion of this social semiotics, the "propriety that determines the relationship between song and merit." Now I will broaden the terms to suggest that the epinician way of speaking itself is constituted by social conventions for speech and performance that we can call a social semiotics, a code for the social practices entailed in the speech event of epinician performance and the speech acts that constitute performance events. The next three chapters of *Pindar's Verbal Art* accordingly present a practical taxonomy for the social semiotics of *epinikion*, detailing what signs (i.e. social conventions) singers and audience heed in the composition and reception of epinician song.

2

Epinikion as Event

For Dell Hymes the notion of a speech community, one of the fundamental notions of the Ethnography of Speaking, addresses how members of a community conceive of language and emphasizes the ethnographic description of language use (1974:47–51). The previous chapter presented evidence to show that, from the point of view of the community of artists and audiences who participated in epinician performance, epinician language is spoken, not written. The principle of intersubjective objectivity urges, then, a philological method that is dialogically responsive to how Pindar's language represents itself. As it turns out, the opening of Pindar's *Pythian* 1 provides a specific point of departure for building our local knowledge of epinician art: there are certain *sâmata* 'signs' that singers follow when they compose and perform *epinikion* and that guide the audience's reception and evaluation of works of epinician art. Pindar's description of composition in terms of reception and the audience's co-creation of the communicative exchange highlight the sharedness of those *sâmata*, so that the signs point to some set of social conventions recognized by singers and audience alike: "communicative activity involves all participants; meaning is constructed within their relationship" (Bonifazi 2004a:391). The remaining chapters of *Pindar's Verbal Art* describe the social conventions that epinician composer and audience use in their relationship, beginning in this chapter with another fundamental notion of the Ethnography of Speaking, the speech event (Hymes 1974:52).

Recalling from the Introduction that a register is a style whose use is dedicated to a particular context of situation in accordance with a community's language conventions, the purpose of this chapter is to describe how Pindar's epinician texts record ethnographic evidence for the relationship between epinician style and the event of epinician performance. Bauman calls such evidence "the keying of performance" (1977:15–24; Foley 1995:11–17 and 2002:85–93). Entextualized records of performance include features, or keys, that frame the speech event of performance and, through such framing, forge the link between an artistic idiom and the event to which it is dedicated. This idiom-event link is characteristic of a linguistic register. Pindar's *epinikia* evidence each performance key that Bauman illustrates: special code, figurative language, parallelism, special paralinguistic features, special formulae, appeal to tradition, and disclaimer of performance. Echoing Bauman, I hasten to stress the suggestive nature of his performance keys, which ultimately are to be discovered ethnographically.

Special Code

Jakobson (1960:353) and Hymes (1974:10, 13, and 59), who adapts Jakobson's model of language to the Ethnography of Speaking, apply the term "code" to a communicative vehicle shared by participants in the typical speech events that make up a community's speech economy. In this sense, a linguistic code is a language—say, ancient Greek. In terms of verbal art, a special linguistic code is a communicative vehicle reserved for use in performance events. The difference between a special code and a register is one of relationality: the special code is one performance key among others that calls attention to the existence of a register. The features of *epinikion*'s special code include a blend of varieties of ancient Greek, archaizing morphological and lexical features, and prosodic patterning.[1]

We can witness the development of a conventionalized Doric specifically dedicated to choral lyric that enables the reception of choral art by a Panhellenic audience.[2] Doric features distinguish the medium of choral song from all other non-choral types of verbal art, even if this medium also retains formal features of Ionic and Aeolic varieties.[3] The impact of this can be observed in what Leonard Palmer refers to as the "dilution of the Doric element" in choral idiom (Palmer 1980:124). After the mid-fifth century BCE the composition of choral song declines, with the exception of choral odes in tragedy, which retain traces of the Doric dialect (Cf. Horrocks 1997:20). In the

1 For special code as a performance key, see Bauman 1977:17, Foley 1995:11–12, 83–85, and 93, 1999:23–25, and 2002:85–86. For descriptions of Pindar's language, see, among many others, Gildersleeve 1890:lxiii–cxv, Dornseiff 1921, Forssman 1966, Horváth 1976, Palmer 1980:123–127, and Hummel 1993.

2 On the blend of ancient Greek varieties in Pindar's language as artificial and reserved for literary usage, see Gildersleeve 1890:lxxvi–lxxvii, Palmer 1980:123, Hummel 1993:415–416, and Horrocks 1997:18. On the relationship between choral song and Panhellenic institutions, see Nagy 1979:7. Cf. Bowra 1964:197 and Horrocks 1997:19.

3 But see Davies 1988 for another view.

Classical Period the occurrence of lexical and morphological Doric features, however limited, by convention links verbal art forms that evidence such features with the event of choral performance. A common feature of Doric is the use of the segment α (*a*) where η (*ê*) occurs in other ancient Greek varieties.[4] In Pindar's special code this alternation occurs in certain words: for example, Doric ναός (*naos*) 'temple' and λαός (*laos*) 'the people' for Ionic νηός (*nêos*) and ληός (*lêos*); and in certain morphological forms, particularly the genitive plural noun and adjective ending of the first declension, Doric -ᾶν (*-ân*) compared to Ionic -ῶν (*-ôn*).

Aeolic features give archaizing color to the special code associated with choral performance.[5] This archaizing effect derives in part from the fact that Aeolic forms in Pindar are specifically of the Lesbian variety, a species of Aeolic associated with the poetry of Alcaeus and Sappho, whose work predates Pindar. Examples of Aeolicism in Pindar's choral poetry include -οισ- (*-ois-*), which occurs, for example, in the feminine participle ending -οισα (*-oisa*) instead of Ionic -ουσα (*-ousa*); in third declension dative plural endings Pindar has Aeolic -οισι (*-oisi*) where Ionic -ουσι (*-ousi*) occurs;[6] Pindar has Aeolic Μοῖσα (*Moisa*) 'Muse' for Ionic Μοῦσα (*Mousa*).[7] Pindar's third-person plural active endings are an example of what Nagy refers to as "the dialectal synthesis of Pindaric diction," where Doric -οντι (*-onti*) and Aeolic (specifically Lesbian) -οισι (*-oisi*) occur "to the exclusion of -ουσι [*-ousi*]," the Ionic form (1990:417).[8]

The mere occurrence of prosodic patterning distinguishes epinician language as a special artistic idiom.[9] The basic metrical building blocks for Pindar's *epinikia*, (1) dactylo-epitrite meter, associated with Doric rhythms, but betraying traces of influence from Ionic traditions, and (2) Aeolic meters, echo the art form's conventionalized integration of Doric, Aeolic, and Ionic varieties of ancient Greek—with the characteristic dominance of Doric meters. Nagy

4 On the α (*a*)/η (*ê*) alternation, see Gildersleeve 1890:lxxviii–lxxix, with examples, Gentili 1988:58–59, and Horrocks 1997:21.

5 Note that Horrocks 1997:20 voices the concern that the evidence for Aeolic features may result from the influence of interpolations inserted by Alexandrian scholars in the process of textual transmission.

6 On Aeolic morphology in Pindar's songs, see Gildersleeve 1890:lxxxv and Palmer 1980:124 and 126.

7 Note further that Pindar does not use the attested Doric form Μῶσα (*Môsa*).

8 See also Gildersleeve 1890:lxxxv and Palmer 1980:124–125.

9 The point of departure on Pindar's prosody is Maehler 1989:178–188. See also Gildersleeve 1890:lxiii–lxxvi, Bowra 1964:317–321, West 1982:60–76, Race 1986:11–13, and Nagy 1990:416–418 and 439–464. With few exceptions the choral poetry of Simonides, Bakkhulides, and Pindar possesses a strophic structure that West (1982:60) associates with a "Dorian tradition of composition."

has observed "that this proportion of Doric/Aeolic/Ionic meters in Pindaric composition corresponds to the dialectal synthesis of Pindaric diction: again we see a pattern of dominant Doric, recessive Aeolic, and residual Ionic" (Nagy 1990:417). Further, the particular features of epinician prosody reinforce what I have said above about the connection between Pindar's special code and the event of performance: the dominance of Doric features of prosody marks Pindar's language as available for choral performance, specifically, a distinctive speech event with its idiomatic ways of speaking, interacting, and meaning.

Figurative Language

Pindar's intricately carved opening lines of *Olympian* 11 are typical of the way in which the poet's language is foregrounded and semantically dense:[10]

> Ἔστιν ἀνθρώποις ἀνέμων ὅτε πλείστα
> χρῆσις· ἔστιν δ' οὐρανίων ὑδάτων,
> ὀμβρίων παίδων νεφέλας.
>
> *Olympian* 11.1–3

> Sometimes people have the greatest need for winds;
> other times, their greatest need is for waters of the heavens,
> rainy children of a cloud.

The ornate description of rainfall as "waters of the heavens" and appositionally as "rainy children of a cloud" is a figurative gesture whose meaning is context-sensitive. Bundy explains the images of wind and rain as a socially conventional "occupational type" of foil: "here sailors and farmers, who have need of wind and rain, respectively, are foil for achievement in general" (1962:10). This interpretation hinges upon background information shared by the epinician performer and his audience and highlights how meaning is context-specific. By calling attention to the situatedness of the social meaning in *epinikion*, Bundy's observation of the "occupational type" of foil indicates how Pindar's figurative language keys performance: *Olympian* 11.1–3 is not a statement about rain and winds, taken literally, but has a context-specific function, to serve as a foil for the central message of *Olympian* 11's performance.

[10] On figurative language as a performance key, see Bauman 1977:17–18 and Foley 1995:12, 64, 85–86, 93, and 2002:87–88. See Bowra 1964:219–236 and 239–277 on Pindar's word choices and imagery; Steiner 1986 and Loscalzo 2003:125–160 on Pindar's metaphors.

Praise and blame poetics is another example of how figurative language has more than denotational meaning.[11] One word that Pindar uses to refer to *epinikion* is *ainos* 'praise';[12] cognate verbal forms are *ainein* 'to praise'[13] and *epainein* 'to praise'.[14] Opposing this designation for the poetics of praise is the designation for blame poetics, *psogos* 'fault-finding'.[15] Also indicative is *psogeros* 'bitter-tongued'; Nagy describes the passage in which this epithet occurs, *Pythian* 2.55–56, as "a programmatic description of blame poetry...as the opposite of praise poetry, in the specific context of rejecting blame within a poem of praise" (Nagy 1990:24): "bitter-tongued [*psogeros*] Archilochus with heavy-worded hatred fattening himself..." (ψογερὸν Ἀρχίλοχον βαρυλόγοις ἔχθεσιν / πιαινόμενον). While the opposition between praise and blame is explicit here, Nagy shows that this opposition is implicit even if it is not expressed: the potential of praise is blame, and vice versa.[16] In other words, praise and blame poetics entails an implicated meaning that contrasts with the literal, strictly denotational meaning of *ainos* and semantically related language. Since composer and audience share the same special code in order to carry off the communicative exchange, such implicated meaning indicates how figurative language partitions the performance event as a special context in which that implicated meaning makes sense, keying performance.

Parallelism

Bauman defines parallelism as "the repetition, with systematic variation, of phonic, grammatical, semantic, or prosodic structures, the combination of invariant and variant elements in the construction of an utterance" (Bauman 1977:19).[17] *Epinikion* exhibits elaborate and mutually imbricated patterns of regularity: prosodic structure and the patterned repetition of

11 For the benchmark description of praise and blame poetics, see Nagy 1979:147–150 and 222–242. See also Kirkwood 1984, Hubbard 1985:72 and 80, Gentili 1988:107–114, and Nagy 1990:147–150, 196–200, 203–206, 424–433, and passim. See Bonifazi 2004c:292–294 on the implicit connotations of the deictic demonstrative adjective (*e*)*keinos* in the context of blame poetics.

12 *Olympian* 2.95, 6.12, 11.7; *Nemean* 1.6.

13 *Olympian* 4.14, 7.16, 9.14, 9.48, 10.100; *Pythian* 1.43, 3.13, 4.140, 9.95; *Nemean* 1.72, 3.29, 4.93, 7.63, 8.39; *Isthmian* 5.59, 7.32, 8.69.

14 *Olympian* 13.2; *Pythian* 2.67, 4.168, 4.189, 5.107, 10.69; *Nemean* 5.19, 11.17.

15 Pindar *Nemean* 7.61, which Nagy 1990:223 discusses.

16 Kirkwood 1984 explicitly rejects Nagy's view that a poetics of praise implies a (rejected) poetics of blame in the context of *epinikion*. Steiner 2002 explores the link between poetics of blame and characterizations of consumption as gluttonous in *Olympian* 1, confirming Nagy's position.

17 On parallelism as a performance key, see also Foley 1995:12–13, 86–87 and 2002:89–90. On parallelism generally, see Jakobson 1960:358, 1966, and Waugh 1980:64–65.

words, sounds, or themes.[18] Such patterned regularities enable an audience to evaluate a performer's communicative competence on the basis of how well or poorly she creates and sustains a pattern of expectancy, while also artfully manipulating it within conventionally established parameters (Bauman 1977:19). In all epinician songs, prosody involves at least three patterns of repetition: (1) the basic metrical structure of an individual song is either dactylo-epitrite or Aeolic; (2) there is patterned repetition among individual lines; (3) there is patterned repetition at the level of strophic structure. For further examples of parallelism, Carola Greengard has described in detail aspects of formal arrangement in *epinikion* that involve the "adaptation and derivation of the archaic structure of ring composition" (1980:15):[19] framing, chiasmus, and recurrent diction. Devices that shape frames are recurrent diction, tautometric responsion, "cases in which similar rather than identical words are involved," compound words, and "repeated patterns of sound and/or rhythm" (Greengard 1980:19–22). Although Greengard does not identify them as such, these structural features are forms of parallelism: they key—or re-key for the modern audience—epinician performance.

Special Paralinguistic Features

In its entextualized state epinician language retains few paralinguistic features, such as "rate, length, pause duration, pitch contour, tone of voice, loudness," which are superimposed on or co-occurring with ordinary phonetic features of language (Bauman 1977:20). A feature of Pindar's special code and an example of parallelism, prosody is also a paralinguistic feature that organizes the flow of speech according to artistic rules for vocal sound patterns. Although we have no record for the mode of epinician song—no information about paralinguistic features that may have been associated with singing—the mere fact that *epinikion* is a sung form of communication indicates that such paralinguistic features serve by convention to key epinician performance.[20]

18 On lexical, phonic, and thematic repetition, see Stockert 1969, Schürch 1971, and Greengard 1980.

19 On ring composition in Pindar's songs see Illig 1932, Hamilton 1974:8, 56–71, 112–113, and Gerber 1982:xi (on *Olympian* 1, specifically). I discuss ring composition at greater length in Chapter 5 below.

20 For an admirable attempt to overcome this gap in our record of epinician performance, see Mullen 1982.

Special Formulae

Special formulae are, "in effect, markers of specific genres, and insofar as these genres are conventionally performed in a community, the formulae may serve as keys to performance" (Bauman 1977:21).[21] Bundy gives the following formulaic elements of *epinikion*:

- a "transitional formula" signals the end of a descriptive passage and moves a song from a foil to the central topic, the *laudandus*'s achievement (1962:2–3);
- ἴσθι νῦν (*isthi nun*) 'know now': νῦν (*nun*) 'now' frequently occurs "in the introduction of climactic terms" of a priamel and ἴσθι (*isthi*) 'know' is "the regular asseveration" that follows a summary priamel (20);
- "the formulaic designation of the *laudandus*'s home city" (21n48 and 23n53);
- the "gnomic climax" of a summary foil, through which the composer asserts the importance of propriety (37);
- ἀλλά (*alla*) 'but' and καὶ νῦν (*kai nun*) 'and now' are "formulaic" in climaxes to a name priamel (37–38);
- the "σιγά [*siga* 'silence'] motive" which "implies that to overdo a subject brings the speaker little pleasure, and...to know when to cease may actually increase it" and "concerns itself with the advantage or disadvantage of the *speaker* in terms of audience reaction" (75, emphasis in original);[22]
- the "χρέος-τεθμός [*khreos-tethmos* 'necessity-assignment'] motive," through which the composer expresses the necessity of sticking to his topic, the "assignment" (42);
- motifs associated with the theme of the "praise of wealth and its proper use": "(1) εὐεργεσία [*euergesia* 'act of kindness'] (good works, liberality, indifference to gain); (2) human expectations (shared humanity, human dependence on God or fate); and (3) enduring fame (occasionally literal immortality)" (86–87).

None of these are formulae in the sense of "special phrases," as described in Foley's discussion of performance keys in *How to Read an Oral Poem*: "the *guslar*'s (and Bishop Njegoš's) 'well-wrought tower' or 'shaggy brown horse' or Homer's

[21] On special formulae as a performance key, see also Foley 1995:13–14, 81, and 2002:90–91.

[22] Cf. Kyriakou 1996:18 on "hush passages" in Pindar's *epinikia* and Burnett 2005:68-69 and 86 on "[t]he melodramatic choral trick of self-imposed silence."

'wine-dark sea' or the Old English poet's 'foamy-necked ship'" (Foley 2002:90). If we consider verbal art as performance cross-culturally, then we should not expect that special formulae will always be phraseological words, like the Homeric epithet, or that they are "of equal importance in all oral poetries," as Foley stipulates (Foley 2002:90). I will show in Chapters Three and Four that the *ways* of epinician speaking—stylistic patterns that constitute the epinician *way* of speaking—are discursive formulae that are conventional to *epinikion*.[23] The Appendix to *Pindar's Verbal Art* presents evidence suggesting that the use of these ways of epinician speaking are so highly patterned that deviations from such patterns can be artistically meaningful. When special formulae occur, even conceived in terms of the list of Bundy's formulaic conventions of *epinikion*, they serve, along with other performance keys, to segment performance as a specially framed speech event.[24]

Appeal to Tradition

An appeal to tradition keys performance by referring to traditional conventions as a standard for the audience's evaluation of the performer's verbal artistic competence (Bauman 1977:21). "Either explicitly or implicitly," as Foley describes this key to performance, "oral poets are constantly establishing and reestablishing the authority of their words...by reaffirming their ties to an ongoing way of speaking, to an expressive mode larger than any one individual" (Foley 2002:91). Pindar's use of *humnos* 'song of praise' illustrates his explicit appeals to tradition. As Calame has argued, the example of Pindar's *Nemean* 5, whose mythological narrative depicts the Muses, led by Apollo, performing during the wedding of Peleus and Thetis, shows that *humnos* "defines itself as a song in which gods and heroes are celebrated" (2001:75). Calame goes on to make the important observation that the diversity of ways in which Archaic Greek forms of song use the term *humnos* indicates that it is not considered a lyric genre until the Alexandrian period (2001:78). As a strategy in a song of praise, rather than a genre of verbal art, Pindar at times appeals to the tradition of *humnos*. *Olympian* 2, for example, begins with an invocation addressed to *humnoi*:

23 The existence of discursive formulae in *epinikion* will corroborate the research of Martin (1984 and 1989), who has demonstrated that the formulaic quality of Archaic Greek poetry can be identified at the discursive and speech act level of communication in addition to that of prosodically defined phraseological word formulae.

24 On framing of performance events see Bauman 1977:9; Foley 1995:14–15 and 87 and 2002: 91–92.

Ἀναξιφόρμιγγες ὕμνοι
τίνα θεόν, τίν' ἥρωα, τίνα δ' ἄνδρα κελαδήσομεν;

Olympian 2.1–2

Lyre-ruling *humnoi*,
of what god, of what hero, of what man shall we sing in praise?

This passage is an appeal to tradition, serving to locate *Olympian* 2 in relation to existing conventions for praise associated with the strategy of *humnos*. Rather than resorting to literal exegesis to interpret Pindar's references to song and dance, we can more empirically interpret them as explicit appeals to tradition that key performance, as in the passage's opening, where Pindar aligns his composition with the traditional *humnos*. Some examples of other explicit appeals to tradition include references to Homer, a past authority who demonstrates the power of persuasive speech to create an enduring record of action (*Pythian* 4.277, *Nemean* 7.21, and *Isthmian* 4.37);[25] one reference to Arkhilokhos (*Olympian* 9.1) positively compares that poet's art with epinician praise;[26] another, discussed above, specifically contrasts Pindar's praise poetry with Arkhilokhos' blame poetry (*Pythian* 2.55).

We have already seen examples of implicit appeals to tradition: (1) the Doric features of the epinician way of speaking are an implicit appeal to traditions of choral song; (2) the prosodic features of Pindar's *epinikia* are an implicit appeal to traditions of Archaic Greek song as opposed to poetry;[27] (3) Aeolic features of epinician language are an implicit appeal to tradition that connects Pindar's songs with older predecessors; (4) Pindar's praise and blame poetics is an implicit appeal to the traditional poetics of *ainos*. Whether explicit or implicit, Pindar's appeals to tradition key epinician performance by inviting an audience to interpret and evaluate his songs on the basis of conventional and communal standards for performance.

Disclaimer of Performance

A first-person voice often interrupts the course of Pindar's songs, a phenomenon that is part of the motivation for the hypothesis that Pindar uses an "oral

25 See Nisetich 1989:22–23 and passim on the ways in which Pindar's treatment of Homer reflect more Pindar's conception of his own poetry than of Homer's poetry.

26 The scholia report that the opening lines of *Olympian* 9 refer to the *tênella kallinike* cry. Originally in a hymn to Herakles composed by Arkhilokhos, *tênella kallinike* was used as an impromptu victory song. For a recent discussion of the passage, with sources, see Thomas 2007:144–145.

27 Here I am drawing from Nagy's distinction between song and poetry (1990:17–51).

subterfuge" to represent his putatively written compositions as spontaneous speech.[28] These *Abbruchsformeln* 'break-off formulas' can be thought of as saying one thing and doing another, in the sense that Foley (2002:93) explains disclaimers of performance: "saying you can't means asserting that you can and you will."[29] Here is an example of such a break-off:

> ἐμοὶ δ' ἄπορα γαστρίμαργον μακάρων τιν' εἰπεῖν· ἀφίσταμαι.
>
> *Olympian* 1.52
>
> For me it is impossible to say that any of the blessed ones is
> gluttonous; I stay away from that.

In this passage Pindar displays his observance of the conditions for appropriate speech expressed by gnomic statements that occur earlier in the song:

> ἦ θαυματὰ πολλά, καί πού τι καὶ βροτῶν
> φάτις ὑπὲρ τὸν ἀλαθῆ λόγον
> δεδαιδαλμένοι ψεύδεσι ποικίλοις ἐξαπατῶντι μῦθοι.[30]
>
> *Olympian* 1.28–29
>
> Truly wondrous are many things, and, as it seems, mortals'
> speech in excess of a true account,
> stories crafted with ornate lies, are utterly deceptive.

One example of "stories crafted with ornate lies" is the story that Pelops' ivory shoulder replaced the flesh and bone shoulder eaten by Demeter in another version of the Pelops story. By refusing to tell such a story (*Olympian* 1.52), Pindar observes the conditions for propriety communicated at *Olympian* 1.28–29. This is one sense in which Pindar says one thing and does another: by *saying* that he will not tell a deceptive story, he *performs* a display of his competence in the appropriate use of speech. In this respect, we can see the

28 See Bauman 1977:21–22 and Foley 1995:15, 87, and 2002:92–93 on the disclaimer of performance as a performance key. On Pindaric *Abbruchsformeln*, see Schadewaldt 1928:267–268, 286, 312, Hamilton 1974:16–17, Race 1990:41–57, Kyriakou 1996, and Mackie 2003:9–37.

29 Mackie (2003:6, 9–37) explains Pindaric break-offs as "a safeguard against κόρος [*koros*] 'excess'." See also Race 1980 on rhetorical functions of break-offs.

30 Here I follow Bowra's edition of Pindar (1935). Snell and Maehler's edition (1997) has the noun θαύματα (*thaúmata*) 'wonders.' Their critical apparatus does not acknowledge the readings of the major MSS., which have either the unusual adjective θαυματά (*thaumatá*) 'wondrous' or the singular noun θαῦμα (*thauma*) with the neuter plural article τά (*ta*). The *Codex Vaticanus* evidences the prior reading, and Bowra identifies this manuscript as the most reliable at this locus (1935:v and 2). Gildersleeve, who maintains that he made no emendations to his edition, also accepts the reading θαυματά (*thaumatá*) (1890:132). So does Fisker 1990:35.

break-off at *Olympian* 1.52 as an example of Bundy's *siga*-motif, a Pindaric formula that corresponds to Bauman's characterization of the disclaimer of performance, which "serves as a moral gesture, to counterbalance the power of performance to focus heightened attention on the performer, and a key to performance itself" (1977:23).

There is another sense in which Pindar says one thing and does another at *Olympian* 1.52 because this disclaimer occurs after Pindar has actually told the deceptive story that he refuses to tell (*Olympian* 1.46–51). Although Pindar distances himself from this deceptive story with the statement at line 52, through the strategy of reporting the story in indirect discourse, and by attributing it to an untrustworthy source, "a jealous neighbor" (line 48), it is still a component of his composition; he *says* one thing and *does* another.[31] In the context of *Olympian* 1 as a whole, Pindar reproduces the deceptive story about how Pelops got his ivory shoulder to heighten the contrast with his own version of the story. To report the deceptive story is an implicit appeal to tradition through which Pindar displays his ability to produce the famous version of the story that he de-selects.

Performance Keys Conclusion

A crucial implication of the dedicated use of epinician language in epinician performance, the consequence of the fact that epinician language is a register, is that *epinikion* entails culture-specific ways of meaning. The communicative means used in epinician performance key that performance event as such, and this keying sets up a special frame for the interpretation of messages, so that it "contrasts with at least one other frame, the literal" (Bauman 1977:9).[32] Epinician performance keys enable an audience, ancient or modern, to evaluate and interpret *epinikion* in terms of the art form's idiomatic, connotative

31 Thus Mackie 2003:13 does not account for the fact that Pindar actually does tell the story. With respect to Pindar's attribution of the de-selected story about Pelops to a jealous neighbor, Bulman 1992:13 writes that "Pindar demonstratively rejects φθόνος [*phthonos*], damning it in others and quelling it in himself."

32 Closely resonant with Bauman is Nagy's view that "performance frames composition, and we cannot fully grasp the role of composition without knowing about this frame" (1994–1995:14; cf. 1994–1995:19). On frame analysis, I draw from Goffman 1974. Cf. Steiner's comments: "The breakdown of literal levels of meaning sets us on the road to rediscovery and rediscription, allowing poet and audience both to step back from a world of ordinary reference where words function as signs, to one of symbols, where words become significant in themselves. This symbolic language is notoriously dense, making words into a more substantial matter which does not merely represent, but expresses. Such opaque discourse replaces denotation with connotation, the hallmark of metaphoric speech" (1986:149–150).

meaning. Given that *epinikion* is a speech event, as the epinician performance keys indicate, our recognition of the existence of a conventional event-idiom link supports a further conclusion: Pindar is an oral poet. The special code, figurative language, forms of parallelism, and special paralinguistic features unambiguously cue audiences, both ancient and modern, to treat *epinikion* as a speech event, not a writing/reading event. Special formulae, appeals to tradition, and disclaimers of performance regulate the reception of each epinician song according to song and performance traditions and according to participation rules for performance—especially the participation of the audience as critical and highly competent evaluators of *epinikion*. In the next two chapters I will describe the ways of epinician speaking that constitute the epinician way of speaking, paving the way toward an understanding of the strategies of epinician oral composition.

3

Ways of Epinician Speaking I

The first chapter of *Pindar's Verbal Art* urged a fundamental analytical reorientation to the epinician text, from words written to words spoken. Here a further analytical shift is motivated, that from text to context—more specifically, from text to speech event—as the object of analysis. Chapter Two demonstrated that the epinician text records features that key the speech event of epinician performance—or rhetorically re-key it from the perspective of a modern audience. Chapters 3 and 4 of *Pindar's Verbal Art* will describe the speech acts that constitute the event of epinician performance. In this phase of my study of epinician style I draw from Bakhtin's highly influential essay "The Problem of Speech Genres" (1986:60–102), following the lead of folklorists and linguistic anthropologists who have adapted Bakhtin's theory of the utterance to the study of texts and contexts whose constitutive features and social dynamics can be described in terms of intertextuality, the dialogical interaction between two or more instances or fields of discourse.[1] The rubric "speech genres" applies to the typical *ways* of speaking that constitute the epinician *way* of speaking. In Pindar's songs, gnomic statements, lyric passages, prayers, *angeliai* 'victory announcements', and mythological narratives are the simple speech genres or ways of epinician speaking that constitute the complex genre *epinikion*.[2] In this chapter I will first explain my philological method-

1 See generally Bauman 1992, Briggs and Bauman 1992, Hanks 1987 and 1996b, and Tarkka 1993. See Bauman 1992:138–139 specifically on "dialogic genres" and Briggs and Bauman 1992 and Tarkka 1993 on intertextuality. For applications of speech genre studies in linguistic anthropology and folklore to Archaic Greek verbal art, see Martin 1984 and 1989:42–44, 85, and 171. In contrast to the dialogical and dynamic approach to intertextuality modeled by these scholars, Morrison applies intertextuality in the close-cropped sense of "verbal echoes, parallel myths, similar passages, and recurring imagery/language" among Pindar's Sicilian odes (2007:20).

2 Bakhtin 1986:61–62 distinguishes between primary or simple speech genres and secondary or complex speech genres. Hanks 1987:671 describes the relationship between simple and complex genres as "a matter of relative inclusiveness." On primary and secondary genres

ology and then apply that methodology to a description of epinician lyric passages, *gnômai*, *angeliai*, and mythological narratives. Chapter 4 will focus on epinician prayers and conclude my study of the ways of epinician speaking by making some observations about how such a practical taxonomy of epinician speech acts can inform our understanding of epincian art. The Appendix to *Pindar's Verbal Art* records the findings of my description of the ways of epinician speaking for all of Pindar's victory songs.

By referring to ways of epinician speaking, I frame the study of Pindar's simple speech genres in terms of an ethnographic conception of style, as described by Hymes in his influential essay "Ways of Speaking" (1989).[3] Like Bakhtin, Hymes identifies a relationship between simple and complex genres; he understands genres as "stylistic structures," the "elementary, or minimal" forms of which include, by way of example, "riddles, proverbs, prayers, but also minimal verse forms, such as the couplet, and such things as greetings and farewells, where those have conventional organization" (1989:442–443).[4] *Pindar's Verbal Art* has so far looked at how epinician language is a register, a speech style dedicated to epinician performance.[5] In this chapter and the next I am going a step further to demonstrate that the epinician register is a composite of other registers. Each of the simple speech genres of *epinikion*—gnomic statements, lyric passages, prayer, *angelia*, and mythological narrative—has domains of use outside of *epinikion*, including, certainly, other (complex) genres of verbal art and, very likely, speech situations arising in the course of social life. These simple speech genres, then, are discrete stylistic structures, each possessing a characteristic voicing in its own right.

---

see also Bauman 1992:132 and Briggs and Bauman 1992:145. While my method of description differs significantly from his, Fränkel identifies the following typical elements of *epinikion*: "Victory odes are concerned with the victor, his family and his country [corresponding to *angelia*]; the poet also speaks of his own skill and of the particular poem [corresponding to what I refer to as the lyric speech genre]; he makes general reflexions on life and the powers that determine the course of events [corresponding to what I refer to as gnomic statements]; finally, he turns his eyes on the divine in prayer and meditation [corresponding to what I refer to as the precatory speech genre]... There is another specific element in a fifth class of material...namely myths of the gods and legends of the heroes [corresponding to what I refer to as mythological narrative]" (1973:440–441).

3 See Bakhtin 1981:259–422 and 1986:63–67 and passim on the relationship between genre and style.

4 See Briggs and Bauman 1992:140–141 on the relationship between style and genre "in the conceptual repertoire of the ethnography of speaking."

5 Again Hymes (1989:440) defines registers as "major speech styles associated with recurrent types of situations" within a community. Cf. Bakhtin's observation that "language, or functional, styles are nothing other than generic styles for certain spheres of human activity and communication" (1986:64).

Each simple speech genre of *epinikion* has a distinctive timbre, and epinician art entails, in part, orchestrating these autonomous voicings into the truly symphonic art of epinician performance. To describe the simple speech genres of *epinikion* enables us to pull apart, in abstract, the discursive threads that form the fabric of epinician art in order to understand how they combine with one another in practice. To pursue this description in terms of an ethnographic conception of style, specifically, foregrounds the communicative process as the object of analysis, where we can view epinician art as dynamic social action.[6] By contrast, existing studies of the structure or unity of Pindar's songs treat features like mythological narrative and gnomic statements as discursive chunks that can be manipulated on a page.[7] When we realize that *epinikion* is performed verbal art that entails speech and situated interaction between composer and audience, such formalism proves inadequate to the task of discovering how Pindar's art works.

Chapters 3 and 4 of *Pindar's Verbal Art* will describe how each simple speech genre of *epinikion* is constituted by the following features:

> *Speech Subject* (i.e. who speaks?)
> *Addressee*[8]
> *Speech Object*[9]

6 Cf. Hymes explanation of the rubric "ways of speaking": "My second reason for favoring *ways of speaking* is that it has analogy with 'ways of life,' on the one hand, and Whorf's term 'fashions of speaking,' on the other. The first analogy helps remind anthropologists that the ways of mankind do include ways of speaking, and helps remind linguists that speaking does come in ways, that is, shows cultural patterning" (1989:446, emphasis in original). See Hanks 1987:681 on the "organic link between style, genre, and action"—a link that is a central to *Pindar's Verbal Art*.

7 E.g. Hamilton 1974 and Greengard 1980. Hanks offers a more inclusive descriptive domain: "In a purely formal approach, genres consist of regular groupings of thematic, stylistic, and compositional elements. Generic types differ by the features or configurations by which they are defined, irrespective of the historical conditions under which the types come to exist and of the social values attached to them in a given context. On the other hand, genres can be defined as the historically specific conventions and ideals according to which authors compose discourse and audiences receive it. In this view, genres consist of orienting frameworks, interpretive procedures, and sets of expectations that are not part of discourse structure, but of the ways actors relate to and use language" (1987:670). See also Hanks 1987:676–677 and Briggs and Bauman 1992:146–147.

8 Bakhtin stresses the relationship between addressivity and genre: "Each speech genre in each area of speech communication has its own typical conception of the addressee, and this defines it as a genre" (1986:95). See Hanks 1987:682 for an application of Bakhtin's concept of addressivity.

9 I conceive of the speech object of epinician simple speech genres as analogous to the "semantic exhaustiveness of the theme," a factor of the finalization of the utterance (Bakhtin 1986:76–77). See Hanks (1987:692) for a discussion of Bakthin's concept of the finalization of the utterance in terms of "*kinds* of completeness" and "*levels* at which completion is achieved" (emphasis in original).

Speech Plan[10]
Spatial Dimension of the utterance
Temporal Dimension of the utterance

Note that I have referred to the "speech subject" as such both to be consistent with Bakhtin's descriptive terms and because I wish to foreground the importance of human agency in social practice.[11] From this point of view, the designation "speech subject" is a reminder that, according to the principle of intersubjective objectivity and an ethnographic mode of philology, my analysis aspires to describe epinician speech and performance from the subjective perspective of participants in the event of performance. For Bakhtin (1986:67–76) the "change of speaking subjects" is a feature of the utterance that especially distinguishes the descriptive methodology of his translinguistics from grammar and structural linguistics. The designation "speech subject" is also useful for distinguishing between the speaker or addresser of an utterance and what the utterance is about, the "speech object." It turns out that in ancient Greek this distinction may correspond to the difference between the grammatical subject of a sentence and the grammatical object of a sentence. In most cases, the speech plan of an utterance is to pursue or, better, perform its speech object. For example, the speech object of one type of prayer is an entreaty, and the speech plan of such a prayer is to perform that entreaty. I qualify below how I identify the spatial and temporal dimensions of each speech genre.

The main strategy that I use to discover the features constitutive of the simple genres of *epinikion* is the analysis of deictic features of epinician language.[12] Deixis is the descriptive term for the set of structural units in a language that pick out aspects of a speech event such as participants, time of the event, place of the event, objects referred to, and the relationships among

10 Cf. Bakhtin's (1986:77–78) definition of "the speaker's *speech plan* or *speech will*," a factor in the finalization of an utterance.

11 Bakhtin elaborates as follows: "The terminological imprecision and confusion in this methodologically central point of linguistic thinking [the concept of "speech"] result from ignoring the *real unit* of speech communication: the utterance. For speech can exist in reality only in the form of concrete utterances of individual speaking people, speech subjects. Speech is always cast in the form of an utterance belonging to a particular speaking subject, and outside this form it cannot exist" (1986:71, emphasis in original).

12 The main influences for my approach to deixis include: Bühler 1934:34–39, Jakobson 1957, Benveniste 1971:195–204 and 217–230, Levinson 1983:54–96, Hanks 1987, 1990, 1992, 1993, 1996a passim, 1996b, and Urban 1989. Studies that involve applying deixis to Pindar's songs include Felson 1984, 1999, and 2004c, D'Alessio 2004, Athanassaki 2004, Bonifazi 2004a, and Martin 2004. See also Danielewicz 1990, Calame 2004, Felson 2004b, and Peponi 2004 for studies of deixis in Greek poetry.

these aspects of speech; as Hanks describes them, deictics "are morphemes (or strings of morphemes) that in most languages make up closed paradigmatic sets": pronouns, demonstratives, articles, spatial adverbs, temporal adverbs, and presentative adverbs (1992:46–47). The "basic communicative function" (Hanks 1992:47) of deictics is to mark off the boundaries of a speech framework, to locate participants and other referents in relationship to that framework.[13] Using deixis as a descriptive basis for identifying the constitutive features of each simple speech genre of *epinikion* enables us to see how these speech genres are schemas for interaction between performer and audience. With its focus upon human agency and interaction, deixis, coupled with Bakhtin's approach to the study of speech behavior, makes it possible to pursue a truly participant-centered analysis.[14]

On the basis of deixis I identify three key dimensions of relationality among the features of simple speech genres. These patterns of relationality provide a basis for empirical description and for discovery of how simple speech genres combine to organize the complex genre of *epinikion*. My assumption is that, at the level of the complex genre of *epinikion*, the speech subject is Pindar and the addressee is the audience. In the context of performance a composition's author, the speech subject, is the event-participant principally accountable to the audience's evaluation. The composer-audience relationship then provides the communicative and interactional frame within which the emergent frameworks of simple speech genres occur. For this reason, I identify the composer-audience relationship as the origo of epinician performance, the interactional focal point. [15] The features of speech genres are relative to this origo in either of two senses: *inclusively* or *exclusively*.[16] Components of a speech genre may be in an inclusive or exclu-

13 Cf. Levinson: "Essentially deixis concerns the ways in which languages encode or grammaticalize features of the context of utterance or speech event, and thus also concerns ways in which the interpretation of utterances depends on the analysis of that context of utterance" (1983:54).

14 Cf. the view of folklorist Lotte Tarkka: "Situatedness of meaning, or the emergence of meaning in performance..., implies an act of communication, and thus persons (or a person) in the concrete sense of the word" (1993:180). See also Hanks 1987 and 1996b.

15 Here I am drawing from Hanks 1992:51 on the origo of an indexical framework. Mine is a highly simplified statement of the situation. Yet my description stands as a basis for discovering more precisely how, as Hanks writes, "a single deictic word stands for minimally two objects: the referent is the thing, individual, event, spatial or temporal location denoted; and the indexical framework is the origo ('pivot' or zero-point) relative to which the referent is identified (the speech event in which the act of reference is performed, or some part of this event)."

16 These are broadly gauged rubrics for what Hanks 1992:48–50 describes as relational features of deictics. See Bonifazi 2004a:394–407 for a classification of epinician deixis.

sive relationship relative to the origo of performance, and some features of a speech genre may be inclusive or exclusive relative to other features of the same speech genre. For example, the speech object of mythological narrative (events and figures reported in mythological narrative) is exclusive relative to the speech subject (composer in a third-person voice) and addressee (the audience) of the mythological narrative: events and figures described in an instance of mythological narrative occur in a framework that is exclusive relative to the frame of interaction between composer and audience. As I show below, the fundamentally constitutive feature of what I identify as the lyric speech genre is reflexivity: the speech subject is a participant in the current speech event, and the speech object is regularly some aspect of the current speech event (e.g. song or music or praise); such features of the lyric speech genre are inclusive relative to the frame of interaction between composer and audience.

These relations of inclusivity and exclusivity can be identified in terms of a central concept in Bakhtin's philosophy of language and literature: the chronotope.[17] As the word's Greek roots suggest, the word *chronotope* "expresses the inseparability of space and time" and is "a formally constitutive category of literature" (Bakhtin 1981:84). My ethnographic description of style in Pindar's *epinikia* captures the form of the chronotope by identifying the spatial and temporal dimensions of each simple speech genre.[18] In my analysis of epinician speech genres, three terms serve to identify how Pindar's language blocks out the chronotopic relations among speech genres:[19]

Immediate: a framework sharing the same, current frame of interaction between the subject and addressee of a given speech genre;

Non-immediate: a framework not sharing the same frame of interaction between speech subject and addressee;

Mythological: a mythological framework for events that do not share the same framework of interaction between speech subject and addressee.

17 Bakhtin explains: "We will give the name *chronotope* (literally, 'time space') to the intrinsic connectedness of temporal and spatial relationships that are artistically expressed in literature" (1981:84, emphasis in original).

18 Bakhtin writes: "The chronotope in literature has an instrinsic *generic* significance. It can even be said that it is precisely the chronotope that defines genre and generic distinctions, for in literature the primary category in the chronotope is time" (1981:84–85, emphasis in original).

19 Here too I adopt the rubrics for these categories from what Hanks 1992:48–50 identifies as relational features of deictics.

Mythological narrative, for example, always refers to events and figures that are exclusive, in terms of chronotope, relative to the event of performance.[20]

The following description of the ways of epinician speaking is necessary because, as Hanks has written, "[w]hether we read a text as fiction, parody, prayer, or documentary is a generic decision with important consequences for interpretation" (1987:670). With the increased fluency in the epinician way of speaking that we gain through our knowledge of the ways of epinician speaking, we become more fully competent audience members to Pindar's art.[21] This description of speech genres is ultimately based on my analysis of Pindar's entire epinician corpus. Because it is a work relatively familiar to a general audience of classicists, I use *Olympian* 1 as an illustrative example in this and the next two chapters of *Pindar's Verbal Art*. This song commemorates the victory of Hieron, tyrant of Syracuse, in the single horse race at the Festival for Olympian Zeus in 476 BCE.

Gnomic Style

The dominantly constitutive stylistic feature of Pindar's gnomic style is its inclusive indefiniteness.[22] The rubric "inclusive indefiniteness" captures the

20 However, this is a valid observation only at the level of simple speech genre. At the level of the complex speech genre of *epinikion*, the act of doing mythological narrative is inclusive relative to the event of performance. On the temporal relationship between narrated events and the act of narration see Bauman 1986a:54–77 and Hansen 1990.

21 As Briggs and Bauman write: "a crucial part of the process of constructing intertextual relations may be undertaken by the audience" (1992:157).

22 Aristotle's characterization of *gnômai* identifies both its indefinite quality and its situatedness (*Rhetoric* 2.21.2). Mackie captures this quality of gnomic statements, observing: "A gnome is...by nature a general statement, designed to apply to any number of different situations" (2003:18). Boeke 2007 is the current point of departure on Pindar's *gnômai*; she approaches this speech genre from the point of view of the referential function of language, as described in my Introduction above. See earlier Bischoff 1938. Bowra 1964:224 identifies the gnomic statement as a "traditional part of choral song" and elsewhere writes: "The strength of Pindar's maxims lies in his ability to take a common theme and make it uncommon by putting it into the most suggestive and provocative terms. In substance his maxims have often been uttered before, but his presentation of them is new and striking through the personal touch which he gives to them" (1964:226; cf. 229–230). Hamilton 1974:16 defines the gnomic statement as "an aphorism...a concise statement of a generalized truth." See also Hamilton 1974:115–116 on "Gnomic Clusters," Slater 1979:65–66 on "gnomic progression." Bundy 1962:7–8 describes gnomic statements as a foil in a summary priamel; see Bundy 1962 passim for other formal functions of gnomic statements. Hubbard 1985:143–145 treats gnomic statements in the context of what he identifies as the subject/object relation. I agree with Race (1986:29–30) in linking Pindar's use of gnomic statements with a "didactic tradition which includes Hesiod (especially the *Works and Days*), Theognis, Phokylides, and a lost work containing

fact that the deictic features of gnomic style do not indicate a specific speech subject, addressee, spatial dimension, and temporal dimension (thus the indefinite quality of gnomic statements), but must bear upon the composition in which they occur (thus the inclusive quality of gnomic statements). To clarify this point, I draw from William Hansen's distinction between structural and applied messages in storytelling, where a structural message is "the central message or point of a text taken by itself as a text without a particular context" and an applied message "is the message that a teller actually employs the story to communicate on a particular occasion, the point he or she wishes to make with it" (1982:101). The aphoristic quality of gnomic statements may tempt us to interpret them as structural messages about social, religious, or moral views that transcend particular contexts and stand (structurally) on their own.[23] Indeed, the pragmatic indefiniteness of the ethnographic features constitutive of gnomic style is implicitly indicative of how *gnômai* are statements that are of general import and concern humans, again, in general.[24] Although gnomic statements, stylistically, are not anchored to a particular context, the messages of actual gnomic statements are to be understood as applied to the local and emergent context in which they are embedded: the indefiniteness of gnomic style and the practical meaning of *gnômai* in the emergent context of performance apply to participants in the performance of the song in which they occur.[25] The following is a summary of the gnomic statement's features:

---

the 'sayings of Cheiron.'" On the question of the influence of the *Kheironos Hupothêkai* 'Sayings of Cheiron' upon Pindar's *epinikia*, see Chapter 4. My view of Pindar's gnomic statements resonates with Steiner's: "[a]long with praise, gnomic reflections play an important role within the epinician song, pointing out the relevance of the particular event to all men and satisfying the didactic role that poetry also fills" (1986:22–23). Currie 2005:78–81 explores the question of whether Pindar's gnomic statements communicate the possibility of literal immortality through hero cult for the *laudandus* or the symbolic immortality of *kleos*.

23 Boeke 2007 abstracts Pindar's *gnômai* from their local communicative contexts in order to to develop a cosmological map (29–101), which she then applies as an interpetive vantage point upon *Olympian* 12, *Isthmian* 4, *Olympian* 13 (103–159), and upon the role of the epinician poet (161–194). I am wary of such absolutizing approaches to messages in Pindar because they risk casting him more as a philosopher or hierophant than a performer of traditional art, a danger compellingly addressed by Nisetich 1989:27–35. Nisetich 1988 also nicely captures how intimations of religion in *Olympian* 2 can be best grasped by interpreting them in light of the occasionality of the song.

24 In this connection I agree with Hubbard's caution concerning "the critical bias [that] has resulted from an overemphasis on individual gnomic statements" (1985:7) and "the danger of taking such gnomes out of context and privileging them as the poet's doctrine" (108).

25 This description of gnomic statements resonates closely with Hubbard's description of Pindar's first-person indefinite: "a generalized, gnomic first person that includes poet, patron, audience, and all men who participate in the same community of values" (Hubbard 2002:257–258).

Speech Subject: third-person voice of composer in an inclusive relation to speech object;

Addressee: indefinite, but inclusive of all participants in performance event;

Speech Object: statements about appropriate speech and/or actions; formal features of the speech object are indefiniteness, deictic (e.g. indefinite article) and lexical (e.g. neuter forms of adjectives used substantively);

Speech Plan: to express socially conventional rules for appropriate speech and action;

Spatial Dimension: indefinite, but inclusive; the utterance's addressivity and speech object extend to all participants in the performance event, which, either actually or by convention and rhetorically, occur in face-to-face interaction among Pindar, chorus, and audience;

Temporal Dimension: indefinite, but inclusive.

A stretch of gnomic statements at *Olympian* 1.28–35 illustrates that Pindar's *gnômai* are constituted by these ethnographic features. Consider first the following passage:

> ἦ θαυματὰ πολλά, καί πού τι καὶ βροτῶν
> φάτις ὑπὲρ τὸν ἀλαθῆ λόγον
> δεδαιδαλμένοι ψεύδεσι ποικίλοις ἐξαπατῶντι μῦθοι.
>
> *Olympian* 1.28–29

> Truly wondrous are many things, and, as it seems, mortals'
> speech in excess of a true account,
> stories crafted with ornate lies, are utterly deceptive.

The features of the speech genre *gnôma* occurring in this passage are:

Speech Subject: third-person voice of composer, as indicated by third-person verb ἐξαπατῶντι (line 29) in an inclusive relationship to the speech object;

Hubbard cites *Pythian* 11.50–54 as an example of the first-person indefinite, but my description of the ways of epinician speaking leads to the conclusion that the two-word utterance (*phthoneroi d' amunontai* "jealous people are driven off") at the end of line 54 is the only gnomic utterance in the passage (see Appendix). Young 1968:58–59 and Fränkel 1975:475n12 and 514 identify the first-person indefinite as a conventional feature of the victory song. See also Köhnken 1971:209–210 and Kyriakou 1996:24–25.

Addressee: all participants in the speech event; there is no evidence of qualified addressivity;

Speech Object: appropriate speech; features of indefiniteness include: θαυματὰ πολλά (line 28), neuter plural adjectives used substantively; βροτῶν (line 28) is a generic reference to humans; the adverb που with indefinite pronoun τι (line 28);

Speech Plan: to express a basis for evaluating whether mortals' speech is true or appropriate;

Spatial Dimension: indefinite, but inclusive;

Temporal Dimension: indefinite, but inclusive; the present tense verb ἐξαπατῶντι (line 29) does not limit the temporal scope of the evaluation to the here and now.

The dominant characteristic of the gnomic statement in lines 28–29 is an inclusive indefiniteness, evidenced by the passage's speech subject, addressee, speech object, speech plan, and spatial and temporal aspects. Because my focus is upon the epinician text as a record of epinician speech practices, I interpret the force of gnomic statements in terms of the dominantly constitutive framework of social interaction in epinician performance, namely the relationship between composer and audience. From the point of view of this relationship, the speech object of the gnomic statement is inclusive relative to speech subject and addressee. The regular speech object of *gnômai*, socially conventional rules for appropriate speech and action, guides the composer's composition and the audience's reception and evaluation of it. This is another way of explaining how gnomic statements are very often forms of metacommunication that, in a sense, comment upon aspects of epinician speech and performance.

Inclusive indefiniteness is also characteristic of the following lines:

> Χάρις δ', ἅπερ ἅπαντα τεύχει τὰ μείλιχα θνατοῖς,
> ἐπιφέροισα τιμὰν καὶ ἄπιστον ἐμήσατο πιστόν
> ἔμμεναι τὸ πολλάκις.
>
> *Olympian* 1.30–32

> But grace, which provides all mild things for mortals,
> bringing honor, it makes the unbelievable believable,
> often.

The ethnographic features constituting this passage as a gnomic statement are:

Speech Subject: third-person voice of composer, as evidenced by third-person verbs τεύχει (line 30) and ἐμήσατο (line 31) in an inclusive relationship to the speech object;

Addressee: all participants in the speech event; there is no evidence of qualified addressivity;

Speech Object: *kharis* and how it effects or jeopardizes appropriate speech; features of indefiniteness include ἅπαντα...τὰ μείλιχα (line 30), a phrase with neuter plural adjectives used substantively; θνατοῖς (line 30); ἄπιστον (line 31) neuter singular adjective used substantively;

Speech Plan: to express how *kharis* benefits mortals and effects appropriate speech;

Spatial Dimension: indefinite, but inclusive;

Temporal Dimension: indefinite, but inclusive; the present tense of the verb τεύχει (line 30) and the aorist tense (by convention treated as present tense) of the verb ἐμήσατο (line 31) do not limit the temporal scope of this utterance.

This passage too is an example of a gnomic statement that communicates rules for appropriate speech. In this case *kharis* 'grace, favor, charm' (line 30), which serves as a principle of reciprocity throughout *Olympian* 1, is the force behind persuasive speech. In the case of the performance of *Olympian* 1 the implication of this general principle is that, if the composition of the song observes the rules for reciprocity entailed in *kharis*, then the composition is trustworthy. This general principle for appropriate speech sets up another basis (along with lines 28–29, discussed above) for evaluating the composer's competence. Thus the message communicated by these gnomic statements is not strictly structural but applies to the speech event of *Olympian* 1's performance.

Lines 33–34 contain another gnomic statement that contributes to the argument about appropriate speech in the series of *gnômai* at lines 28–35:

> ἁμέραι δ' ἐπίλοιποι
> μάρτυρες σοφώτατοι.
>
> *Olympian* 1.33–34

> days to come
> are the wisest witnesses.

The ethnographic features of this *gnôma* are:

Speech Subject: third-person voice of composer, as indicated by understood third-person plural verb in an inclusive relationship to the speech object;

Addressee: all participants in the speech event; there is no evidence of qualified addressivity;

Speech Object: the testimony of time, with the implication that time evaluates whether speech is appropriate or not;

Speech Plan: to communicate that time assesses whether speech is appropriate or not;[26]

Spatial Dimension: indefinite, but inclusive;

Temporal Dimension: indefinite, but inclusive.

Lines 33–34 contribute to the gnomic passage's emergent argument (i.e. lines 28–35) about rules for appropriate speech that apply to participants in the event of *Olympian* 1's performance; they apply inclusively to the composer's composition of a song and to the audience's reception of that song.

This is the last in the series of gnomic statements that we have been considering:

> ἔστι δ' ἀνδρὶ φάμεν ἐοικὸς ἀμφὶ δαιμόνων καλά· μείων γὰρ αἰτία.
>
> *Olympian* 1.35

> It is appropriate for a man to say upright things about the gods;
> for fault is less.

The features occurring in this *gnôma* are:

Speech Subject: third-person voice of composer, indicated by the third-person singular verb ἐστί in an inclusive relationship to the speech object;

Addressee: all participants in the speech event; there is no evidence of qualified addressivity;

Speech Object: appropriate speech about the gods and the consequences for observing this social convention; features of indefiniteness include: ἀνδρὶ, used here like the indefinite pronoun τινί; the impersonal use of third-person singular verb ἐστί with infini-

26 I would suggest, then, that lines 33–34 imply that subsequent reperformance would signal time's affirmative evaluation of *Olympian* 1's performance.

tive φάμεν; the occurrence of neuter plural adjective καλά used substantively;

Speech Plan: to express social conventions for appropriate speech about the gods;

Spatial Dimension: indefinite;

Temporal Dimension: indefinite, but inclusive.

Line 35 focuses upon one particular dimension of *kharis*, understood in *Olympian* 1 as a principle of reciprocity: the reciprocal relationship between gods and humans. To read the passage as a moralizing statement or as an expression of Pindar's religious views does not account for how the passage *applies* in performance. Given the patterning of features generic to gnomic statements, this passage, like other *gnômai*, is generalizing in a way that is inclusive of participants in the event of *Olympian* 1's performance. From this point of view line 35 expresses a criterion for the audience's evaluation of the composer's observance of rules for appropriate speech. Positive evaluation of Pindar's speech about the gods affirms that Pindar does *kharis* well, with the further implication, based upon lines 30–32, that his speech is true (*piston* 'believable', line 31) and the still further implication that when Pindar praises Hieron, this praise is valid.

Line 35 concludes the argument of lines 28–35 about appropriate speech. The ideas, points of view, and values that these lines express can be understood in their emergent sense not as Pindar's philosophical outlooks or moral attitudes but as artistic messages. At a formal level, Pindar's gnomic statements are wholly couched in the artistic idiom of *epinikion*: lines 28–35 are keyed to epinician performance. In addition, the content of the lines is artful because its argument about appropriate speech applies in a particular (pragmatic) way to praise poetics: as a means for evaluating the performance of *Olympian* 1 as a work of verbal art.

The Lyric Speech Genre

The dominant feature of this speech genre is its self-reflexive quality,[27] which characteristically has a first-person speech subject so that it is, in part, "lyric" in

[27] Bowra 1964:322 identifies "personal remarks, especially about the poet and his patrons" as a traditional element of the victory ode. I roughly separate these into the lyric speech genre—Bowra's remarks about the poet—and *angelia*, remarks about patrons. However, I stress that the basis for my description is the ethnographic/deictic features of each type of utterance; I do not define the simple speech genres solely in terms of content. What I am referring to as the lyric style embraces passages labeled by Hamilton 1974:16–17 as "Poet's Task," defined "as

Jakobson's sense of lyric poetry as "oriented toward the first person" (1960:357). Pindar regularly describes composition or speech or performance using the lyric speech genre, so that it is reflexive in the sense that its speech object and/or speech plan typically has something to do with the current moment of communication. The rubric "lyric" has the further advantage of being consistent with Nagy's demonstration (1990:35), on the basis of historical linguistics, that the designation of "lyric poetry" or "melic poetry" is applicable to Pindar: it is appropriate that the simple speech genre characterized by reflexive features (representing communication, from the point of view of the individual epinician song) should correspond to the broader generic category of Archaic Greek song types to which it belongs. The lyric speech genre has the following features:

Speech Subject: first person, singular (composer) or plural (chorus), in an inclusive relation to the speech object;

Addressee: audience as participant in framework of lyric speech genre and in speech object of that framework (not always indicated in the text, but implicit to social interaction among composer, chorus, and audience);

Speech Object: epinician language, epinician performance, participants in the event of epinician performance, or the speech plan of *epinikion*;

Speech Plan: to praise, to sing, or to describe epinician language, conventions, and performance;

Spatial Dimension: immediate, "here";

Temporal Dimension: immediate, "now."

The following passage is one example of the lyric speech genre:

ἐμοὶ δ' ἄπορα γαστρίμαργον μακάρων τιν' εἰπεῖν· ἀφίσταμαι.

Olympian 1.52

For me it is impossible to say that any of the blessed ones is gluttonous; I stay away from that.

the poet introducing himself into the poem to talk about his obligations," and Hamilton identifies the Pindaric *Abbruchsformel* as a "subdivision of Poet's Task." Hornblower 2004:361 identifies *egô*-asyndeton as a Pindaric strategy for making self-reflexive comments about the poetic process.

The features of the lyric speech genre occurring in this passage are:

Speech Subject: first person, indicated deictically by the pronoun ἐμοί and by the verb ἀφίσταμαι;

Addressee: not indicated;

Speech Object: appropriate speech about the gods and the expression of the composer's observance of this convention of propriety;

Speech Plan: to communicate the composer's observance of propriety concerning speech about the gods;

Spatial Dimension: immediate, as indicated by reference to a participant in performance, the composer (ἐμοί and the first-person singular verb ἀφίσταμαι refer to the composer);

Temporal Dimension: immediate, as indicated by the present tense of the implied verb ἐστί and by the present tense of the verb ἀφίσταμαι.

The features of this lyric passage have the dominantly organizing feature of reflexivity: they refer to features constitutive of the current speech genre—the speech subject, speech object, speech plan, spatial dimension, and temporal dimension. Although there is no explicit reference in the passage to an addressee, the accumulated evidence of my analysis of speech genres in Pindar's *epinikia* indicates that, on the basis of the very facts that line 52 is a lyric speech genre and that the lyric speech genre has a reflexive quality, the passage can be understood to take place within the framework of interaction between epinician performer/composer and the epinician audience.[28] Pindar's expression of willingness to observe social conventions about appropriate speech implies the audience's evaluation of his song on the basis of criteria for appropriate speech, anchoring the utterance in the origo of performance, the composer-audience interaction.

A second lyric passage in *Olympian* 1 also has the dominantly organizing feature of reflexivity:

ἐμὲ δὲ στεφανῶσαι
κεῖνον ἱππίῳ νόμῳ

28 To further support this claim, according to principles of linguistic pragmatics the very use of first-person pronouns and other forms of first-person reference implies (pragmatically) that there is an addressee who is a participant in the currently happening speech event. The use of 'I' implies an addressee that is 'not-I' and, so, 'you', and the use of 'you' implies a speaker, a 'not-you' and so 'I' who addresses 'you'. Cf. Benveniste 1971:225.

Αἰοληΐδι μολπᾷ
χρή· πέποιθα δὲ ξένον
μή τιν᾽ ἀμφότερα καλῶν τε ἴδριν †ἅμα καὶ δύναμιν κυριώτερον
τῶν γε νῦν κλυταῖσι δαιδαλωσέμεν ὕμνων πτυχαῖς.

Olympian 1.100–105

It is necessary for me to crown
that man with a rider's measure
in Aeolic song.
I am persuaded that there is not any host
both skilled in upright things and at the same time more sovereign in power
among people today to ornament with famous layers of hymns.

The features of the lyric speech genre occurring in this passage are:

Speech Subject: first person, indicated by the first-person pronoun ἐμέ (line 100) and by the first-person verb πέποιθα (line 103);

Addressee: not explicitly indicated;

Speech Object: (1) song and epinician language, indicated by ἱππίῳ νόμῳ (line 101), Αἰοληΐδι μολπᾷ (line 102), and κλυταῖσι... ὕμνων πτυχαῖς (line 105); (2) to decorate, that is, celebrate, Hieron (κεῖνον, line 101), indicated by στεφανῶσαι (line 100) and δαιδαλωσέμεν (line 105);

Speech Plan: to communicate the necessity for the composer to perform the speech object, indicated by χρή (line 103) and δαιδαλωσέμεν (line 105);

Spatial Dimension: immediate, indicated by reference to participants in the performance event, the composer (indicated by the first-person pronoun ἐμέ (line 100) and by the first-person verb πέποιθα (line 103) and Hieron, whose victory the poem commemorates, indicated by the deictic demonstrative κεῖνον (line 101);[29]

[29] Here I am making the assumption that Hieron would have been pragmatically present, whether physically or symbolically, at the original performance of *Olympian* 1. Intrepreting the function of *keinon* (line 101) in *Olympian* 1.100–103, Bonifazi explains that "different pragmatic positions of 'I' and of 'κ.' [for *keinon*] are made close, to underscore at the same time the physical—or symbolic—distance between the two, *and the possibly common frame shared by them*" (2004c:290, my emphasis). The common frame shared by the epinician composer and, in this case, the *laudandus*, is indicative of the self-reflexive quality of the lyric speech genre.

Temporal Dimension: immediate, indicated by reference to participants in speech event of the performance of this song and by present tense of χρή (line 103); πέποιθα (line 103) is regularly treated as a perfect with present meaning.[30]

As with line 52, lines 100–105 also possess the dominantly organizing feature of reflexivity: all of the passage's features explicitly concern the current speech event and participants in that event.

The example passages illustrate that in the lyric speech genre the fields of relationality have a reflexive quality: the chronotope is the here and now of performance; the relationship between the speech object—epinician language, epinician performance, participants in the event of epinician performance, or the speech plan of *epinikion*—is inclusive relative to both the participant framework (composer and audience) and to the chronotope (i.e. what is happening here and now is epinician speech). The reflexive quality of the lyric speech genre, then, can be seen in the social interaction among participants, its chronotopic configuration, and the contiguity of the speech object and speaking itself.

Angelia, Victory Announcement

Angelia is a simple speech genre that replicates what scholars identify as a conventional mode of discourse associated with athletic competition, the formal announcement of the athlete's victory. The conventional victory announcement may have included the athlete's name, his ancestry (often identified by the athlete's patronymic), the name of his home, and the event in which he was victorious. Pindar frequently uses words such as *angelia* 'message, news, announcement',[31] *angellein* 'to proclaim',[32] and *angelos* 'messenger'[33] to describe *epinikion* as the action of proclaiming the achievement of an athlete. Here I cite Laura Nash, whose book, *The Aggelia in Pindar*, is dedicated to the study of the relationship between Pindar's *epinikion* and the conventional victory announcement (1990:15):

> Pindar has at hand at least one fixed outline for determining the facts relevant to the victory and for giving them a structural foundation in the ode: the ἀγγελία [*angelia*]. Like the herald's proclamation at the festival, the epinician ἀγγελία [*angelia*] announces the

30 Cf. Gildersleeve 1890:138.

31 *Olympian* 3.28, 4.5, 8.82, 9.25, 14.21; *Pythian* 2.4, 2.41, 4.279, 8.50; *Isthmian* 8.41; *Fragment* 169.34.

32 *Olympian* 7.21; *Pythian* 1.32, 9.2. Cf. *Paean* 2.77.

33 *Olympian* 6.90; *Pythian* 4.278; *Nemean* 1.59, 6.57. Cf. *Paean* 6.101.

> victor's name, father, and city. The exact point at which the ἀγγελία [*angelia*] was pronounced in the games is unclear, but it is most likely to have been recited at the end of each event and/or at the final crowning of the victor. Pindar picks up the actual reference point for the victory announcement, the festival and specific contest, and usually includes these details in his poetic *angelia*.[34]

The relationship between the conventional victory announcement at the site of the games and the epinician *angelia* is a case of what Bakhtin calls heteroglossia.[35]

34 Bowra 1964:322 identifies "personal remarks...about...patrons" as a traditional element of the victory ode. Hamilton 1974:15 identifies two elements of what he refers to as the "Naming Complex" of the victory song: "the name of the victory and the name of the place of victory"; "name of the event, homeland, and father" often occur with the name of the victory and the name of the place of the victory, but only these two regularly occur in the "Naming Complex." Citing Hamilton, Most 1985:62–63 observes that "there are three elements which are found in every Pindaric epinician without exception: the name of the victor, the name of his city, and the name of the games in which the victory was won." He goes on to compare this epinician phenomenon to the formal victory announcement (where he gives at 63n18 Pindar's *Pythian* 1.29–33, the Olympian victor list [*Oxyrhynchus Paypyri* 222], and fragments of Phlegon of Tralles [F. Jacoby, *Fragmente der griechischen Historiker*, 257 F 1–34] as ancient sources for the victory announcement's standard content): "the same elements...almost certainly comprised the herald's announcement of victory at the games themselves—victor's name, city and discipline—and add one further element which, because it is implied by the very situation of utterance of the herald, the herald himself did not need to mention but the poets evidently must: the location of the games" (Most 1985:63). The content of the speech genre *angelia* includes what Race 1986:26 identifies as the "essential information" of the victory song. Steiner 1986:21 observes: "The epinician genre demands that the poet mention the critical factors of the event he celebrates. He must refer to the name of the victor, his father and city, the Games where he competed and the particular contest in which he achieved triumph." Miller 1993a:113 equates the conventional components of the victory announcement—in his terms, "facts of identity" and "facts of achievement"—with the raw material that provides the basis for the rhetorical organization of the victory song. Hubbard draws a nice connection between literary and material records, but for reasons that become clear below I disagree with his interpretation of that connection: "Indeed, the earliest inscribed bases of victory statues and other commemorative offerings, such as votive plaques and cauldrons, provide the formulaic elements naming the victor, father, city, contest, and divine patron, from which elements the genre of epinician epigram and ultimately epinician lyric developed" (2004:76). Kurke 1993:142–149 and Thomas 2007:158–159 also observe the similarities between inscriptions on victory monuments and Pindar's victory songs.

35 Hubbard's observation (2004:77) that "Pindar frequently presents his song as a re-enactment of the victor's crowning and proclamation by the herald of the games" is another way of stating that *angelia* is a form of heteroglossia in Pindar's *epinikia*. Hubbard goes on to make the observation that "an epinician poem is always already a reperformance and re-evocation of a ritualized moment that transpired in a pan-Hellenic space." I disagree, however, with Hubbard's view that such a correspondence between the victory announcement and *epinikion* suggests, in itself, that the performance venue for *epinikion* was the site of a victory.

Heteroglossia is a form of dialogization in which a work of verbal art organizes within itself a multiplicity of registers and speech genres conventional to other contexts and events of communication.[36] In the case of *angelia*, we witness uniquely and unambiguously a form of social heteroglossia in which Pindar organizes within his epinician composition a speech type, *angelia*, that belongs to a speech situation with its own constellation of schemes and strategies for communication. No other simple speech genre constitutive of the complex genre of *epinikion* draws such a direct connection between epinician performance and a historically attested domain of social practice as *angelia* does. *Angelia* is a discursive bridge between an epinician song and the achievement that it commemorates. Indeed, this connection between art and reality is one impetus to read Pindar as a historical record. In terms of my overall project, then, the simple speech genre *angelia* is a point of analysis that especially calls attention to philological methodology. The limitation of existing studies of epinician performance can be described as an inability to come to terms with what I think of as a fact of human social practice, that art *is* reality.[37] So the context of epinician performance is not—neither in the first instance, nor for the purposes of description and interpretation of the epinician texts—the historical backdrop understood as dates, names, and places, but, as it turns out, epinician performance itself. The

36 For the sake of consistency, in this definition I have couched Bakhtin's formulation in terms that I have been using in the course of *Pindar's Verbal Art*. In Bakhtin's words: "The novel can be defined as a diversity of social speech types (sometimes even diversity of languages) and a diversity of individual voices, artistically organized. The internal stratification of any single national language into social dialects, characteristic group behavior, professional jargons, generic languages, languages of generations and age groups, tendentious languages, languages of authorities, of various circles and of passing fashions, languages that serve the special socio-political purposes of the day, even of the hour (each day has its own slogan, its own vocabulary, its own emphasis)—this internal stratification present in every language at any given moment of its historical existence is the indispensable prerequisite for the novel as a genre. The novel orchestrates all its themes, the totality of the world of objects and ideas depicted and expressed in it, by means of the social diversity of speech types and by the differing individual voices that flourish under such conditions. Authorial speech, the speech of narrators, inserted genres, the speech of characters are merely those fundamental compositional unities with whose help heteroglossia can enter the novel; each of them permits a multiplicity of social voices and a wide variety of their links and interrelationships (always more or less dialogized). These distinctive links and interrelationships between utterances and languages, this movement of the theme through different languages and speech types, its dispersion into the rivulets and droplets of social heteroglossia, its dialogization—this is the basic distinguishing feature of the stylistics of the novel" (1981:262–263). See also Bakhtin 1981:301–331 on heteroglossia in the novel.

37 This is not intended as a philosophical statement that valorizes art, but as a more pedestrian observation that, from the point of view of practice, if things, including art, happen in social life, then they are real and available for description as such.

recognition that heteroglossia is characteristic of epinician art draws attention to the need for a mode of description that aspires to discover, not only the cause-and-effect relationship between the conventional victory announcement and *epinikion*, but also the artistic effects of dialogization. To that end, I present here a summary of the ethnographic features of the epinician *angelia*:

Speech Subject: composer in third-person voice exclusive from speech object (i.e. the composer is not a participant in the events that he describes);

Addressee: audience as a participant in framework of speech genre;

Speech Object: athlete, athlete's family, athlete's home state, and events that have occurred in a frame of social interaction temporally and spatially non-immediate relative to performance, such as the athlete's victory and/or prior victories, athletic victories of members of the athlete's family, and other achievements of the athlete or his family; the athlete whom an epinician song commemorates and/or his family members are potentially participants in the reported events as well as the event of performance;

Speech Plan: to report to the audience events that have occurred in a frame of social interaction non-immediate relative to performance event;

Spatial Dimension: usually non-immediate relative to performance event;

Temporal Dimension: usually non-immediate relative to performance event, but can track from non-immediate to immediate relative to the performance event.

The following passage contains what were probably the conventional elements of the formal victory announcement that occurred at the site of a victory:

ὅτε παρ᾽ Ἀλφεῷ σύτο δέμας
ἀκέντητον ἐν δρόμοισι παρέχων,
κράτει δὲ προσέμειξε δεσπόταν,
Συρακόσιον ἱπποχάρμαν βασιλῆα· λάμπει δέ οἱ κλέος
ἐν εὐάνορι Λυδοῦ Πέλοπος ἀποικίᾳ.

Olympian 1.20–24

> ...when beside the Alpheos River the horse drove,
> extending its ungoaded body in the race,
> and united its master with dominance,
> the Syracusan king and horse rider. His renown shines bright
> in the colony with noble people, the colony of Lydian Pelops.

This passage includes reference to the athlete Hieron (lines 22–23), to his home, Syracuse (line 23), and the event in which he was victorious, the single horse race (lines 20–22). To identify Syracuse as the "colony of Lydian Pelops" (line 24) describes Hieron's home in a way that serves simultaneously to refer to its mythological foundation and to introduce the segment of mythological narrative that begins in line 25. The ethnographic features of *angelia* in this passage are:

Speech Subject: composer-performer(s) in a third-person voice, indicated by third-person verbs προσέμειξε (line 22) and λάμπει (line 23);

Addressee: audience as the hearer of this *angelia*; audience does not participate in reported events;

Speech Object: the event of athletic competition at Olympia (a frame non-immediate relative to performance), the athlete's victory, and Hieron's *kleos* 'renown' (line 23);

Speech Plan: to report to the audience events that have occurred in a frame of social interaction that is non-immediate and/or distinctive from the current composer-audience interaction;

Spatial Dimension: the events connected with the athletic competition are spatially non-immediate relative to the performance frame, but the description of Hieron's *kleos* (line 23) may be seen as relevant to a spatially contiguous (i.e. immediate) frame;

Temporal Dimension: the events connected with the athletic competition are temporally non-immediate relative to the performance frame, but the description of Hieron's *kleos* (line 23) is in a temporally contiguous frame, as indicated by the present tense verb λάμπει (line 23).

Even in cases where there may be contiguity with respect to spatial and temporal dimensions of the event of performance and events reported during performance in the *angelia* speech genre, the respective frames of interaction entailed in performance and reported events remain distinct. In the following passage Pindar uses present tense verbs, which locate events described in the *angelia* as temporally contiguous with the event of performance, to describe Hieron as a ruler in Sicily, the location of the athlete's home *polis* of Syracuse:

> ...Ἱέρωνος...
> θεμιστεῖον ὃς ἀμφέπει σκᾶπτον ἐν πολυμήλῳ
> Σικελίᾳ δρέπων μὲν κορυφὰς ἀρετᾶν ἄπο πασᾶν,
> ἀγλαΐζεται δὲ καί
> μουσικᾶς ἐν ἀώτῳ.
>
> *Olympian* 1.11–15

> ...Hieron...
> who tends the traditional scepter in Sicily, full of flocks,
> who, while he plucks the flower of every virtue,
> is also adorned
> with the peak of musical craft.

The features of *angelia* occurring in this passage are:

Speech Subject: composer in third-person voice, indicated by the third-person verbs ἀμφέπει (line 12) and ἀγλαΐζεται (line 14);

Addressee: audience, which hears the report, but does not participate in action described (here, ruling in Sicily);

Speech Object: Hieron, participant in event of performance, indicated deictically by the relative pronoun ὅς (line 12), whose antecedent is Hieron (line 11), and his rule in Sicily;

Speech Plan: to report and to commemorate, indicated by the verb ἀγλαΐζεται (line 14), whose subject is ὅς (line 12);

Spatial Dimension: indeterminate, but distinctive frame from event of performance, as indicated principally by the third-person voice of the speaker;

Temporal Dimension: immediate relative to, but distinctive from, the event of performance.

To conclude this description of Pindar's *angelia*, a practical taxonomy of the ethnographic features of the speech genre is valuable for identifying the connection between the commemorating event of performance and the achievement that epinician performance celebrates—the connection between the deed of victory and the word of performance. Further, our knowledge of the stylistic boundaries of the *angelia* speech genre enable us to identify how Pindar's compositions can artfully integrate diverse ways of speaking into the epinician way of speaking. The identification of such dynamics of heteroglossia is an important component to our fluency in epinician art and, in Chapter Five, will help us to discover novelistic features of epinician style.

Mythological Narrative

While there are many existing studies of myth in Pindar's *epinikia* that focus upon formal qualities, such as the length of mythological narrative and its position in an ode,[38] and mythological content,[39] none consider the generic quality of the *style* of mythological narratives. Indeed, Richard Hamilton, author of an often-cited work on the structure of the victory ode, has written that "there appears to be no standard pattern governing its structure" (1974:56). But it is possible to identify the ethnographic features of the style of mythological narrative in even the briefest passages:[40]

Speech Subject: performer in third-person voice exclusive from speech object;

Addressee: audience, exclusive from the speech object;

Speech Object: actor(s) and actions excluded from the performance frame of interaction;

Speech Plan: to narrate traditional stories or to display portions of them;

Spatial Dimension: mythological; interactive framework for participants in narrated events is in an exclusive relation to performance;

38 Bowra identifies "a myth or myths from the heroic past" as a traditional element of the victory ode (1964:322). Young writes that myth "usually occupies a central position in the ode; many of the myths appear in ring form; most are introduced by a mere relative word" (1971:35). Hamilton 1974:14–15 distinguishes between "two types of mythic material...the long type... Myth...and the short type...Mythic Example." See also Köhnken 1971.

39 Young writes that "myths may serve a programmatic purpose extolling some subject connected with the victor, such as his genealogy or city. Most scholars have argued that many myths, whether they arise from the program or not, function as paradigms or exempla to illustrate some contemporary subject, usually, but not necessarily pertaining to the victor" (1971:35). See also Hubbard 1985:133–140 on Pindar's myths as paradigms for *laudator* and *laudandus*.

40 Cf. Segal on Pindar's *Pythian* 4: "He may sketch a myth in four words, as he does the story of the Titans ([*Pythian* 4] 291), or tell it in two hundred lines, as he does the story of Jason" (1986:135–136). Young 1971:44–46 advocates for a broader application of the designation "myth" in the analysis of Pindar's songs—an appeal that I hope my analysis answers.

Temporal Dimension: mythological, which ranges from the mythological past to immediate, relative to the performance event.

Mythological narrative is constituted by a mode of pastness that distinguishes it from that of *angelia*: mythological narrative concerns events in which possible participants in the event of performance (e.g. the athlete, members of the athlete's family, the audience) do not participate.[41] The chronotope "mythological" serves to indicate this exclusive relation of the speech object(s) of mythological narrative relative to the event of performance. Mythological narrative is temporally transcendent in that the telling of events occurring in a mythological chronotope can bear upon the present of performance, in part, by virtue of the fact that performance is the nexus between the event of narration and narrated events.[42]

The first brief stretch of mythological narrative occurring in Pindar's *Olympian* 1 focalizes the song's treatment of the Pelops myth upon a particular facet—the story of how Pelops got his ivory shoulder:

> τοῦ μεγασθενὴς ἐράσσατο Γαιάοχος
> Ποσειδάν, ἐπεί νιν καθαροῦ λέβητος ἔξελε Κλωθώ,
> ἐλέφαντι φαίδιμον ὦμον κεκαδμένον.
>
> *Olympian* 1.25–27

> ...whom [i.e. Pelops] the earth-embracing, mighty Poseidon desired,
> after Klotho removed him from the purified cauldron.
> And Pelops was well furnished with a shoulder bright with ivory.

The features occurring in these lines are:

Speech Subject: composer in third-person voice, indicated by third-person verbs ἐράσσατο (line 25) and ἔξελε (line 26);

Addressee: audience, non-participant in, and so excluded from, the speech object (the narrated events);

Speech Object: Poseidon's desire for Pelops and how Pelops got his ivory shoulder;

[41] Thus the demarcation between the "story worlds" of myth and encomium (Athanassaki 2004:319, following Felson 1984) can be identified on the basis of the ethnographic approach to style that I propose.

[42] See Berge 2007 for a recent study of chronological arrangement of mythological narratives *Pythian* 10 and *Olympian* 3.

Speech Plan: to narrate Poseidon's desire for Pelops and how Pelops got his ivory shoulder;

Spatial Dimension: mythological;

Temporal Dimension: mythological, indicated by the speech object (a traditional story) and by aorist verbs ἐράσσατο (line 25) and ἔξελε (line 26).

The longest segment of mythological narrative in *Olympian* 1 recounts the deeds of Pelops. In the context of the poem as a whole, Pindar sets up the mythological figure of Pelops as an exemplar in the fulfillment of the principle of reciprocity conveyed by the word *kharis*:

τοὔνεκα {οἱ} προῆκαν υἱὸν ἀθάνατοί <οἱ> πάλιν
μετὰ τὸ ταχύποτμον αὖτις ἀνέρων ἔθνος.
πρὸς εὐάνθεμον δ' ὅτε φυάν
λάχναι νιν μέλαν γένειον ἔρεφον,
ἑτοῖμον ἀνεφρόντισεν γάμον
Πισάτα παρὰ πατρὸς εὔδοξον Ἱπποδάμειαν
σχεθέμεν. ἐγγὺς {δ'} ἐλθὼν πολιᾶς ἁλὸς οἶος ἐν ὄρφνᾳ
ἄπυεν βαρύκτυπον
Εὐτρίαιναν· ὁ δ' αὐτῷ
πὰρ ποδὶ σχεδὸν φάνη.
τῷ μὲν εἶπε· "Φίλια δῶρα Κυπρίας ἄγ' εἴ τι, Ποσείδαον,
    ἐς χάριν
τέλλεται, πέδασον ἔγχος Οἰνομάου χάλκεον,
ἐμὲ δ' ἐπὶ ταχυτάτων πόρευσον ἁρμάτων
ἐς Ἆλιν, κράτει δὲ πέλασον.
ἐπεὶ τρεῖς τε καὶ δέκ' ἄνδρας ὀλέσαις
μναστῆρας ἀναβάλλεται γάμον
θυγατρός. ὁ μέγας δὲ κίνδυνος ἄναλκιν οὐ φῶτα λαμβάνει.
θανεῖν δ' οἷσιν ἀνάγκα, τά κέ τις ἀνώνυμον
γῆρας ἐν σκότῳ καθήμενος ἕψοι μάταν,
ἁπάντων καλῶν ἄμμορος; ἀλλ' ἐμοὶ μὲν οὗτος ἄεθλος
ὑποκείσεται· τὺ δὲ πρᾶξιν φίλαν δίδοι."
ὣς ἔννεπεν· οὐδ' ἀκράντοις ἐφάψατο
ἔπεσι. τὸν μὲν ἀγάλλων θεός
ἔδωκεν δίφρον τε χρύσεον πτεροῖσίν τ' ἀκάμαντας ἵππους.
ἕλεν δ' Οἰνομάου βίαν παρθένον τε σύνευνον·
ἔτεκε λαγέτας ἓξ ἀρεταῖσι μεμαότας υἱούς.

νῦν δ' ἐν αἱμακουρίαις
ἀγλααῖσι μέμικται,
Ἀλφεοῦ πόρῳ κλιθείς,
τύμβον ἀμφίπολον ἔχων πολυξενωτάτῳ παρὰ βωμῷ· τὸ δὲ
κλέος
τηλόθεν δέδορκε τᾶν Ὀλυμπιάδων ἐν δρόμοις
Πέλοπος, ἵνα ταχυτὰς ποδῶν ἐρίζεται
ἀκμαί τ' ἰσχύος θρασύπονοι.

Olympian 1.65–96

For that reason the immortals sent Tantalos' son back
again among the quick-fated race of men.
When at the flowering age
whiskers covered his chin with dark,
he turned his thoughts to ready marriage,
to have from her father, the man from Pisa, the widely renowned
Hippodameia.
After going near the gray sea alone in darkness,
he called upon the heavy-pounding god
with the good trident.
Near at his feet the god appeared.
Pelops addressed him: "Come on, Poseidon, if at all the cherished
gifts of Kypria result in grace,
restrain the bronze spear of Oinomaos,
bear me on the swiftest chariot
to Elis, and bring me to dominance.
After killing thirteen men,
suitors, he delays the marriage
of his daughter. Great risk does not fall to a mortal who lacks
strength.
Among those for whom it is necessary to die, why would anyone
sit in darkness and foolishly boil off a nameless old age
and be without a share in all upright things? But this contest lies
before me.
May you grant the desired deed."
Thus he spoke and did not use unfulfilled
words. Glorifying him, the god
gave both a golden chariot-board and untiring horses with wings.
Then Pelops took Oinomaos's might and the virgin for a bride.

He fathered six sons, leaders of the people and eager for virtue.
Now Pelops has been included
in splendid blood offerings,
reclining at the course of the Alpheos River,
having an often-visited tomb beside an altar that hosts many
people.
In the races of Pelops the renown of the Olympic Games
radiates from far off,
where swiftness of feet
and the boldly working peaks of strength contend.

The ethnographic features occurring in this passage are:

Speech Subject: composer, exclusive from speech object (the narrated events), in third-person voice, indicated by third-person verbs (e.g. προῆκαν [line 65] and ἔρεφον [line 68]) and third-person pronoun νιν (line 68);

Addressee: audience;

Speech Object: Pelops' deeds: his chariot race with Oinomaos, the winning of Hippodameia, and the signs of his renown;

Speech Plan: to narrate Pelops' deeds;

Spatial Dimension: mythological and exclusive relative to the performance event;[43]

Temporal Dimension: mythological, but inclusive of the performance event because the narrated events follow a temporal trajectory from remote past, indicated by past tense verbs (e.g. προῆκαν [line 65] and ἔρεφον [line 68]) and by the etiological quality of the narrative (the story of Pelops' chariot race with Oinomaos is an etiology for athletic competitions at the Festival of Zeus Olympios [Nagy 1990:116–135]), to immediate, indicated principally by the deictic νῦν, initial word of line 90.

43 If the original performance frame's origo was at Olympia, then the space of narrated events is contiguous with the space of narration (Pelops prays to Poseidon to bear him to Elis [line 78] the region in the western Peloponnesus where Olympia is located; the narrative refers to the Alpheos River [line 92] near the cult site of Olympia; to Pelops' tomb and cult site, located at Olympia [about 50 meters from the temple of Zeus Olympios; line 93]; and to the Festival of Zeus Olympios and the "races of Pelops" [lines 93–96]). If the original performance frame's origo was at Hieron's home of Syracuse, then the narrated events are spatially non-immediate relative to performance. At a still more abstract level it is possible in any case simply to describe narrated events as "there" relative to the "here" of performance.

The examples of mythological narrative from *Olympian* 1 serve to illustrate the stylistic patterns of the speech genre and to identify an overall pattern to the variety of mythological references and passages in Pindar's *epinikia*. This ethnographic description of mythological narrative opens up the possibility of describing an individual epinician song as a dynamic communicative process, as we will see in Chapter Five.

In the next chapter I will continue to describe the ways of epinician speaking, focusing on the last speech genre of prayer. Because Pindar's prayers have diverse forms and because my ethnographic study of them bears upon the salient Pindaric problems of first-person futures and praise poetics, I have dedicated Chapter 4 entirely to this topic.

4

Ways of Epinician Speaking II

The forms of prayer in Pindar's *epinikia* are diverse, but they have converging stylistic features that indicate an overall pattern, a speech genre. The multiformity of precatory speech acts in Pindar's *epinikia* complicates the preliminary question involved in the description of every simple epinician speech genre—how to define the domain of analysis. If the objective is to describe the patterning of ethnographic features constitutive of the speech genre of prayer, how do we decide what passages of Pindar's *epinikia* to include in such an analysis? One tendency in existing scholarship on Pindar's prayers has been to assume that the question of whether or not Pindar addresses his prayers to a deity is a relevant domain of analysis.[1] But methodologically the assumption of the relevance of religion to Pindar's prayers results from a deductive analysis that foregrounds the referential function of language and inserts the prayer-deity equation into the mix of considerations in an exegetical analysis of Pindar's style. From the perspective of a speech- and performance-centered

[1] Bowra 1964:322 identifies "prayers or praise to the gods" as a traditional element of the victory ode. Similarly for Gerber 1982:115 the category "religious nature" explicitly informs his interpretation. Bundy 1962:76–83 and passim is an exception to the tendency and treats Pindar's prayers as an epinician convention. Although Hamilton 1974:17 acknowledges that Pindar's prayers may or may not be addressed to a deity, this is still a category of description relevant to his analysis; he identifies "two main kinds [of prayer] with two distinct types in the second category": "Poetic Invocation," which "usually takes the form of an elaborate and lengthy invocation of some particularly relevant but not panhellenic divine figure" and is characterized by the use of an imperative verb; "Future Prayer," which "takes the form either of an invocation of a major panhellenic god...or of a simple prayer with the optative, with or without *theos*." See also Hamilton 1974:115 and Gerber 1982:175, who cites Hamilton 1974:20 and 24n30. Mackie also makes the prayer-god equation: "I suggest that we should read the future-oriented wishes and prayers in conjunction with [the] other epinician convention of crediting the gods for the victory" (2003:102). Race 1990:85–117 describes opening hymns, distinguishing between "two basic forms of hymns, rhapsodic and cultic." On Pindar's prayers see also Greengard 1980:54–62 (on "invocational framing"), Hubbard 1985:141–142, Race 1986:29 and 1990:119–140, and Mackie 2003:77–106.

analysis, the relevant descriptive criteria are to be discovered ethnographically. Observing the principle of intersubjective objectivity, I take my descriptive cues from Pindar's own language practices to determine the domain of analysis for epinician prayers. My first step will be to look at the forms of metalanguage that Pindar uses to name epinician prayers in order to identify the scope of the speech genre's speech plan. In support of this approach, I cite Bakhtin's elaboration of his concept of speech plan, one of the features constitutive of speech genres: "[t]his plan determines both the choice of the subject itself (under certain conditions of speech communication, in necessary connection with preceding utterances), as well as its boundaries and semantic exhaustiveness. It also determines, of course, the choice of a generic form in which the utterance will be constructed" (1986:77).[2] On the basis of an empirical description of the functional load of Pindar's prayers, we can discover syntactic patterns associated with the utterances that fulfill those functions. This is the second step in my analysis. I stress, however, that syntax is not constitutive of speech genres; syntax includes deictic information about the constitutive features of speech genres—speech subject, addressee, speech object, and their spatio-temporal dimensions.[3] By identifying what gets included in the domain of analysis on the basis of speech plan and syntax, it is possible, finally, to discover the ethnographic features of prayer style that co-occur in every Pindaric prayer.

2 Bakhtin's concept of speech plan closely correlates with Hymes's "'use' functions," which Hymes contrasts with "'structural' functions" (1989:439).

3 A fundamental motivation for the Ethnography of Speaking and Bakhtin's translinguistics is the limited utility of grammar and structural linguistics for describing language as dynamic practice. As Martin has written, "[i]n literature, as in life, individual sentences do not matter" (2004:345). Cf. Bakhtin: "The sentence as a language unit is grammatical in nature. It has grammatical boundaries and grammatical completedness and unity. (Regarded in the whole of the utterance and from the standpoint of this whole, it acquires stylistic properties.) When the sentence figures as a whole utterance, it is as though it has been placed in a frame made of quite different material. When one forgets this in analyzing a sentence, one distorts the nature of the sentence (and simultaneously the nature of the utterance as well, by treating it grammatically). A great many linguists and linguistic schools (in the area of syntax) are held captive by this confusion, and what they study as a sentence is in essence a kind of *hybrid* of the sentence (unit of language) and the utterance (unit of speech communication). One does not exchange sentences any more than one exchanges words (in the strict linguistic sense) or phrases. One exchanges utterances that are constructed from language units: words, phrases, and sentences" (1986:74–75, emphasis in original). So too Hymes: "In Kenneth Burke's terms, there has been a tendency to treat language and its use as matters of 'motion' (as if of the purely physical world), rather than as matters of 'action' (as matters of the human dramatistic world of symbolic agency and purpose)... With all the difficulties that notions of purpose and function entail, there seems no way for the structural study of language and communication to engage its subject in social life in any adequate, useful way, except by taking this particular bull by the horns" (1974:21). See Hymes 1989:433 on the hegemonic effects of "the genre of grammars."

The Speech Plan of Epinician Prayers

To identify the scope of the speech plan associated with Pindar's prayers, I have analyzed the following forms of metalanguage:

> ἀπύειν (*apuein*) 'to invoke'[4]
> ἀρά (*ara*) 'prayer'[5]
> ἐπεύχεσθαι (*epeukhesthai*) 'to utter a prayer'[6]
> εὐχά (*eukha*) 'prayer'[7]
> εὔχεσθαι (*eukhesthai*) 'to pray' or 'to vaunt'[8]
> εὖχος (*eukhos*) 'vaunt'[9]
> λίσσεσθαι (*lissesthai*) 'to entreat'[10]
> λιτά (*lita*) 'entreaty'[11]
> λιτανεύειν (*litaneuein*) 'to entreat'[12]
> λιτός (*litos*) 'supplicatory'[13]

I will first describe the prayer functions named by forms of metalanguage characterized by the stem *eukh*- and then go on to describe functions named by other forms of prayer metalanguage.

Eukhos 'Vaunt'

To deal first with what might appear to be the form of language use most tenuously attributed to the category of prayer, the word *eukhos* occurs three times in Pindar's *epinikia*:

> τίς δὴ ποταίνιον
> ἔλαχε στέφανον
> χείρεσσι ποσίν τε καὶ ἅρματι,

4 *Olympian* 1.72, 5.19; *Pythian* 2.19, 5.104, 10.4.

5 *Isthmian* 6.43.

6 *Pythian* 3.77; cf. *Paean* 7b.15.

7 *Olympian* 4.13; *Pythian* 9.89; *Isthmian* 6.44. Cf. εὐχωλά (*eukhôla*) 'prayer', which does not occur in the *epinikia*, at *Fragment* 122.2.

8 *Olympian* 3.2, 6.53, 7.23, 8.86, 14.5; *Pythian* 3.2, 4.97, 4.293, 5.124, 8.67, 9.100; *Nemean* 8.37, 9.54; *Isthmian* 6.14. Cf. *Paean* 6.64, 16.3; *Partheneion* 1.11; *Dithyramb* 1.15, 2.26; *Fragment* 39.

9 *Olympian* 10.63; *Pythian* 5.21; *Nemean* 6.59.

10 *Olympian* 12.1; *Pythian* 1.71, 4.207; *Nemean* 3.1; *Isthmian* 6.45. Cf. *Paean* 6.3.

11 *Olympian* 2.80, 8.8, and *Pythian* 4.217. Note that I follow Race 1997a:286–287 and take *litas* at *Pythian* 4.217 to be a form of *lita* 'entreaty', but Slater 1969b:305 identifies it as a form of the adjective *litos* 'supplicatory'.

12 *Nemean* 5.32 and 8.8; cf. *Paean* 9.38.

13 *Olympian* 6.78; cf. *Fragment* 21.

ἀγώνιον ἐν δόξᾳ θέμενος εὖχος, ἔργῳ
καθελών;

Olympian 10.60–63

Who took the latest
victory wreath
by hand, by foot, by chariot,
first imagining a contestant's vaunt [*eukhos*], then achieving
it in deed?

μάκαρ δὲ καὶ νῦν, κλεεννᾶς ὅτι
εὖχος ἤδη παρὰ Πυθιάδος ἵπποις ἑλών
δέδεξαι τόνδε κῶμον ἀνέρων,
Ἀπολλώνιον ἄθυρμα.

Pythian 5.20–23

And you are blessed now because,
after you gained a vaunt [*eukhos*] with your horses from the
renowned Pythian Games,
you have received this reveling group of men,
Apollo's delight.

ἑκόντι δ' ἐγὼ νώτῳ μεθέπων δίδυμον ἄχθος
ἄγγελος ἔβαν,
πέμπτον ἐπὶ εἴκοσι τοῦτο γαρύων
εὖχος ἀγώνων ἄπο, τοὺς ἐνέποισιν ἱερούς,
Ἀλκίμιδα, τέ γ' ἐπαρκέσαι
κλειτᾷ γενεᾷ.

Nemean 6.57–61

Taking a double burden on my willing back,
I have come as a messenger,
announcing that this twenty-fifth
vaunt [*eukhos*] from the contests that they call sacred,
you, Alkimidas, convey
to your famous family.

At *Olympian* 10.63 *eukhos* occurs in the context of what I described in Chapter 3 as the simple speech genre *angelia*. The composer represents himself as deliberating about whose victory the current composition celebrates and represents the *laudandus* as contemplating an *agônion eukhos* 'competitor's vaunt'.[14] To characterize the composition and performance of an individual song in the language of prayer proves to be a highly salient pattern in Pindar's use of this speech genre. The occurrence of *eukhos* at *Pythian* 5.21 also refers to the song and its performance. This reference is further articulated by the phrase δέδεξαι τόνδε κῶμον ἀνέρων "you have received this reveling group of men" (line 22). As the choral-monody debate in Pindar scholarship makes clear, *kômos* is a word that Pindar regularly uses to describe epinician performance. Lines 20–23 of *Pythian* 5 juxtapose the *kômos* with *eukhos*. Especially relevant to identifying the ethnographic features of Pindar's prayers is the second-person address to *Pythian* 5's *laudandus*, Arkesilas, at lines 20 and 22. At *Nemean* 6.57–61 the composer represents himself as an *angelos* who announces that the *laudandus* is conveying an *eukhos*, which we can understand as both the prestige of athletic victory and the commemoration of it in epinician performance. As in *Pythian* 5.20–23, *Nemean* 6.57–61 includes a second-person address to the song's *laudandus*, Alkimidas. Taken together, these passages indicate that *eukhos* can refer to the prestige of victory and to the performance of *epinikion* itself. This turns out to be one of the ways that Pindar uses the verb *eukhesthai*, indicating that this latter form of metalanguage for epinician prayers has applications that embrace those of *eukhos*.

Eukhesthai 'To Pray' or 'To Vaunt'

In comparison to other forms of metalanguage for epinician prayers, Pindar applies *eukhesthai* to name the broadest range of functions for the speech genre. To first illustrate Pindar's uses of *eukhesthai* in the sense of 'to vaunt', I cite two passages:

> ἐθελήσω τοῖσιν ἐξ ἀρχᾶς ἀπὸ Τλαπολέμου
> ξυνὸν ἀγγέλλων διορθῶσαι λόγον,
> Ἡρακλέος
> εὐρυσθενεῖ γέννᾳ. τὸ μὲν γὰρ πατρόθεν ἐκ Διὸς εὔχονται· τὸ δ'
> Ἀμυντορίδαι
> ματρόθεν Ἀστυδαμείας.
>
> *Olympian* 7.20–24

[14] I take *agônion eukhos* to be a reference to the performance of *Olympian* 10 itself.

From the beginning, starting with Tlapolemos I wish
by making an announcement to set the well-known story straight for them,
for Heracles'
mighty line.[15] On their father's side, they boast [*eukhontai*] to be from Zeus, on their mother's side, to be descendents
of Amuntor, through Astudameia.[16]

κλέπτων δὲ θυμῷ
δεῖμα προσήνεπε· "Ποίαν γαῖαν, ὦ ξεῖν', εὔχεαι
πατρίδ' ἔμμεν; καὶ τίς ἀνθρώπων σε χαμαιγενέων πολιᾶς
ἐξανῆκεν γαστρός; ἐχθίστοισι μὴ ψεύδεσιν
καταμιάναις εἰπὲ γένναν."

Pythian 4.96–100

Concealing fear in his heart,
Pelias addressed Jason: "What land, stranger, do you boast [*eukheai*]
is your homeland? And what earthborn people produced
you from a grey womb? Without tainting your reply with hateful lies,
tell your descent."

As with *eukhos* at *Nemean* 6.57–61 (quoted above), Pindar's use of *eukhesthai* at *Olympian* 7.20–24 occurs in a context where the composer represents himself as a messenger. As with *eukhos* at *Pythian* 5.20–23 and *Nemean* 6.57–61, the use of *eukhesthai* at *Pythian* 4.97 occurs in a (represented) context characterized by second-person address. In both passages, *Olympian* 7.20–24 and *Pythian* 4.96–100, *eukhesthai* has the sense of 'to boast', parallel to the meaning of *eukhos* 'vaunt'. Clustering around these uses of *eukhesthai* in the sense of 'to boast' are syntactic constructions in which Pindar tends to couch his prayers: a second-person imperative verb *eipe* 'tell' (*Pythian* 4.100) and *ethelein* 'to wish, to be willing' + infinitive (*Olympian* 7.20–21).

15 I.e. the family of the *laudandus*, Diagoras.

16 Astudameia was Amuntor's daughter, who married Tlapolemos, son of Herakles, son of Zeus.

The function of *eukhesthai* at *Pythian* 4.96–100 and *Olympian* 7.20–24, to perform a *eukhos*, contrasts with the most frequently occurring use of the verb, which is to make a request, to pray. Here I cite examples:[17]

> Τυνδαρίδαις τε φιλοξείνοις ἁδεῖν καλλιπλοκάμῳ θ' Ἑλένᾳ
> κλεινὰν Ἀκράγαντα γεραίρων εὔχομαι.
>
> *Olympian* 3.1–2

> To please the descendents of Tyndareus, who are kind to friends,
> and to please Helen, whose hair is lovely,
> I pray [*eukhomai*], as I honor famous Akragas.

> ἀλλ' εὔχεται οὐλομέναν νοῦσον διαντλήσαις ποτέ
> οἶκον ἰδεῖν, ἐπ' Ἀπόλλωνός τε κράνᾳ συμποσίας ἐφέπων
> θυμὸν ἐκδόσθαι πρὸς ἥβαν πολλάκις, ἔν τε σοφοῖς
> δαιδαλέαν φόρμιγγα βαστάζων πολίταις ἡσυχίᾳ θιγέμεν,
> μήτ' ὦν τινι πῆμα πορών, ἀπαθὴς δ' αὐτὸς πρὸς ἀστῶν·
> καί κε μυθήσαιθ', ὁποίαν, Ἀρκεσίλα,
> εὗρε παγὰν ἀμβροσίων ἐπέων, πρόσφατον Θήβᾳ ξενωθείς.
>
> *Pythian* 4.293–299

> But after enduring his wretched sickness, he [Damophilos] prays
> [*eukhetai*]
> to see his home one day, and taking part in the symposium at
> Apollo's spring,
> he prays that he often give his heart to youth's enjoyments, and
> among wise
> citizens picking up the intricately designed lyre, he prays that he
> may touch peace,
> bringing pain to none, and that he may be without affliction
> among the townspeople.
> Damophilos would tell the story, Arkesilas, of what
> a spring of ambrosial words he found when he was recently a
> guest in Thebes.

[17] Other occurrences of *eukhesthai* in the sense of 'to pray' with the function of making a request include: *Olympian* 8.86 (with optative of wish type prayer at lines 87–88); *Pythian* 3.2, 8.67, 9.100 (with second person address to the song's *laudandus*); *Nemean* 8.37, 9.54 (with second person address to Zeus); and *Isthmian* 6.14.

> εὔχομαί νιν Ὀλυμπίᾳ τοῦτο δόμεν γέρας ἔπι Βάττου
> γένει.
>
> *Pythian* 5.124
>
> I pray [*eukhomai*] that he [i.e. Zeus] grant this prize at Olympia for
> the race of Battos.

In each of these passages, the construction *eukhesthai* + infinitive expresses a request in the sense of 'to pray for' or 'to pray that'. This function of *eukhesthai* is analogous to that of the set of prayer-metalanguage characterized by the stem *lit-*: *lissesthai* 'to entreat', *lita* 'entreaty', *litaneuein* 'to entreat', and *litos* 'supplicatory'. At *Olympian* 3.1–2 and *Pythian* 5.124, where *eukhesthai* in the sense of 'to pray for' or 'to pray that' occurs, Pindar represents his song in terms of a prayer uttered in a first-person voice. At *Pythian* 4.298–299 Pindar represents his composition as Damophilos' discovery, in the context of describing the latter's prayers at lines 293–297. I note as well the use of potential optative at *Pythian* 4.298, in the context of Pindar's use of *eukhesthai* in the sense of 'to pray for' or 'to pray that'. The fact that this syntactic construction occurs in the context of prayers—both the reported prayers of Damophilos and the prayer style indicated by the second-person address to the *laudandus* of *Pythian* 4, Arkesilas (line 298)—suggests that a potential optative is to be included among the possible syntactic constructions in which Pindar may nest his prayers.

Two functions of *eukhesthai* remain to describe. The first suggests that *eukhos* and *eukha* are to be described as the main subcategories of *eukhesthai*:

> Καφισίων ὑδάτων
> λαχοῖσαι αἵτε ναίετε καλλίπωλον ἕδραν,
> ὦ λιπαρᾶς ἀοίδιμοι βασίλειαι
> Χάριτες Ἐρχομενοῦ, παλαιγόνων Μινυᾶν ἐπίσκοποι,
> κλῦτ᾽, ἐπεὶ εὔχομαι· σὺν γὰρ ὑμῖν τά <τε> τερπνὰ καί
> τὰ γλυκέ᾽ ἄνεται πάντα βροτοῖς,
> εἰ σοφός, εἰ καλός, εἴ τις ἀγλαὸς ἀνήρ.
>
> *Olympian* 14.1–7
>
> You who possess the Kephisian waters,
> who dwell in a realm with beautiful foals,
> revered for your singing, you Queens of bright
> Orchomenos, Graces, you keepers of the long line of
> Minyans,

hear when I pray [*eukhomai*]; for, thanks to you,
every delight,
every sweetness is a joy to mortals,
if one is wise, if beautiful, if full of splendor.

In this passage *eukhesthai* could mean either 'to pray' or 'to vaunt'; the phrase *klut', epei eukhomai* could as reasonably be translated "Hear me, when I pray" as "Hear me, when I make a vaunt." Like his uses of *eukhos* at *Pythian* 5.20–23, *Nemean* 6.57–61, and *Olympian* 10.60–63, I interpret Pindar's use of *eukhesthai* at *Olympian* 14.5 as a way of describing the composition and performance of the song itself. The fact that Pindar describes epinician song, the complex speech genre, in terms of the language of prayer, a simple speech genre, as we have seen, suggests that the very use of that prayer language may by convention imply an act of commemorating, honoring, or celebrating the addressee of a prayer.[18] As a final observation about *Olympian* 14.1–7, the intransitive use of *eukhesthai* in line 5 has a second-person addressee, the Kharites, as indicated by vocative forms (lines 3–4) and by second-person plural forms (line 5).

The final type of function to which Pindar applies *eukhesthai* is to express a vow. The relevant passage occurs in a mythological narrative about the birth of Iamos to Apollo and Euadne; when Apollo searches for his newborn son, the members of Euadne's home claim not to know the child's whereabouts:

τοὶ δ' οὔτ' ὦν ἀκοῦσαι
οὔτ' ἰδεῖν εὔχοντο πεπταῖον γεγενημένον.

Olympian 6.52–53

That they neither heard
nor saw the boy, they swore [*eukhonto*], though it had been five
days since his birth.

The occurrence of *eukhesthai* at *Olympian* 6.53 in the sense of 'to swear that' (a subcategory of *eukhesthai* in the sense of 'to pray for' or 'to pray that') involves the syntactic structure of *eukhesthai* with a complementary infinitive. More important for identifying the scope of the speech plan of Pindar's prayers is the observation that this use of *eukhesthai* is analogous to one of the uses of *eukha* 'prayer', to name a vow.

18 See pp. 114–115.

Eukha 'Prayer'

This form of metalanguage applies to functions that are analogous to Pindar's use of *eukhesthai* in the broad sense of 'to pray' (in contrast to 'to make a vaunt'); Pindar uses *eukha* 'prayer' to name speech acts such as vows, prayers, or entreaties. The first example of *eukha* that I will describe is analogous to the use of *eukhesthai* in the sense of 'to swear that' at *Olympian* 6.53 (Gildersleeve 1890:345):

> τοῖσι τέλειον ἐπ' εὐχᾷ κωμάσομαί τι παθών
> ἐσλόν. Χαρίτων κελαδεννᾶν
> μή με λίποι καθαρὸν φέγγος.
>
> *Pythian* 9.88–90
>
> Because I experienced something good in fulfillment of a vow
> [*eukha*], I will make a victory revel for them [Herakles and
> Iphikles].
> May the resounding Kharites'
> clean light not leave me!

In addition to observing the parallel uses of *eukha* in the sense of 'vow' at line 88 and of *eukhesthai* in the sense of 'to swear that' at *Olympian* 6.53, cited above, note that *Pythian* 9.88–90 includes a reference to performance (*kômasomai*, line 88, an example of a first-person future type prayer) and an utterance in the optative of wish syntactic construction. Alternatively, if we understand *eukha* at *Pythian* 9.88 as a prayer in the sense of a request rather than a vow, then here we have an application of the word that is analogous to its uses in the next examples.[19]

Pindar uses two occurrences of *eukha* in the context of uttering an entreaty, a use that is analogous to *eukhesthai* in the sense of 'to pray for' or 'to pray that' and to *lissesthai* 'to entreat', *lita* 'entreaty', *litaneuein* 'to entreat', and *litos* 'supplicatory'. This is the first example:

> Ἐλατὴρ ὑπέρτατε βροντᾶς ἀκαμαντόποδος Ζεῦ· τεαὶ γὰρ
> Ὧραι
> ὑπὸ ποικιλοφόρμιγγος ἀοιδᾶς ἑλισσόμεναί μ' ἔπεμψαν
> ὑψηλοτάτων μάρτυρ' ἀέθλων·
> ξείνων δ' εὖ πρασσόντων

19 Slater 1969b:213 and Gentili 1995:612 take *eukha* at *Pythian* 9.88 in the broad sense of 'prayer', but Race 1997a:351 translates it as 'wish'.

ἔσαναν αὐτικ' ἀγγελίαν ποτὶ γλυκεῖαν ἐσλοί·
ἀλλὰ Κρόνου παῖ, ὃς Αἴτναν ἔχεις
ἶπον ἀνεμόεσσαν ἑκατογκεφάλα Τυφῶνος ὀβρίμου,
Οὐλυμπιονίκαν
δέξαι Χαρίτων θ' ἕκατι τόνδε κῶμον
χρονιώτατον φάος εὐρυσθενέων ἀρετᾶν. Ψαύμιος γὰρ ἵκει
ὀκέων, ὃς ἐλαίᾳ στεφανωθεὶς Πισάτιδι κῦδος ὄρσαι
σπεύδει Καμαρίνᾳ. θεὸς εὔφρων
εἴη λοιπαῖς εὐχαῖς·
ἐπεί νιν αἰνέω.

Olympian 4.1–14

You are the driver of thunderbolts with indefatigable feet, highest Zeus; for, your Hôrai,
circling to songs guided by the multisonic lyre, sent me
as witness to most sublime contests.
Whenever friends succeed,
right away good people share in the joy of a sweet victory announcement.
But son of Kronos, you who hold windy Aitna,
the crushing burden above terrible hundred-headed Typhon,
according to the will of the Kharites, accept this Olympian victor's revel
as the most everlasting light of enduring virtues; it's [the *kômos*] on its way,
thanks to Psaumis'[20] chariot. Now that he's been crowned with Pisa's olive wreath,
he yearns to waken prestige for Kamarina.[21] May a god be favorable
to future prayers [*eukhai*],
since I praise him.

The characterization of a god as possessed of a responsive position (*euphrôn* 'favorable', line 12) helps us to see that a form of request is entailed in the function of *eukhai* (line 13). As often occurs in Pindar's prayers, at *Olympian* 4.1–14 the composer represents the performance of the song in terms of

[20] The *laudandus* of *Olympian* 4.
[21] Psaumis' *polis*.

prayer: he describes himself as a "witness to the sublimest contests" (line 3), a statement that is qualified by the following gnomic statement (lines 4–5), which expresses the propriety of performing an *angelia* 'victory announcement'; the second-person imperative address to Zeus (lines 8–10) entreats the god to "accept this Olympian victor's revel"; at line 14, the composer represents the performance of *Olympian* 4 as the performance of *ainos* 'praise' (line 14) in the sense of the conventional poetics of praise and blame, as described in Chapter Two. To record the syntactic constructions associated with prayer in *Olympian* 4.1–14, there is a second-person imperative type prayer (lines 8–10) and an optative of wish (lines 12–13, where the instance of *eukha* in the sense of 'entreaty' occurs).

The final example of *eukha* occurs in the context of direct discourse in a mythological narrative, where Herakles utters a prayer while making libations at the request of Telamon:

> ὁ δ' ἀνατείναις οὐρανῷ χεῖρας ἀμάχους
> αὔδασε τοιοῦτον {τι} ἔπος· "Εἴ ποτ' ἐμᾶν, ὦ Ζεῦ πάτερ,
> θυμῷ θέλων ἀρᾶν ἄκουσας,
> νῦν σε, νῦν εὐχαῖς ὑπὸ θεσπεσίαις
> λίσσομαι παῖδα θρασὺν ἐξ Ἐριβοίας
> ἀνδρὶ τῷδε ξεῖνον ἀμὸν μοιρίδιον τελέσαι."
>
> *Isthmian* 6.41–46
>
> He stretched his unconquerable hands toward heaven
> and uttered some such speech as this: "If ever, Father Zeus,
> you have heard my prayers [*arai*] with a willing heart,
> now I request [*lissomai*] of you, now with divine entreaties
> [*eukhai*],
> bring from Eriboia[22] this man's[23] bold son
> to make him our destined friend."

This example of prayer is especially illustrative because Pindar represents a prayer in direct discourse and the passage includes three forms of metalanguage for prayer. *Eukhai* (line 44) has the sense of 'entreaty', especially when considered in the context of the use of a form of *lissesthai* 'to entreat' (line 45). The only epinician instance of *ara* 'prayer' (line 43) is the most inclusive term for the forms of prayer metalanguage that occur in this passage. Given

22 Wife of Telamon.
23 Telamon.

the richness of this example, the second-person address to Zeus stands out as a feature embracing and organizing the multiple forms of metalanguage for prayer in the passage.

Lita 'Entreaty'

Recalling that the metacommunication about appropriateness rules for the epinician way of speaking can be a useful heuristic device for discovering stylistic patterns in Pindar's songs, I cite a gnomic statement that expresses norms about the use of the word *lita* 'entreaty':

> ἄνεται δὲ πρὸς χάριν εὐσεβίας ἀνδρῶν λιταῖς·
> ἀλλ' ὦ Πίσας εὔδενδρον ἐπ' Ἀλφεῷ ἄλσος,
> τόνδε κῶμον καὶ στεφαναφορίαν δέξαι· μέγα τοι κλέος
> αἰεί,
> ᾧτινι σὸν γέρας ἕσπετ' ἀγλαόν.
>
> *Olympian* 8.8–11

> Men's entreaties [*litai*] are fulfilled in reciprocity for reverence.
> But grove of Pisa, you with your lovely trees beside the Alpheos River,
> accept this victory revel and the bringing of the crown. Renown is always great
> for whomever your splendid prize attends.

In the context of *Olympian* 8's performance, the gnomic statement at line 8 bears upon the audience's evaluation of the composer. To fulfill the rules for appropriate speech communicated by this gnomic statement merits a positive evaluation of the song's performance. Immediately following this gnomic statement about one condition for favorable response to *lita*, the composer utters a *lita* in the next two lines (9–10). As we will see, the justification for labeling this utterance a *lita* 'entreaty' follows from the fact that the use of *lissesthai* 'to entreat' is regularly accompanied by a second-person imperative verb in the form of, "I entreat you, do X." Based upon this, I identify prayers in the form of a second-person imperative, like that at *Olympian* 8.9–10, as *litai*. By implication, that particular *lita* enacts the principle of reciprocity communicated by the gnomic statement; by further implication, the entreaty, which entails positive evaluation of the song's performance, assumes that the composer fulfills the criterion of *eusebia* 'reverence' (line 8). In this context I understand the entreaty as a way to identify competent performance of the epinician way of speaking because it correlates to Bundy's observation of the conventional "propriety that determines the relationship between song and merit" (1962:11). In this passage, then, there is a form of metacommunication whereby the composer expresses a criterion for assessing his composition and Pindar immediately fulfills that criterion. We should note as well the following grammatical (deictic) features of the passage: vocative address (line 9), second-person imperative (line 10), and second-person singular possessive adjective (line 11). In addition, like other epinician prayers we have considered, in this passage Pindar represents the song's performance in terms of prayer.

Other examples of Pindar's use of *lita* 'entreaty' illustrate the persuasive power of the speech act they name. In the first example, the context is a description of the Isle of the Blessed; after listing some of those who dwell there, Pindar tells of Achilles:

> Ἀχιλλέα τ᾽ ἔνεικ᾽, ἐπεὶ Ζηνὸς ἦτορ
> λιταῖς ἔπεισε, μάτηρ.
>
> *Olympian* 2.79–80

> His mother[24] brought Achilles after she
> persuaded Zeus' heart with entreaties [*litai*].

The second example also illustrates the persuasive power of *lita*, this time in the context of describing how Jason learned magical arts from Aphrodite:

> πότνια δ᾽ ὀξυτάτων βελέων
> ποικίλαν ἴυγγα τετράκναμον Οὐλυμπόθεν
> ἐν ἀλύτῳ ζεύξαισα κύκλῳ
> μαινάδ᾽ ὄρνιν Κυπρογένεια φέρεν
> πρῶτον ἀνθρώποισι λιτάς τ᾽ ἐπαοιδὰς ἐκδιδάσκησεν σοφὸν
> Αἰσονίδαν·
> ὄφρα Μηδείας τοκέων ἀφέλοιτ᾽ αἰδῶ, ποθεινὰ δ᾽ Ἑλλὰς αὐτάν
> ἐν φρασὶ καιομέναν δονέοι μάστιγι Πειθοῦς.
>
> *Pythian* 4.213–219

> The queen of the sharpest arrows,
> after joining a mottled wryneck to four spokes
> of an inescapable wheel, from Olympus
> the Cyprus-born goddess brought this maddening bird

[24] Thetis.

to men for the first time and she taught the son of Aison how to be knowledgeable in entreaties [*litai*] and incantations,
in order to remove Medea's shame before her parents and so that desirous Hellas
would disturb her when she is burning in her mind under the lash of Persuasion.

We also witness the persuasive power of *lita* in a passage that uses the adjectival for *litos* 'supplicatory':

εἰ δ᾽ ἐτύμως ὑπὸ Κυλλάνας ὄρος, Ἁγησία, μάτρωες ἄνδρες
ναιετάοντες ἐδώρησαν θεῶν κάρυκα λιταῖς θυσίαις
πολλὰ δὴ πολλαῖσιν Ἑρμᾶν εὐσεβέως, ὃς ἀγῶνας ἔχει μοῖράν τ᾽ ἀέθλων,
Ἀρκαδίαν τ᾽ εὐάνορα τιμᾷ· κεῖνος, ὦ παῖ Σωστράτου,
σὺν βαρυγδούπῳ πατρὶ κραίνει σέθεν εὐτυχίαν.

Olympian 6.77–81

Hagesias,[25] if the men on your mother's side of the family, who live near Mount Kullana,[26]
truly and many times gifted the herald of the gods with many supplicatory [*litai* (adj.)] sacrifices,
reverently—Hermes, who keeps the trials of contests as his portion
and who honors Arkadia as a land with noble men, then he it is, son of Sostratos,[27]
who, along with the loudly thundering father, fulfills your good fortune.

In this occurrence of *litos* 'supplicatory' (line 78), as with each of the uses of *lita* 'entreaty' that illustrate the persuasive power of the speech act that the word names, I suggest that there is a connection between the poetics of prayer (lines 79–80) and the poetics of praise that is reflected in the two main senses in which Pindar uses the word *eukhesthai*, 'to pray' and 'to make a vaunt'. I call attention to the second-person address evidenced by the vocative forms for the song's *laudandus*, Hagesias (lines 77 and 80).

25 The *laudandus* of *Olympian* 6.

26 Near Stymphalos in Arkadia.

27 Father of Hagesias.

Lissesthai and *Litaneuein* 'To Entreat'

Corresponding to the persuasive power of *lita* 'entreaty', the speech plan of *lissesthai* 'to entreat' is to make a request. Each of the following uses of *lissesthai* occur in the pattern described above: *lissesthai* 'to entreat' with a second-person imperative verb in the form of, "I entreat you, do X":

> Λίσσομαι, παῖ Ζηνὸς Ἐλευθερίου,
> Ἱμέραν εὐρυσθενέ' ἀμφιπόλει, σώτειρα Τύχα.
>
> *Olympian* 12.1–2
>
> I entreat [*lissomai*] you, child of Zeus the Deliverer,
> saving Tukha,[28] keep well mighty Himera.[29]

> λίσσομαι νεῦσον, Κρονίων, ἥμερον
> ὄφρα κατ' οἶκον ὁ Φοίνιξ ὁ Τυρσανῶν τ' ἀλαλατὸς ἔχῃ,
> ναυσίστονον ὕβριν ἰδὼν τὰν πρὸ Κύμας,
> οἷα Συρακοσίων ἀρχῷ δαμασθέντες πάθον.
>
> *Pythian* 1.71–73
>
> I entreat you [*lissomai*], son of Kronos, nod in agreement,
> so that the Phoenician and the battle cry of the Etruscans may
> stay peacefully at home, after seeing the hubris of theirs
> that brought shipwreck before Cumae—
> such things they suffered when subdued by the dominance of the
> Syracusans.

> Ὦ πότνια Μοῖσα, μᾶτερ ἁμετέρα, λίσσομαι,
> τὰν πολυξέναν ἐν ἱερομηνίᾳ Νεμεάδι
> ἵκεο Δωρίδα νᾶσον Αἴγιναν· ὕδατι γάρ
> μένοντ' ἐπ' Ἀσωπίῳ μελιγαρύων τέκτονες
> κώμων νεανίαι, σέθεν ὄπα μαιόμενοι.
>
> *Nemean* 3.1–5
>
> Royal Muse, our mother, I entreat you [*lissomai*],
> come in the Nemean sacred month to the much visited

28 I.e. Fortune.

29 Sicilian *polis* of Ergoteles, the *laudandus*.

> Dorian island of Aigina; for at the waters
> of Asopos, constructors of sweetly voiced
> victory revels, young men, are waiting, seeking your voice.

The patterned use of *lissesthai* 'to entreat' with a second-person imperative verb in the form of "I entreat you, do X" necessarily means that each of these examples involves second-person address. Further, two of the passages quoted above, *Olympian* 12.1–2 and *Pythian* 1.71–73, commemorate the *polis* of each song's *laudandus* in the form of a prayer. *Nemean* 3.1–5 is another case where Pindar represents epinician performance in the context of a prayer. Thus, in all of the occurrences of *lissesthai* presented above, some aspect of epinician praise is couched in the form of prayer.

For a final example of *lissesthai* 'to entreat', Pindar depicts the Argonauts making a request to Poseidon for safe travel through the Symplegades:

> ἐς δὲ κίνδυνον βαθὺν ἱέμενοι δεσπόταν λίσσοντο ναῶν,
> συνδρόμων κινηθμὸν ἀμαιμάκετον
> ἐκφυγεῖν πετρᾶν.
>
> *Pythian* 4.207–209

> Heading into great risk they entreated [*lissonto*] the lord of
> ships
> to escape the unyielding movement
> of the colliding rocks.

This use of the verb is in reported speech and of the type "I entreat you, do X," but the indirect statement requires an infinitive instead of an imperative verb. Functionally analogous to the use of *lissesthai* at *Pythian* 4.207–209, Pindar uses *litaneuein* 'to entreat' to report an entreaty in a third-person voice:

> ψεύσταν δὲ ποιητὸν συνέπαξε λόγον,
> ὡς ἦρα νυμφείας ἐπείρα κεῖνος ἐν λέκτροις Ἀκάστου
> εὐνᾶς· τὸ δ᾽ ἐναντίον ἔσκεν· πολλὰ γάρ νιν παντὶ θυμῷ
> παρφαμένα λιτάνευεν. τοῖο δ᾽ ὀργὰν κνίζον αἰπεινοὶ λόγοι.
>
> *Nemean* 5.29–32

> She contrived a false, made-up story,
> that he [Peleus] tried for her bridal "favors" in Akastos' bed.
> But the opposite happened. Repeatedly and with all her heart
> she spoke deceptively and begged him [*litaneuen*]. Her headlong
> words incited his anger.

ἔβλαστεν δ' υἱὸς Οἰνώνας βασιλεύς
χειρὶ καὶ βουλαῖς ἄριστος. πολλά νιν πολλοὶ λιτάνευον ἰδεῖν.

Nemean 8.7–8

A son [Aiakos] was born to be king of Oinona
best in strength and strategies. Many often begged [*litaneuon*] to see him.

Apuein 'To Invoke'

Next I present examples of Pindar's use of *apuein* 'to invoke':

ἐγγὺς {δ'} ἐλθὼν πολιᾶς ἁλὸς οἶος ἐν ὄρφνᾳ
ἄπυεν βαρύκτυπον
Εὐτρίαιναν· ὁ δ' αὐτῷ
πὰρ ποδὶ σχεδὸν φάνη.

Olympian 1.71–74

After going near the gray sea alone in darkness,
he called upon [*apuen*] the heavy-pounding god
with the good trident.
Near at his feet the god appeared.

Σωτὴρ ὑψινεφὲς Ζεῦ, Κρόνιόν τε ναίων λόφον
τιμῶν τ' Ἀλφεὸν εὐρὺ ῥέοντα Ἰδαῖόν τε σεμνὸν ἄντρον,
ἱκέτας σέθεν ἔρχομαι Λυδίοις ἀπύων ἐν αὐλοῖς,
αἰτήσων πόλιν εὐανορίαισι τάνδε κλυταῖς
δαιδάλλειν, σέ τ', Ὀλυμπιόνικε, Ποσειδονίοισιν ἵπποις
ἐπιτερπόμενον φέρειν γῆρας εὔθυμον ἐς τελευτάν
υἱῶν, Ψαῦμι, παρισταμένων.

Olympian 5.17–23

Savior Zeus, high in the clouds, dwelling on Kronos' hill,
honoring the widely flowing Alpheos and the holy cave on Mount Ida,
as your suppliant I come, invoking you [*apuôn*] with Lydian pipes,
to ask that you adorn this city with renowned nobility among its men—

and to ask you, Olympian victor who delights in Poseidon's horses,
to bear the gladdening prize to the finish
with your sons, Psaumis, standing around you.

σὲ δ', ὦ Δεινομένειε παῖ, Ζεφυρία πρὸ δόμων
Λοκρὶς παρθένος ἀπύει, πολεμίων καμάτων ἐξ ἀμαχάνων
διὰ τεὰν δύναμιν δρακεῖσ' ἀσφαλές.

Pythian 2.18–20

You, son of Deinomenes, Zephurian Lokris, the maiden,
calls on [*apuei*] before her home, now that from the unconquerable troubles of war
she has seen security through your power.

These examples of *apuein* 'to invoke' suggest that the verb names the essence of what it means to make a Pindaric prayer; *apuein* can be validly glossed as 'to make a second-person address'. *Olympian* 1.71–74 frames Pelops' prayer to Poseidon, a passage of direct discourse characterized by the hero's second-person address to the god. As I will illustrate in Chapter Five, Pelops is a model of appropriate speech in *Olympian* 1. In light of this, it is interesting to juxtapose Pindar's use of *apuein* at *Olympian* 1.72, which describes Pelops' performance of a prayer, with Pindar's use of the verb at *Olympian* 5.19, where he represents the performance of *Olympian* 5 in terms of prayer. This juxtaposition illustrates how *apuein*, like uses of other forms of metalanguage for prayer, can be used to describe epinician performance itself.[30] With this in mind, note that *Olympian* 5.17–23, includes vocative addresses to Zeus (line 17) and to the song's *laudandus*, Psaumis (lines 21 and 23), an instance of prayer that suggests the neutralization of the functional difference between *eukha* 'prayer' and *eukhos* 'vaunt', the main subcategories of *eukhesthai* 'to pray' or 'to vaunt'. At *Pythian* 2.18–20 Pindar represents the *laudandus*'s *polis* invoking the athlete at the same time as the composer himself addresses the *laudandus*, as indicated by second-person forms (lines 18 and 20) and vocative forms (line 18).

Epeukhesthai 'To Utter a Prayer'

There is only one epinician occurrence of *epeukhesthai* 'to utter a prayer', the last instance of metalanguage for prayer that I will examine:

30 This possibility may motivate Currie's claim that "[t]he verb ἀπύειν [*apuein*] is generally used of choral singing" (2004:67).

> ἀλλ᾽ ἐπεύξασθαι μὲν ἐγὼν ἐθέλω
> Ματρί, τὰν κοῦραι παρ᾽ ἐμὸν πρόθυρον σὺν Πανὶ μέλπονται
> θαμά
> σεμνὰν θεὸν ἐννύχιαι.
>
> *Pythian* 3.77–79
>
> But I wish to utter a prayer [*epeuxasthai*]
> to the Mother,[31] the holy goddess of whom, along with Pan, the
> girls often
> sing at night.

In this passage an example of the grammatical construction of the type *ethelein* 'to wish, to be willing' + infinitive occurs. I would also suggest, on the basis of *Pythan* 3.77–79, that the function of *epeukhesthai* 'to utter a prayer' is analogous to that of *apuein* 'to invoke'. Since we have seen that *eukha* 'prayer' and *eukhos* 'vaunt' identify contrasting functional domains in Pindar's use of the speech genre *eukhesthai* and since *eukhos* has a marked functional domain, it seems that in Pindar's usage the functional domain of *eukha* embraces *epeukhesthai* and *apuein*.

Discussion

To summarize this analysis of the functions indicated by the speech plan of Pindar's metalanguage for epinician prayers, I will begin by reiterating my initial observation, that *eukha* 'prayer' and *eukhos* 'vaunt' are subcategories of *eukhesthai* 'to pray' or 'to vaunt', with *epeukhesthai* 'to utter a prayer' a subcategory of *eukha* 'prayer'. In the course of the foregoing analysis, it became clear that the functional load of *eukha* 'prayer' can include that borne by *lissesthai* 'to entreat', *litaneuein* 'to entreat', *lita* 'entreaty', and *litos* 'supplicatory'. On the basis of the functional, contextual, and grammatical parallels to other occurrences of metalanguage of prayer, it is appropriate to describe *eukhos* 'vaunt' as a form of metalanguage for epinician prayers. This is recommended by uses of *eukhesthai* in the sense of 'to vaunt' (*Olympian* 7.20–24 and *Pythian* 4.96–100) and by the strong tendency among the examples of epinician prayers that I have presented for Pindar to describe the performance of his praise poetry in terms of prayer. As a final point of summary, the function of *epeukhesthai* 'to utter a prayer' is parallel to that of *apuein* 'to invoke'. I am now prepared to

[31] The exact reference is unclear, but it is thought to be Magna Mater or Rhea. Σ *Pythian* 3.78 (Drachmann 1910:81), and Pausanias 9.25.3 tell us that Pindar had a shrine to the Mother of the gods and to Pan near his home. See Gildersleeve 1890:275 and Race 1997a:252n2.

summarize this analysis in the form of a diagram representing the relationships among forms of metalanguage for Pindar's prayers:

Diagram 1: Epinician Prayers

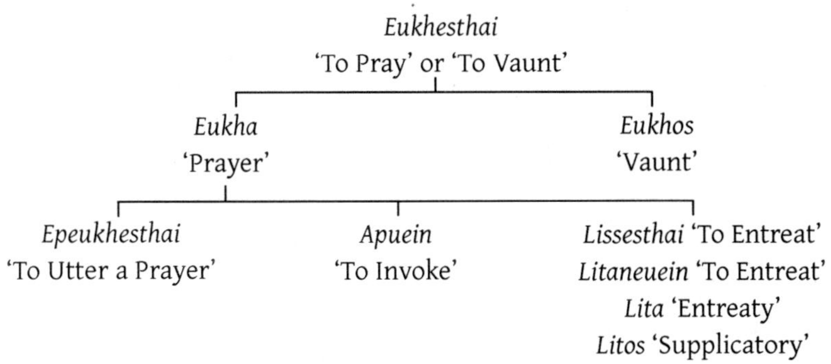

As this diagram suggests, patterns of metalanguage recommend labeling Pindar's prayers in terms of the word he uses to describe most categorically this speech genre, namely *eukhesthai*. To summarize the parameters for the speech plan discovered through the analysis of Pindar's metalanguage for *eukhesthai*, I offer the following list of functions:

To make a vaunt
To make a request or entreaty[32]
To make a vow
To express a wish[33] or intention[34]
To invoke

In the course of my analysis I have noted syntactic patterns associated with *eukhesthai*. Although to describe speech and performance in terms of grammar is of limited utility for the purposes of discovering the shape of the precatory

32 Cf. Race 1986:29, who elsewhere describes (1) requests in the context of illustrating how Pindar uses the effect of climax in hymnal invocations (1990:16–20) and (2) negative expressions in Pindar's prayers (1990:78–80).

33 Hubbard 1985:141 defines prayers as "wishes for future prosperity" and gives the opening lines of *Pythian* 12 and *Olympian* 7.87–90 and 13.24–30 as examples of prayers. See also Hubbard 1995 on Pindar's implied wishes. Mackie 2003:77–106 analyzes wishes and prayers for the future, describing them as an epinician convention, but I disagree with her position that Pindar's concern with the future suggests that he conventionally aligns his artistic craft with the arts of prophecy. Loscalzo 2003:73–75 also discusses Pindar's role as "profeta delle Musa." My view is that a prophet's stance is one among many strategies for traditionalization that Pindar may adopt.

34 Race (1990:106) claims that when uttering a "poetic intention" in "rhapsodic hymns" the poet adopts the role of composer, in "cultic hymns," the role of suppliant.

speech genre and for identifying social and artistic schemes and strategies associated with Pindar's prayers, a taxonomy of syntactic forms for epinician prayers serves to illustrate the range of possibilities. As such a taxonomy illustrates, Pindar composes *eukhesthai* using a wide range of syntactic forms. To summarize the possible syntactic constructions in which Pindar couches his prayers:

Second-person imperatives[35]
ethelein 'to wish, to be willing' + infinitive[36]
elpesthai 'to hope, to desire' + infinitive[37]
Independent optatives: optative of wish[38] and potential optative[39]
First-person future verbs that express intention, wish, or request[40]
Hortatory subjunctive[41]

35 E.g. *Olympian* 4.8–10, addressed to Zeus in the context of the use of *eukha* at *Olympian* 4.13; *Olympian* 8.9–10, addressed to the sacred grove of Pisa in the context of the use of *lita* 'entreaty' at *Olympian* 8.8; *Olympian* 12.1–2, addressed to Tukha in the context of the use of *lissesthai* 'to entreat' at *Olympian* 12.1; *Olympian* 14.5, addressed to Kharites in the context of a use of *eukhesthai* at *Olympian* 14.5; *Pythian* 1.71, addressed to Zeus in the context of the use of *lissesthai* 'to entreat' at *Pythian* 1.71; *Nemean* 3.3, addressed to the Muse in the context of the use of *lissesthai* 'to entreat' at *Nemean* 3.1; *Isthmian* 6.46, addressed to Zeus in context of a use of *lissesthai* 'to entreat' at *Isthmian* 6.45. Cf. Hamilton's definition of "Poetic Invocation," which "usually takes the form of an elaborate and lengthy invocation of some particularly relevant but not panhellenic divine figure" and is characterized by the use of an imperative verb (1974:17).

36 E.g. *Olympian* 7.20–22, in the context of a use of *eukhesthai* at *Olympian* 7.23; *Pythian* 3.1–5, which involves the *ethelein* 'to wish, to be willing' + infinitive pattern in a present contrafactual conditional clause; *Pythian* 3.77, where *epeukhesthai* occurs. Slater 1969a:86 identifies *ethelein* + infinitive as a variation of the encomiastic future, but Pelliccia 1995:327–328 disputes this claim.

37 E.g. *Olympian* 1.109–111 (cited below).

38 E.g. *Olympian* 4.12–13, in the context of the use of *eukha* at *Olympian* 4.13; *Olympian* 8.87–88, in the context of the use of *eukhesthai* at *Olympian* 8.86; and *Pythian* 9.89–90, in the context of the use of *eukha* at *Pythian* 9.89. Cf. Hamilton 1974:17, who gives as a type of prayer in Pindar, "Future Prayer," which "takes the form either of an invocation of a major panhellenic god or of a simple prayer with the optative, with or without *theos*."

39 E.g. *Pythian* 4.298 (with vocative address to the song's *laudandus*), in the context of an occurrence of *eukhesthai*, *Pythian* 4.293. Note that I do not claim that potential optative constructions (or any other syntactic construction for that matter) are characteristically forms of *eukhesthai*.

40 E.g. *Pythian* 9.89, in the context of a use of *eukha*, *Pythian* 9.89. Cf. Hamilton 1974:17 on "Future Prayer" and Mackie 2003:77–106. Pelliccia 1995:317–332 engages closely with interpretations of Pindar's use of future verbs, especially Bundy 1962 and Slater 1969a, and identifies three types of rhetorical futures in Pindar: "the intra-carminal programmatic future," "performative utterance," and the "extra-carminal" encomiastic future. Pfeijffer (1999b:15) finds Pelliccia's study "too much determined by the prerogatives of the Bundian framework" and refutes the claim that there is an encomiastic future conventional to Pindar's art (Bundy 1962:21–22; Slater 1969a). Race 2004 reasserts the validity of Bundy's convention-centered approach to Pindar, generally, and in particular, the performative quality of the encomiastic future (86–92).

41 I include this syntactic construction because it can be a way to express intention, as e.g. at *Pythian* 1.60: "Come on, then, let's compose a cherished hymn for the king of Aitna" (ἄγ' ἔπειτ' Αἴτνας βασιλεῖ φίλιον ἐξεύρωμεν ὕμνον).

Now that I have explored the speech plan of the simple speech genre *eukhesthai*, before turning to the description of its ethnographic features, I pause to make a point of methodological qualification. My present interest is to discover the convergent features of the speech genre *eukhesthai*, the ethnographic rules of co-occurrence, which I describe below. As my analysis of the speech plan for *eukhesthai* suggests, the speech acts identified by Pindar's metalanguage for prayer also exhibit patterns of alternation.[42] The rules of co-occurrence indicate the existence of a stylistic pattern for precatory speech acts in the broader sense of acts of speaking that constitute speech events. The rules of alternation in Pindar's use of the precatory speech genre indicate the existence of speech acts in the Austinian sense of performative speech acts (1975). As we have already seen, one pattern of alternation that I identify in Pindar's prayers is that, given an opposition between speech acts identified in epinician usage by *eukha* 'prayer' and those identified by *eukhos* 'vaunt', *eukhos*-acts are marked and *eukha*-acts are unmarked. While we can also observe that markedness relationships obtain among the speech acts within the domain of *eukhai* (identified in Pindar's usage by *lissesthai* 'to entreat', *lita* 'entreaty', *litaneuein* 'to entreat', *litos* 'supplicatory', *apuein* 'to invoke', and *epeukhesthai* 'to utter a prayer'), the marked quality of *eukhos* in opposition to *eukha* is especially noteworthy in the context of praise poetry. As a strategy of praise poetics, an authoritatively and effectively performed *eukha* is finally a performative speech act that I would identify as *eukhos*, a vaunt. In such a speech act, any opposition between *eukhos* and a form of *eukha* is neutralized, and the performative force of *eukhos* becomes dominantly constitutive of the speech act. To illustrate this I will briefly describe how a genre of poetry, the Instruction of Princes, which Richard Martin has explored, evidences *eukhesthai* style.

The Instruction of Princes is a cross-culturally attested genre of discourse in which a king or advisor communicates to a prince the "rules for proper legal, religious, political, and social behavior" (Martin 1984:32–33). Hesiod's *Works and Days* and the *Kheirônos Hupothêkai* (*Precepts of Kheiron*) attributed to Hesiod (*Fragments* 283–285) are examples of the Instruction of Princes genre in ancient Greek poetry.[43] Martin compares an Old Irish genre called *tecosc* 'instruction'

42 On sociolinguistic rules of co-occurrence and alternation, see Ervin-Tripp 1972 and Hymes 1989.

43 Boeke 2007:11–12 discusses the *Kheirônos Hupothêkai* as a literary antecedent to Pindar's use of popular wisdom in the *epinikia*, but sees only a loose connection between the two, apparently disagreeing with the point in Kurke 1990, whom Boeke cites, about Pindar's self-conscious alignment with traditional wisdom.

to these ancient Greek versions of Instruction of Princes. The earliest text of *tecosc* is the *Audacht Morainn* (*Testament of Morann*, 700 CE), which "purports to be the death-bed instructions of the mythical first Irish lawmaker, Morann, to Neire, his foster-son, for transmission to the young king Feradach Find Fechtnach" (Martin 1984:33). For present purposes, I want to highlight that, as Martin explains, this text records admonitions addressed to a king. Martin gives another Irish parallel from the twelfth century as evidence "that a king actually recited or assented to proverbial statements and injunctions of a *tecosc* during his inauguration ceremony" (Martin 1984:35). Since Martin also cites Pindar's *Pythian* 6.19–26 as evidence for the high value accorded to the *Kheirônos Hupothêkai* in antiquity (1984:32), it is fitting that Leslie Kurke (1990) has described how the tradition of advice poetry influences the song.

In her study of *Pythian* 6 Kurke tells us that "[t]he genre of *hypothêkai* would be characterized by a proem, an address to a specific addressee, sometimes by mythological material, but mainly by a collection of injunctions and traditional wisdom loosely strung together with gnomic material" (1990:60).[44] As with the Irish parallel cited by Martin, in Kurke's description of *hupothêkai* the stylistic features of Pindar's speech genre *eukhesthai* come to bear: "address to a specific addressee" is second-person address, which is characteristic of injunctions. Among her evidence to demonstrate that ancient Greeks recognized the *Kheirônos Hupothêkai* as a "distinctive type of poetry," Kurke gives sources that treat *parainesis* 'advice' as a synonym for *Kheirônos Hupothêkai*, including Pindar's only uses of the verb *parainein* 'to advise' (*Pythian* 6.23 and *Isthmian* 6.68) where the word "signals to its audience the introduction of ὑπόθηκαι [*hupothêkai*] into Pindar's poem" (1990:91):

> σύ τοι σχεθών νιν ἐπὶ δεξιὰ χειρός, ὀρθὰν ἄγεις ἐφημοσύναν,
> τά ποτ' ἐν οὔρεσι φαντὶ μεγαλοσθενεῖ
> Φιλύρας υἱὸν ὀρφανιζομένῳ
> Πηλεΐδᾳ παραινεῖν· μάλιστα μὲν Κρονίδαν,
> βαρύοπαν στεροπᾶν κεραυνῶν τε πρύτανιν,
> θεῶν σέβεσθαι. ταύτας δὲ μή ποτε τιμᾶς
> ἀμείρειν γονέων βίον πεπρωμένον.
>
> *Pythian* 6.19–27

> You hold him[45] in your right hand
> and practice the direct command,

[44] On proverbs as a performed genre of verbal art, see Martin 1993.
[45] The father of Thrasyboulos (the second-person addressee), *laudandus* of *Pythian* 6.

the things they say one time in the mountains
the son of Philura to the mighty son of Peleus,
when he was deprived of his parents, advised [*parainein*]: most of
all the gods the son of Kronos,
booming-voiced ruler of thunder and lightning,
revere and of the same honors never
to deprive parents throughout their fated lifetime.

Λάμπων δὲ μελέταν
ἔργοις ὀπάζων Ἡσιόδου μάλα τιμᾷ τοῦτ᾽ ἔπος,
υἱοῖσί τε φράζων παραινεῖ.

Isthmian 6.66–68

Lampon,[46] by applying effort
to his deeds, especially honors this saying of Hesiod's,
and by declaring it to his sons he advises [*parainei*] them
of it.

Kurke's treatment of *parainesis* as synonymous to the genre of *hupothêkai*, in that both entail instruction or admonition in the stylistic form of the speech genre *eukhesthai*, accords well with Martin's study of the Instruction of Princes, where he explains that "the use of vocatives...is a traditional element in Greek poetic *parainesis* from Homer on" (1984:31) and elsewhere describes *parainesis* "as a key genre, one that frames the discourse of didactic, elegiac, and even dramatic poetry in Greece" (2000:53). Kurke (1990:97) offers an illuminating example of the "parainetic mode," Athena's address to Telemakhos: "I will thoroughly instruct [*hupothêsomai*] you, if only you would obey" (σοὶ δ᾽ αὐτῷ πυκινῶς ὑποθήσομαι, αἴ κε πίθηαι, *Odyssey* i 279). Here we see stylistic features of the speech genre *eukhesthai*: second-person address and a first-person future verb expressing intention. I would add here that in his study of Hesiod's metanastic poetics, Martin (1992:16) specifically links prayer style with the poetics of wisdom as represented by Hesiod's *Works and Days* and Phoinix's speech to Achilles (*Iliad* IX 434–603).

As both Kurke and Martin explain, *hupothêkai* include gnomic and mythological material, in addition to forms of speech that I associate with the speech genre *eukhesthai*. Here I characterize why I stress the importance of prayer-vaunt language in *hupothêkai*. First, no other simple speech genre in Pindar's

46 Father of Phylakidas, the *laudandus* of *Isthmian* 6.

epinikia exhibits as many patterns of alternation as *eukhesthai*. Second, one conclusion that I have drawn from my detailed analysis of Pindar's prayers is that all addressees of *eukhesthai* are in some sense authoritative. In terms of the ethnographic features that I have been using to describe the ways of epinician speaking, addressees of *eukhesthai* such as gods, heroes, and personified figures (e.g. Euphrosuna at *Olympian* 14.14) may be the conventional speech objects of mythological narrative. As I will next argue, this correlation is salient in the context of a traditional society in which reperformance, often reperformance of traditional narrative and authoritative speech, or *muthos*, specifically, is a highly valued cultural practice.

The figures whom Pindar's songs commemorate are never the speech objects of mythological narrative, but they are often the addressees of *eukhesthai*. According to the ethnographic rules of the epinician way of speaking that I have been describing, if one criterion for the authoritative status of an addressee of *eukhesthai* is that the addressee may be a speech object of mythological narrative, but a *laudandus* is never a speech object of mythological narrative, then is there another way for us to discover how a *laudandus* comes to be an authoritative addressee? The simple fact that many of the *laudandi* of Pindar's *epinikia* are outstanding members of their communities and possess aristocratic status may establish them as authoritative addressees. The simple fact that communities confer prestige in the form of *kudos* 'talismanic power' (Kurke 1993) on their victorious athletes may also establish Pindar's *laudandi* as authoritative addressees. But such explanations are unsatisfactory —not to say incorrect—because, first, they involve an outside-in approach to context and, second, they do not account for traditional dynamics entailed in the composition and performance of epinician art. In other words, I would like to get at how, in terms of communicative practices, specifically, to identify the authoritative status of an addressee of *eukhesthai* who may not be the speech object of mythological narrative.

If we follow a well-trodden path in the study of Archaic Greek verbal art and take *muthos* as authoritative speech, then I would suggest that the function of an original epinician performance is to establish the status of a song's *laudandus* as an appropriate speech object of *muthos*. The epinician composer performs this function by establishing his song as a model for reperformance, a topic that I address more fully in Chapter 5. To secure a positive evaluation from an audience to an original performance is to introduce Pindar's composition into the word-hoard of tradition and to make it available for reperformance. In order to secure such a positive evaluation, again, the epinician composer must display his competence in his artistic medium. One crucial form that such a display must take is a socially appropriate and effective use of what a community regards as authoritative speech, or *muthos*. Now I suggest that instruction poetry such as *hupothêkai* or *parainesis* is such a form of authoritative speech. When this genre of poetry is addressed to the epinician *laudandus*, the implication, if Pindar's use of it is to be authoritative, is that the addressee must also be authoritative. In such instances of address, the illocutionary act of *eukha* 'prayer' becomes a performative speech act we can call *eukhos* 'vaunt', whose utterance in the context of epinician performance by implication makes the *laudandus* an authoritative addressee. Again, what gets done in such a performative speech act is that the opposition between *eukha* and *eukhos* is neutralized, rendering the prayer a form of praise. As Kurke writes of the last two lines of *Pythian* 6, instruction poetry becomes "transformed by the poet's artifice from admonition to the crowning epinician compliment" (1990:102).[47] In the mode of traditionality evidenced in Archaic and Classical Greece, reperformance is mutually beneficial to poet and *laudandus* in that the word that endures through reperformance conveys the memory and prestige of both artist and athlete to future audiences. As Martin explains in connection with the Irish example of Instruction of Princes, "[t]he Irish king is certified by the poet; reciprocally, the poet is maintained by the king and tribe" (1984:35).

I have taken time to describe dynamics involved in the patterns of alternation in Pindar's prayer-vaunt language only with respect to its connection to instruction poetry. I detect other dynamics that are worth exploring in future research. Yet, given that in a number of Pindar's *epinikia* (*Pythian* 3, 4, 6, 9, and *Nemean* 3) there are mythological passages that depict Kheiron, the instructor of princes *par excellence*, the relationship between *eukhesthai* and Pindar's use of instruction poetry seems to be an especially important application of this speech genre (cf. Kurke 1990:93–94).

Ethnographic Features of Epinician *Eukhesthai*

To resume my description of the rules of co-occurrence evidenced in Pindar's prayers, in the foregoing discussion I have anticipated that the most dominantly constitutive feature of the precatory speech genre is second-person addressivity. It is important to further validate this claim in light of the fact that some of the examples of prayer given above do not provide deictic

47 Kurke accordingly describes *Pythian* 6 as "an appropriation of *hupothêkai* for epinician purposes" (1990:98).

evidence of a second-person addressee. For convenience, I recall here two examples of precatory utterances treated above that do not have an explicit addressee:

θεὸς εὔφρων
εἴη λοιπαῖς εὐχαῖς.

Olympian 4.12–13

May a god be favorable
to future prayers [*eukhai*].

Χαρίτων κελαδεννᾶν
μή με λίποι καθαρὸν φέγγος.

Pythian 9.89–90

May the resounding Kharites'
clean light not leave me!

It may be adequate to make the intuitive observations that at *Olympian* 4.12–13 the unnamed god of line 12 is likely to be the addressee of the *eukhesthai* and that at *Pythian* 9.89–90 the Kharites are likely to be the addressees of that utterance. However, I appeal to the concept of the conative function of language, one of the fundamental components of a speech event in Jakobson's model of communication (summarized in the Introduction), to provide a more methodologically grounded basis for identifying the second-person addressivity in the cases of *eukhesthai* that do not have an explicit second-person reference.

Jakobson explains the conative function as follows: "Orientation toward the ADDRESSEE, the CONATIVE function, finds its purest grammatical expression in the vocative and imperative, which syntactically, morphologically, and often phonemically deviate from other nominal and verbal categories" (1960:355). Jakobson's definition of the conative function of language correlates to epinician prayer types that entail the use of imperative and vocative grammatical forms without further comment. But how do we identify orientation toward the addressee in the case of utterances like those at *Olympian* 4.12–13 and *Pythian* 9.89–90?

In the Introduction I described subfields of linguistics in order to demonstrate that the focus of syntactics is upon the relationships among linguistic signs, whereas in linguistic pragmatics the focus is upon the relationships between linguistic signs and their users. Jakobson highlights the centrality of contexts of participation, versus grammatical contexts, for understanding the conative function by applying a "truth test" to utterances characterized by the relative dominance of the conative function.[48] To illustrate the point, the utterances at *Olympian* 4.12–13 and *Pythian* 9.89–90 are not liable to a truth test: of the utterance "May a god be kind to future prayers," we cannot effectively ask "Is it true?" With respect to such a truth test, then, these utterances are pragmatically akin to utterances with, say, second-person imperative verbs, which are also not liable to a truth test. While this is a starting point, we need sounder evidence to support the claim that second-person addressivity occurs in prayers without explicit second-person deictics.

It is with this problem in mind that I present Jakobson's characterization of poetry types in which the conative function is relatively dominant (but still subordinate to the poetic function): "poetry of the second person is imbued with the conative function and is either supplicatory or exhortative, depending upon whether the first person is subordinated to the second one or the second to the first" (1960:357).[49] This characterization of "poetry of the second person" accords well with what we have seen in the analysis of Pindar's metalanguage for *eukhesthai*. For example, the type of *eukhesthai* that has the form *lissesthai* 'to entreat' + second-person imperative is supplicatory in Jakobson's sense. I suggest that, in the case of Pindaric prayers in which there is no grammatical evidence of a second-person addressee, what we are witnessing is an exhortative type of poetry of the second person in which the second person is subordinated to the first. For example, the optatives of wish at *Olympian* 4.12–13 and *Pythian* 9.89–90 have an exhortative quality. The exhortative quality of first-person future verbs—a possible syntactic environment for Pindaric *eukhesthai*—is implicit in the exegetical convention of positing a short-vowel subjunctive (e.g. Gildersleeve 1890:civ). If such exhortatory utterances subordinate the second person to the first person, how do we locate that subordinated second person?

In the context of epinician performance the always occurring, dominantly constitutive frame of interaction is that between composer and audience. I assume that the traditional artist Pindar would have been mainly (i.e.

48 Jakobson explains a truth test as follows: "The imperative sentences cardinally differ from declarative sentences: the latter are and the former are not liable to a truth test. When in O'Neill's play *The Fountain*, Nano, '(in a fierce tone of command),' says 'Drink!'—the imperative cannot be challenged by the question 'is it true or not?' which may be, however, perfectly well asked after such questions as 'one drank,' 'one will drink,' 'one would drink.' In contradistinction to the imperative sentences, the declarative sentences are convertible into interrogative sentences: 'did one drink?' 'will one drink?' 'would one drink?'" (1960:355).

49 See also Waugh 1980:59.

in consideration of the chorus) subject to evaluation for his epinician compositions. To draw from the example of a supplicatory *eukhesthai*, as in the form *lissesthai* 'to entreat' + second-person imperative, the ethnographic shape of the utterance establishes a framework of interaction; when the composer or the chorus makes a second-person address to Zeus or the Muses, that interaction is played out before the audience, which participates as an overhearer to that speech act. In the case of an exhortative *eukhesthai*, I suggest that the boundaries of emerging frameworks dissolve in such a way that the utterance reaches out, as it were, to embrace the audience; the audience members participate in the speech act as intended listeners and become players in the performance.[50] Such a view is supported by the following explanation of the discursive relationship between the first and second person by Emile Benveniste (1971:225, emphasis in original):

> Language is possible only because each speaker sets himself up as a *subject* by referring to himself as *I* in his discourse. Because of this, *I* posits another person, the one who, being, as he is, completely exterior to 'me,' becomes my echo to whom I say *you* and who says *you* to me. This polarity of persons is the fundamental condition in language, of which the process of communication, in which we share, is only a mere pragmatic consequence. It is a polarity, moreover, very peculiar in itself, as it offers a type of opposition whose equivalent is encountered nowhere else outside of language. This polarity does not mean either equality or symmetry: 'ego' always has a position of transcendence with regard to *you*. Nevertheless, neither of the terms can be conceived of without the other.

Following from Benveniste's observations, we can say that an exhortative prayer uttered by a first-person speaker implies a second-person addressee and, further, we can identify that addressee as the audience, the default and constitutive addressee in the composer-audience frame of interaction.

There is another way to formulate this line of thinking. The features constitutive of speech genres include frameworks of participation, principally the features of speech subject and addressee. On the one hand, we can say that the communication flow from one speech genre to the next during the course of an epinician performance entails the generation of multiple

50 What I am describing here is akin to Bergren's approach to apostrophe in the Homeric hymns: "[t]he poet apostrophizes not simply to elicit the response of the addressee, but also to prove to his 'judging' audience the poetic power of his speech" (1982:85). Cf. Burnett 2005:240–241 on audience involvement in what she identifies as prayers and maxims in Pindar's songs.

frameworks of interaction, each organizing and then yielding to the next framework of interaction that emerges in the unfolding event of epinician performance. On the other hand, given that the dominantly organizing frame of interaction in epinician performance is that between composer and audience, as a postmodern trope, we can see frameworks emerging in the flow of communication as *destructive* of the dominant frame of interaction between composer and audience. To illustrate, in the case of a supplicatory *eukhesthai*, as in the example of the form *lissesthai* 'to entreat' + second-person imperative, the ethnographic shape of the utterance can be said to intrude upon the composer-audience relationship by introducing another framework of interaction constituted by the speech subject and addressee of the supplication; when the composer or the chorus makes a second-person address to Zeus or the Muses, the audience, in a sense, gives over the floor to another participant matrix. By comparison, an exhortative *eukhesthai* reasserts the constitutively dominant composer-audience interaction; the audience members resume the floor. On the basis of the pragmatics of participant frameworks as described in the citation from Benveniste above, then, we can identify the second-person addressivity in an exhortative type of *eukhesthai* in the very subordination of the second person to the first.

As a final illustration of how we can identify the second-person addressivity of Pindar's *eukhesthai* through the conative function of language, I offer an example of a prayer couched in the syntactic form of an optative of wish, but containing an explicit second-person reference:

> εἴη σέ τε τοῦτον ὑψοῦ χρόνον πατεῖν,
> ἐμέ τε τοσσάδε νικαφόροις
> ὁμιλεῖν πρόφαντον σοφίᾳ καθ' Ἕλλανας ἐόντα παντᾷ.
>
> *Olympian* 1.115–116
>
> May it be that you walk aloft for this time
> and that I commune just as long with victorious men
> and be distinguished for wisdom among Greeks everywhere.

Two functions are embedded in this passage: first, the function of expressing a wish, as indicated by the utterance's syntax (the optative of wish construction), a form of *eukha* 'prayer'; second, the function of *eukhos* 'vaunt'. This latter part of the utterance's speech plan is suggested by the preceding discussion of the conative function of language in connection with forms of *eukhesthai* that are not constituted by imperative or vocative forms. We have observed the distinction between supplicatory and exhortative types of prayers and that, in exhortative prayers, the audience is drawn into the participant framework of the utterance. I would suggest, further, that in the context of the performance of praise poetry, a vaunt, in Pindar's language *eukhos*, is appropriate to the exhortative type of prayer: by calling attention to the praiseworthiness of the object of praise through *eukhos*, the performer exhorts the audience to share in his evaluation of the *laudandus*. To stress, these dynamics are identifiable empirically through the description of the pragmatics of speech and performance. In light of these observations, we can interpret *Olympian* 1.115–116 as a distillation of the speech plan constitutive of *eukhesthai*, in that this brief utterance contains the full spectrum of functional capacity of the speech genre, both *eukhos* 'vaunt' (for which the audience is the primary addressee) and *eukha* 'prayer' (for which Hieron is the primary addressee). To point up the relevance of such observations for the philology of Pindar, I would add that here we are able to grasp something of Pindar's verbal art in action; with the methodological and interpretative focus upon practice, no claims of boldness, no intimations of rhetorical flourish, no conjectural history about Pindar's relationship with Hieron are necessary to understand that, at *Olympian* 1.115–116, Pindar displays an incredible fluency in his art form and invites his audience, both ancient and modern, to participate in his song as co-creator of the composition.

I am now prepared to summarize the ethnographic features constitutive of epinician *eukhesthai* as follows:

Speech Subject: first person;

Addressee: second person, explicit or implied by conative function of language;

Speech Object: something boasted, requested, pledged, wished for, or a figure invoked;

Speech Plan: to make a vaunt, to make a request or entreaty, to make a vow, to express a wish or intention, and to invoke;

Spatial Dimension: immediate;

Temporal Dimension: immediate.

The chronotope characteristic of *eukhesthai* is immediate relative to the speech event of performance, but has another quality that distinguishes it from the chronotope of the lyric simple speech genre: because prayers express wishes, requests, advice, and hopes, they possess an orientation toward action subsequent to the moment of speaking. To apply a rubric, we can say that *eukhesthai* has the chronotope "now-address to you about subsequent action."

The following example of *eukhesthai* involves the use of imperatives, a case in which the conative function of language is explicit:

> εἰ δ' ἄεθλα γαρύεν
> ἔλδεαι, φίλον ἦτορ,
> μηκέτ' ἀελίου σκόπει
> ἄλλο θαλπνότερον ἐν ἀμέρᾳ φαεννὸν ἄστρον ἐρήμας δι'
> αἰθέρος,
> μηδ' Ὀλυμπίας ἀγῶνα φέρτερον αὐδάσομεν.
>
> *Olympian* 1.3–7

> But if you wish to sing of victory prizes,
> my heart,
> no longer look
> to another star in the empty ether, shining by day, warmer
> than the sun,
> and we will not sing of a competition tougher than
> Olympia.

The ethnographic features occurring in this passage are:

Speech Subject: composer in a first-person voice, indicated pragmatically (following Benveniste) by the second-person verbs ἔλδεαι (line 4) and σκόπει (line 5); the first-person plural verb αὐδάσομεν (line 7) makes the first-person voice explicit and its future tense communicates speaker's intention;[51]

Addressee: second-person addressivity is explicit in the second-person verbs ἔλδεαι (line 4) and σκόπει (line 5), an instance of self-address by metonymy: the second-person verbs are addressed to φίλον ἦτορ (line 4); the first-person plural verb αὐδάσομεν (line 7) has no explicit addressee, but has an exhortative quality;

Speech Object: (1) entreaty to second-person addressee about what the speech object of the complex utterance of *Olympian* 1 is to be: athletic competition at Olympia; (2) expression of the intent to speak about that speech object;

[51] Gildersleeve 1890:130 interprets αὐδάσομεν 'we will sing' as a short-vowel subjunctive; so too Gerber 1982:24.

Speech Plan: to entreat and to express an intention;

Spatial Dimension: immediate;

Temporal Dimension: immediate, with temporal vector tracking to subsequent, and so to future, speech actions.

At *Olympian* 1.3–7 the second-person address is metonymy for self-reference and indicates that this passage is a hybrid utterance, constituted simultaneously by features of lyric and precatory speech genres. I defer the discussion of hybridization to the next chapter. For the present purposes of description, the second-person addressivity of *Olympian* 1.3–7 constitutes the passage as dominantly a form of *eukhesthai*.

The following example is a prayer of a type similar to *Olympian* 1.3–7, a prayer-lyric hybrid with second-person imperative verbs, and therefore dominantly of the *eukhesthai* speech genre:

ἀλλὰ Δωρίαν ἀπὸ φόρμιγγα πασσάλου
λάμβαν', εἴ τί τοι Πίσας τε καὶ Φερενίκου χάρις
νόον ὑπὸ γλυκυτάταις ἔθηκε φροντίσιν.

Olympian 1.17–19

But take the Dorian lyre from its peg,
if at all the grace of Pisa and Pherenikos
put your mind under the influence of the sweetest thoughts.

The ethnographic features occurring in this passage are:

Speech Subject: composer in a first-person voice; the second-person imperative verb λάμβαν' (line 18) and the second-person pronoun τοι (line 18) pragmatically imply a first-person speaker;

Addressee: second-person singular indicated by the imperative verb λάμβαν' (line 18) and the second-person pronoun τοι (line 18); this second-person addressee is φίλον ἦτορ (line 4), metonymy for speaker's self-address;

Speech Object: entreaty to perform the song as response to the *kharis* (line 18) of Hieron's victory in the single horse race at Olympia;

Speech Plan: to entreat the addressee to perform the song as a response to *kharis* (line 18) of Hieron's victory in the single horse race at Olympia;

Spatial Dimension: immediate;

Temporal Dimension: immediate.

To offer an example of another type of *eukhesthai* that involves the use of a first-person future verb, the following passage is addressed to Pelops:

υἱὲ Ταντάλου, σὲ δ᾽ ἀντία προτέρων φθέγξομαι,
ὁπότ᾽ ἐκάλεσε πατὴρ τὸν εὐνομώτατον
ἐς ἔρανον φίλαν τε Σίπυλον,
ἀμοιβαῖα θεοῖσι δεῖπνα παρέχων,
τότ᾽ Ἀγλαοτρίαιναν ἁρπάσαι,
δαμέντα φρένας ἱμέρῳ, χρυσέαισί τ᾽ ἀν᾽ ἵπποις
ὕπατον εὐρυτίμου ποτὶ δῶμα Διὸς μεταβᾶσαι·
ἔνθα δευτέρῳ χρόνῳ
ἦλθε καὶ Γανυμήδης
Ζηνὶ τωὔτ᾽ ἐπὶ χρέος.
ὡς δ᾽ ἄφαντος ἔπελες, οὐδὲ ματρὶ πολλὰ μαιόμενοι φῶτες ἄγαγον,
ἔννεπε κρυφᾷ τις αὐτίκα φθονερῶν γειτόνων,
ὕδατος ὅτι τε πυρὶ ζέοισαν εἰς ἀκμάν
μαχαίρᾳ τάμον κατὰ μέλη,
τραπέζαισί τ᾽ ἀμφὶ δεύτατα κρεῶν
σέθεν διεδάσαντο καὶ φάγον.

Olympian 1.36–51

Son of Tantalos, in opposition to those of former days I will declare that,
when your father invited the gods to a very well arranged
meal, to his Sipulos,
and offered feasts requiting their hospitality,
then the god with the splendid trident ravished you
because he was beside himself with desire; and that with golden horses
he translated you to the highest home of widely honored Zeus.
At a later time
Ganymede also went there,
to Zeus, for the same obligation.
But when you were nowhere to be seen and people who looked everywhere for you did not lead you to your mother,
a jealous neighbor immediately claimed in secret
that into the peak of water boiling over fire
they cut through your limbs with a sword,
and that around the tables they divided the last bits
of your flesh and ate.

While this prayer is more accurately a stylistic hybrid of *eukhesthai* and mythological narrative, it is dominantly in the style of *eukhesthai*, as indicated by the second-person forms that refer to the addressee, Pelops. The ethnographic features occurring at *Olympian* 1.36–51, are:

Speech Subject: composer in a first-person voice, indicated by φθέγξομαι (line 36);

Addressee: Pelops, indicated by vocative υἱὲ Ταντάλου (line 36), second-person pronouns σέ (line 36) and σέθεν (51), and the second-person singular imperfect verb ἔπελες (line 46);

Speech Object: intention not to tell the traditional story that Pelops got his ivory shoulder as a consequence of his father Tantalos' sacrilegious deception of the gods;

Speech Plan: to express the intention not to tell the story that Pelops got his ivory shoulder as a consequence of his father Tantalos' sacrilegious deception of the gods, indicated by the future singular verb φθέγξομαι (line 36);

Spatial Dimension: immediate (grammatical evidence for second-person address indicates that Pindar pragmatically treats Pelops as a participant in the current speech event);

Temporal Dimension: immediate (grammatical evidence for second-person address indicates that Pindar pragmatically treats Pelops as a participant in the current speech event).

The following example of *eukhesthai* involves direct address to Hieron:[52]

θεὸς ἐπίτροπος ἐὼν τεαῖσι μήδεται
ἔχων τοῦτο κᾶδος, Ἱέρων,
μερίμναισιν· εἰ δὲ μὴ ταχὺ λίποι,
ἔτι γλυκυτέραν κεν ἔλπομαι
σὺν ἅρματι θοῷ κλεΐξειν ἐπίκουρον εὑρὼν ὁδὸν λόγων
παρ' εὐδείελον ἐλθὼν Κρόνιον.

Olympian 1.106–111

A guardian god thinks of your concerns,
taking this on for his responsibility, Hieron.
Unless he should leave soon,

[52] Mackie 2003:92–93 also treats this passage as an example of epinician prayers and wishes for the future.

I hope a still sweeter victory
with the swift chariot to celebrate, after finding an assisting path
of words
and going by the far-seen mound of Kronos.

The ethnographic features occurring in this passage are:

Speech Subject: composer in first-person singular voice. Forms of second-person address imply pragmatically a first-person speaker: the second-person singular possessive adjective τεαῖσι (line 106) and the vocative Ἱέρων (line 107); the first-person singular verb ἔλπομαι (line 109) explicitly indicates a first-person singular speaker;

Addressee: Hieron, indicated by the second-person singular possessive adjective τεαῖσι (line 106) and the vocative Ἱέρων (line 107);

Speech Object: (1) vaunt that a god attends Hieron and his successes; (2) the intention to commemorate Hieron's further successes;

Speech Plan: to vaunt and to express an intention;

Spatial Dimension: immediate, indicated by second-person address to participant in current speech event;

Temporal Dimension: immediate, indicated by second-person address to participant in current speech event.

The following is the final example of *eukhesthai* that occurs in Pindar's *Olympian* 1:[53]

εἴη σέ τε τοῦτον ὑψοῦ χρόνον πατεῖν,
ἐμέ τε τοσσάδε νικαφόροις
ὁμιλεῖν πρόφαντον σοφίᾳ καθ' Ἕλλανας ἐόντα
παντᾷ.

Olympian 1.115–116

May it be that you walk aloft for this time
and that I commune just as long with victorious men
and be distinguished for wisdom among Greeks
everywhere.

53 Hubbard 1985:141–142 identifies this passage as a common type of prayer—the type that concludes an epinician song—and cites the endings of *Olympian* 6, 13, and *Isthmian* 7 as additional examples.

As discussed above, this form of prayer involves the use of an optative of wish with an explicit second-person reference. The ethnographic features occurring in the passage are:

Speech Subject: composer in first-person singular voice indicated by pronoun ἐμέ (line 115b);

Addressee: Hieron, indicated by second-person singular pronoun σέ (line 115), and audience, as suggested by the exhortative quality of the utterance;

Speech Object: a vaunt and wishes for Hieron's current success, for future opportunities for the composer to associate with athletic victors, and hopes for the composer's renown for wisdom;

Speech Plan: to vaunt and to express wishes, indicated by use of independent optative of wish;

Spatial Dimension: immediate, indicated by deictic reference to participants in current speech event;

Temporal Dimension: immediate, indicated by deictic reference to participants in current speech event.

To conclude my treatment of the simple speech genre *eukhesthai*, my analysis here has been more detailed than my description of other simple speech genres of *epinikion*. This was motivated by the need to demonstrate how the speech genre of *eukhesthai* can appropriately be said to constitute a broad range of speech functions expressed in a multiplicity of syntactic constructions. By looking at patterns of alternation in order to define the domain of analysis for epinician prayers, it then became possible to discover patterns of co-occurrence among the features of *eukhesthai* style. Along the way this analysis has addressed the problem of Pindar's first-person futures and explored the relationship between Pindar's *eukhesthai* style and traditional *hupothêkai* or *parainesis*.

In Chapters 3 and 4 I have described the five ways of epinician speaking that constitute the epinician way of speaking. Table 1 summarizes this description:

Table 1: The Ways of Epinician Speaking

	Lyric	Myth	*Angelia*	*Eukhesthai*	*Gnôma*
Speech Subject	First Person, Inclusive Relative to Speech Object	Third Person, Exclusive Relative to Speech Object	Third Person, Exclusive Relative to Speech Object	First Person, Inclusive	Third Person, Inclusive
Addressee	Audience, Inclusive Relative to Speech Object	Audience, Exclusive Relative to Speech Object	Audience, Inclusive	Second Person, Inclusive	Indefinite, Inclusive
Speech Object (Theme)	Reflexive (e.g. Performance, Praise, Language), Inclusive	Actor(s) and Actions, Exclusive Relative to Performance	*Laudandus* *Laudandus*'s Family *Laudandus*'s *Polis* Achievements	Vaunt Entreaty Vow Wish Invocation	Appropriate Speech and Action
Speech Plan	Reflexive (e.g. To Perform, To Praise), Inclusive	To Narrate Traditional Stories	To Report Speech Object	To Perform Vaunt, Entreaty, Vow, Wish, or Invocation	To Express Conventions for Appropriate Speech and Action
Spatial Aspect	Immediate	Mythological	Non-Immediate	Immediate	Indefinite, Inclusive
Temporal Aspect	Immediate	Mythological	Non-Immediate	Immediate	Indefinite, Inclusive

The cumulative evidence of *Pindar's Verbal Art* indicates that Pindar was an oral poet. Chapter 1 demonstrated that, on the basis of intersubjective objectivity, Pindar's communicative medium is unambiguously spoken, not written. Chapter 2 explored how Pindar's text-artifact records certain performance keys that set up the performance frame in such a way that each epinician song is a well-defined speech event. Then Chapters 3 and 4 provided a practical (rather than rigidly formal) taxonomy of the ways of epinician speaking that constitute the epinician way of speaking. The Appendix to *Pindar's Verbal Art* documents just how patterned the ways of epinician speaking and their organization within an individual song are, suggesting that Pindar composes his songs, not by theme like the Homeric singer of tales (Lord 1960:68–98), but by speech genre. While scholars generally accept non-Homeric Archaic Greek poetry as performed and, by implication, oral, *Pindar's Verbal Art* contributes to the project of describing the communicative means employed in such oral poetics. In the next chapter I will continue my study of epinician style by exploring the novelistic features of *epinikion*.

5

Novelistic Features of Epinician Style

To approach *epinikion* as a novelistic form of discourse is an effective basis for stylistic description of the genre and for understanding the art form from the perspective of intersubjective objectivity. To be clear at the outset, I identify Pindar's art as a form of *novelistic discourse* and not as a *novel*, understood as a prose form of verbal art.[1] Continuing to focus upon the example of his most well-known song, *Olympian* 1, I will devote most of this chapter to demonstrating that Pindar's art possesses each of the three characteristics of the novel that Bakhtin identifies (1981:11):

> (1) its stylistic three-dimensionality, which is linked with the multi-languaged consciousness realized in the novel; (2) the radical change it effects in the temporal coordinates of the literary image; (3) the new zone opened by the novel for structuring literary images, namely the zone of maximal contact with the present (with contemporary reality) in all its openendedness.

Before illustrating how *epinikion* possesses these three characteristics, I will first explore how aspects of the ambient cultural context of ancient Greece give rise to the novelistic quality of *epinikion.*

I have stressed throughout *Pindar's Verbal Art* that performance is fundamentally constitutive of epinician composition and reception. When it comes to understanding how *epinikion* is a novelistic form of verbal art and why this

1 Bakhtin also distinguishes the novel from other forms of verbal art in the following way, which highlights another important difference between Pindar's performed oral art and the novel: "All these genres [e.g. epic and tragedy], or in any case their defining features, are considerably older than written language and the book, and to the present day they retain their ancient oral and auditory characteristics. Of all the major genres only the novel is younger than writing and the book: it alone is organically receptive to new forms of mute perception, that is, to reading" (1981:3). Cf. Bakhtin 1981:379.

is important to the study of *epinikion* as an artifact of social history, it is necessary to consider performance in light of reperformance. Just as the dialogical interaction between performer and audience is constitutive of the speech event of epinician performance, and just as the dialogical interaction between speech subject and addressee is dominantly constitutive of each simple speech genre that constitutes *epinikion*, dialogue between the contexts of original performance and reperformance is constitutive of the complex genre of *epinikion*. The medium, as it were, of this dialogue is mimesis. According to Nagy, the performance of ancient Greek poetry is a form of mimesis understood as the reenactment of a model (1996:4 and 39–58).[2] This conception of mimesis derives from Nagy's study of the relationship between myth and ritual,[3] which the following citation illustrates (1996:56, emphasis in original):

> If you *re-enact* an archetypal action in ritual, it only stands to reason that you have to *imitate* those who re-enacted before you and who served as your *immediate* models. But the *ultimate* model is still the archetypal action or figure that you are re-enacting in ritual, which is coextensive with the whole line of imitators who re-enact the way in which their ultimate model acted, each imitating each one's predecessor.

Mimesis, then, entails reenactment through ritual of an archetypal action, which serves as the model to be reenacted, and myth is a reenactment of ritual in the form of poetic performance, where, following Nagy (1990:32–33), I take myth in the broad sense of special speech, such as the acts of speech used in the context of Archaic Greek performance of song and poetry. To illustrate the relationship of myth and ritual to performance by way of an example that is pertinent to choral song, concerning Alkman's *Partheneion*, Nagy "propose[s] that archetypal figures, including the primary archetypal figures named Hagesikhora and Agido, are *models* being acted out by real chorus-members in performances held on a seasonally-recurring basis. Even their names designate models—either divine, like Hagesikhora, or royal, like Agido" (Nagy 1996:57, emphasis in original; cf. Stehle 1997:24). In this scenario the context for reperformance is relatively stable, with Alkman's song, a form of myth in the sense of special speech, reperformed by a chorus and "on a seasonally-recurring basis." Under the influence of Panhellenism, which surrounds the composition and performance of Pindar's songs, however, there are multiple

2 For another consideration of mimesis in Archaic Greek poetry see Gentili 1988:50–60.

3 Among the many possibilities, see Nagy 1990:30–33 on the relationship between myth and ritual.

scenarios possible for the reperformance of *epinikion*, as described recently by Bruno Currie (2004):[4] oral diffusion through informal reperformance (recitation from memory) by those who were present at the original production of an individual song; the transmission of texts, which would have been used in schools for memorization and oral recitation; recitation as informal entertainment during family meals; solo recitation in sympotic context;[5] more formal choral reperformance in a sympotic context; songs or stories derived from, but not exact reproductions of, Pindar's original compositions; production of a song's reperformance by the *laudandus*'s family;[6] "formal choral reperformances organized by the *polis*"; and "regular reperformance at the site of the games."[7] Oral diffusion and recitation are two media of reperformance that entail one of Gentili's conditions for oral poetry: "oral transmission (memorized poetic tradition)" (Gentili 1988:4).[8] Adding this to the argument in Chapter One that Pindar's songs represent themselves as forms of "oral composition (extemporaneous improvisation)" and "oral communication (performance)," we see that *epinikion* satisfies all three of Gentili's conditions for oral poetry.

4 For Pfeijffer (1999a:7–11) the evidence of local references in the *epinikia* "suggests quite the opposite of Pindar's envisaging a Panhellenic audience," but fluency in epinician art depends upon reading the dialogue between the local and the Panhellenic, especially when it comes to understanding the constitutive role that Panhellenic tradition played in the survival of *epinikion* and the athlete's *kleos*.

5 Consideration of the reperformance of *epinikion* often focuses upon the symposium venue. Kurke argues that the transmission of Pindar's poetry through reperformance at symposia "attest[s] to their popularity with the social stratum that tended to perform poetry at symposia—generally speaking, the upper classes" (1991:5). Morrison's view is "that the most likely and most common reperformance scenario for Pindaric and Bacchylidean victory odes was monodic reperformance at symposia" (Morrison 2007:15). Cf. Irigoin 1952:8–20, Herington 1985:28, Clay 1999, Athanassaki 2004:339, and Nicholson 2005:11.

6 Loscalzo 2003:99–100 interprets *Nemean* 4.13–16 as evidence for this reperformance scenario.

7 Herington 1985:26–27 observes similarities between Alkman's *Partheneion* and Pindar's *Partheneion* 2, suggesting perhaps a more stable reperformance scenario for this composition than for the *epinikia*. See Stehle 1997:93–100 for an important discussion of Pindar's *Partheneion* 2, with comparison to Alkman's *partheneia*. Following Loscalzo 2003:104–105, we might add to Currie's list of scenarios reperformance during regular festivals for songs that may have been composed for original performance at such festivals. Loscalzo's example is *Pythian* 5, whose lines 77–81 suggest the Carnea as the performance venue for that song. Carey's explanation, following Morgan 1993:12, for the lack of explicit details in extant *epinikia* about the costumes of epinician performers applies to other circumstances as well: "one obvious effect of the lack of specificity about the physical aspects of the première is to elide the difference between the first and the subsequent performances" (2007:199).

8 Herington 1985:48–50 argues that independent of the technology of writing "an uninterrupted succession of *re-performances*" (emphasis in original) enabled the transmission of Archaic Greek music and choreography into the fourth century BCE (see his Appendix VII for testimonia).

The comparison of reperformance contexts for Alkman's *Partheneion* and Pindar's *epinikia* illustrates the weakening pervasiveness of the connection between myth and ritual.[9] The difference between a relatively stable context for the reperformance of Alkman's *Partheneion* and the diversity of reperformance scenarios for Pindar reflects Nagy's description of Panhellenic poetry as "those kinds of poetry and song that operated not simply on the basis of local traditions suited for local audiences [e.g. Alkman's *Partheneion*]. Rather, Panhellenic poetry would have been the product of traditions, so that the tradition that it represents concentrates on traditions that tend to be common to most locales and peculiar to none" (1990:54). I suggest that the following passage reflects Pindar's awareness of the multiple possibilities for the recontextualization of an original performance—and not only an awareness, but an expressed preference for a fluid translation of his compositions to a variety of reperformance contexts (cf. Ford 2002:120):

> μή νυν, ὅτι φθονεραὶ θνατῶν φρένας ἀμφικρέμανται ἐλπίδες,
> μήτ' ἀρετάν ποτε σιγάτω πατρῴαν,
> μηδὲ τούσδ' ὕμνους· ἐπεί τοι
> οὐκ ἐλινύσοντας αὐτοὺς ἐργασάμαν.
>
> *Isthmian* 2.43–46

> Don't now, because envious hopes are a wet blanket for mortals'
> minds,
> don't ever let a family's virtue go silent,
> nor these *humnoi*, since
> I did not craft them to be fixed in place.

Given that Pindar's *epinikia* were reperformed and, thus, served as a model for reenactment, what accounts for the capacity of an individual epinician song to be available as such a model for reenactment in a wide variety of contexts of situation for reperformance? While Nagy's *Pindar's Homer* (1990) stands a magisterial response to this question, among others, I offer here my own observation that the stylistic diversity of *epinikion* accommodates itself to diverse contexts of reperformance. To stress, this dynamic is dialogical. It is not that *epinikion* is possessed of an inherent complexity that happens to be adaptable from one reperformance context to the next, but in a dialogical fashion an epinician composer anticipates the evaluative responses of poten-

[9] Here I am paraphrasing Nagy: "In complex societies—and the situation in archaic Greece can already be described as such—the pervasiveness of myth and ritual, as well as their connectedness with each other, may be considerably weakened" (1990:31).

tial target audiences to future reperformances in such a way that original performance is constituted by an awareness of multiple potential reperformance venues.[10]

These observations about Panhellenism and the relationship between original performance and reperformance form a backdrop for considering how the dynamics of Panhellenism create cultural and historical factors that are remarkably similar to the contextual surround that, according to Bakhtin, gives rise to the genre of the novel. I will focus on three socio-historical factors that he identifies as crucially contributing to development of the novel: polyglossia, knowledge (versus memory), and contemporaneity (1981:3–40).

Polyglossia involves the interaction of what Bakhtin refers to as "national languages"; while "[p]olyglossia had always existed," it becomes constitutive of the novel when verbal art self-consciously exploits the creative potential that can arise from polyglossia (Bakhtin 1981:12). Whereas other genres appropriate and canonize polyglossia, absorbing it into a "pure language" (e.g. "tragedy is a polyglot genre" [Bakhtin 1981:12] encased in the language of Attic *koinê*), the novel comes to terms with polyglossia and reflects stylistically the linguistic diversity of its socio-historical moment. The process of Panhellenism gave rise to polyglossia, which the epinician way of speaking absorbed into the scope of the art form's expressive capacity. Given the one-time connection between the main varieties of ancient Greek language—Doric, Aeolic, and Ionic—and particular geographic regions, it is appropriate to conceive of these varieties as "national languages" in the sense that these languages were used by members of discrete speech communities in a pre-Panhellenic context, as opposed to dialects or varieties in the context of a Panhellenic speech community.[11] Under the influence of Panhellenism, as discussed in Chapter Two, these varieties of ancient Greek entered "into international and interlingual contacts," to apply

10 This view then is another way of accounting for the fact "that any given Pindaric composition defies the realization of all the signs of occasionality that it gives about itself" (Nagy 1994–1995:19). See Mackie on "how the future functions as a theme in epinician poetry" (2003:77). Her focus is not upon reperformance or considerations of tradition, but looks at how an epinician artist locates the athlete's victory in terms of a temporal scope that embraces past (39–76), present (9–37), and future (77–106).

11 On speech communities, see Hymes 1974:47–51. On varieties of ancient Greek, see Horrocks 1997:7–16, whose discussion makes clear that it is appropriate to associate a relatively discrete speech community with each of the major ancient Greek varieties: "The Ancient Greeks, like speakers of any other language, were sensitive to such dialectal differences, and had divided themselves into three principal 'tribes': Ionians (comprising speakers of Attic and the Ionic dialects); Dorians (speakers of the North West Greek and Peloponnesian Doric dialects); and Aeolians (speakers of Boeotian and Thessalian, together with speakers of the dialects of Lesbos and the adjacent territory on the northern Aegean coast of Asia Minor)."

one of Bakhtin's characterizations of polyglossia (1981:11).[12] As we have seen, *epinikion* is a document of such contacts in the context of Archaic Greece by virtue of its synthesis of Doric, Aeolic, and Ionic in morphology and prosody (Nagy 1990:417).[13] Polyglossia, then, along with the fact that the epinician way of speaking is comprised of ways of epinician speaking, means that we can properly identify *epinikion* as "a multi-styled genre" (Bakhtin 1981:25).

According to Bakhtin, whereas for epic and other "high genres," which include for him Pindar's songs, memory is "the source and power for the creative impulse," "[t]he novel, by contrast, is determined by experience, knowledge, and practice (the future)" (1981:15). Bakhtin's attribution of a primary role to memory in the composition of "high genres" is a function of his conception of tradition, as reflected in his characterization of epic: "The world of epic is the national heroic past: it is a world of 'beginnings' and 'peak times' in the national history, a world of fathers and of founders of families, a world of 'firsts' and 'bests'" (1981:13). While Bakhtin's description of how epic and "high genres" evaluate the past is anachronistic in light of more recent developments in the study of traditional art forms, it is highly resonant with prevailing views of Pindar and how his *epinikia* juxtapose the *laudandus*'s achievement with mythological exemplars.[14] From this point of view, epini-

12 But see also Bakhtin 1981:61–68 where he augments his description of polyglossia in the essay "Epic and Novel" (Bakhtin 1981:3–40) with reference to ancient Greek and Roman literature. Note especially the following: "Out of the heart of this confident and uncontested monoglossia [of ancient Greek life, per Bakhtin] were born the major straightforward genres of the ancient Greeks—their epic, lyric and tragedy. These genres express the centralizing tendencies in language. But alongside these genres, especially among the folk, there flourished parodic and travestying forms that kept alive the memory of the ancient linguistic struggle and that were continually nourished by the ongoing process of linguistic stratification and differentiation" (1981:67). As I show below, Pindar's language is much more stratified and differentiated than centralized. Nagy 1979:7–9 describes the process of Panhellenism as "intersocial organization" and "intercultural synthesis" as represented by such cultural developments as the Olympic Games, the Delphic Oracle, and Homeric epos.

13 See Chapter Two, "*Epinikion* as Event." Cf. Bakhtin 1981: "the novel must represent all the social and ideological voices of its era, that is, all the era's languages that have any claim to being significant; the novel must be a microcosm of heteroglossia" (411).

14 Resonating with Bakhtin here, Carne-Ross 1985:18 claims that the purpose of myth is to explicate the significance of an ephemeral athletic victory in terms of the enduring paradigm of gods and heroes. Mackie comments that "the epinician poet praises men of the present, his athletic victors, by likening them to heroes from the past" (2003:46) but maintains that "the past is introduced not for its own sake but for the sake of the present occasion" (48). In an analogous vein, Mullen demonstrates that when we consider not just time (i.e. present and past) but also space, the *hic et nunc* of performance embodied in choral dancers, "the [central] mythical section [of a given song] as it is being danced will be no less present to us than the beginning or end [of the song]" (1982:88).

cian art is constituted by "the transferal of a represented world into the past, and the degree to which this world participates in the past" (1981:13).

However, an ethnography of epinician speaking locates epinician art in the present of performance, the here and now of oral composition and aural reception (Bakhtin's practice and experience), and, further, accounts for how the dialogical relationship between original performance (the present) and reperformance (the future) is constitutive of *epinikion*. The mode of mimesis exemplified by Alkman's *Partheneion*, with its reenactment of an archetypal model, contrasts markedly with *epinikion*, which variously selects the models that it claims to reenact. In Alkman's song, the figures of Hagesikhora and Agido are models for the chorus in reperformance. In a similar way, Homer is a traditional model in the performance and reperformance of Homeric *epos* and cognate works traditionally attributed to the eponymous singer of tales.[15] Drawing from Nagy's gloss for the meaning of Hesiod's name as "one who emits the voice," Richard Martin has recommended that we "see the poet as a generic figure who embodies the singing power of the Muses" (1992:15).[16] These examples illustrate the outcome of the process through which "the Panhellenic tradition of oral poetry appropriates the poet, potentially transforming even historical figures into generic ones who represent the traditional functions of their poetry" (Nagy 1990:79). By contrast, there is no ritually or traditionally sanctioned archetypal model *generic* to *epinikion*.[17] Pindar was, and remains, from the point of view of subsequent tradition, a historical figure, not an eponymous or legendary one.

Epinician performance is as much a matter of futurity as of tradition. Indeed, tradition is a kind of dialogue across the temporal continuum: the present of an epinician song's original performance draws from the past to legitimate its claims on the present and anticipates future audiences through which reperformance sustains the (now) traditional status of a given song and its composer. This dynamic (dialogical) conception of tradition leads to the observation that, rather than reenacting a specific, generic, or arche-

15 See Foley 1998, 1999:57–61, Nagy 1979:296–300, 1990:22 and 373, and 1996:59–86.

16 For his discussion of the meaning of Hesiod's name, see Nagy 1979:296–297.

17 This view is *contra* Nagy's claim that "epinician represents the *kômos* as its own prototype, to be re-enacted in the here and now of the victory song's mimesis" (1994–1995:24). This difference in interpretation can be reconciled: rather than treating the *kômos* as an absolutized, global model (Nagy 1994–1995:25) for the occasion of epinician performance, I would say that Pindar's representations of epinician performance in terms of a *kômos* are local strategies of traditionalization. Rothwell recently concludes his analysis of literary and plastic testimonia for komastic antecedents to animal choruses in ancient Greek comedy by arguing that the *kômos* was not exclusive to any particular context, such as Dionysiac cult or the symposium (2007:34–35).

typal performance model, Pindar sought to establish himself and his compositions as models for subsequent reperformance.[18] When Pindar deploys strategies of traditionalization, we are witnessing how he authenticates his compositions through a display of competence in traditional material in order to earn a positive evaluation from the audience to original performance and, thereby, to establish those compositions as models for reperformance.[19] Bauman describes traditionalization as "an act of authentication, akin to the art or antique dealer's authentication of an object by tracing its provenience" (1992:137).[20] In my discussion of epinician *eukhesthai*, I touched upon one of Pindar's strategies for traditionalization: his use of the advice tradition characterized by the *Kheirônos Hupothêkai*. For another example, the use of features of a special code conventionally associated with choral performance further aligns *epinikion* with a model for choral performance, such as the Delian Maidens, as depicted in the *Homeric Hymn to Apollo* (Nagy 1996:56).[21] Kurke has recently argued that in Pindar's *Paean* 6 the opening triad serves to characterize the composer "as an outsider and to constitute his special status and authority vis-à-vis the Delphians. Thus, as ἀοίδιμος Πιερίδων προφάτας ["the Pierians' singing prophet," *Paean* 6.6], the speaking subject lays claim to mantic status derived from the Muses, separate from but analogous to that of Pytho herself in the opening invocation" (2005:104).[22]

18 Among scholars of Greek lyric poetry tradition is too often conceived of in limited terms as an ossified container of the past or as the point of reference for innovation on the (ossified) precedent of the past. For a recent example of this trend, see Fearn 2007:9–23 and passim.

19 It would be appropriate to refer to this as a process of entextualization, "the generation of textuality," following Briggs and Bauman: "Even when the content of the discourse lacks a clear textual precedent, generic intertextuality points to the role of recontextualization at the level of discourse production and reception. Genre thus pertains crucially to negotiations of identity and power—by invoking a particular genre, producers of discourse assert (tacitly or explicitly) that they possess the authority needed to decontextualize discourse that bears these historical and social connections and to recontextualize it in the current discursive setting [where recontextualization can be a form of entextualization]. When great authority is invested in texts associated with elders or ancestors, traditionalizing discourse by creating links with traditional genres is often the most powerful strategy for creating textual authority" (1992:147–148). Marshalling evidence that the image of falling leaves is traditional and illustrating how Pindar adapts that traditional image to his poetic purposes in *Olympian* 12, Nisetich 1977 adumbrates my approach to the Pindaric practice of traditionalization.

20 Hansen describes a similar strategy for authenticating ancient popular literature that he calls "pseudo-documentarism, an author's untrue allegation that he (or she) has come upon an authentic document of some sort that he (or she) is drawing upon or passing on to his (or her) readers" (2003:302).

21 See also Gentili 1988:51. Martin observes parallels between the episode in the *Hymn to Apollo* where Apollo leads the chorus of Cretan sailors (lines 515–522) and Pindar's *Pythian* 8 (2004:362–363).

22 Note that Kurke identifies the process involved in *Paean* 6 as "ritualization."

To explain the poetics of the composer's outsider, special, and authoritative status, Kurke applies Martin's term *metanastês*, which he defines as "one who has moved into a new community" (1992:14). In Archaic Greek verbal art "'[m]etanastic' poetics," Martin explains, "is the voice of the immigrant; but it is also the technique of the mystic who returns, as a stranger in his own land, to tell about what he knows" (1992:14). As the composer of *Paean* 6 Pindar is not a member of the local Delphian community, but by virtue of participating in the traffic in praise, which entails the use of conventions of gift economy that are privileged from the point of view of aristocratic ideology, he is very much, in Martin's words, an "exterior insider." For Kurke, then, metanastic poetics in *Paean* 6 involves the composer's self-representation as "a figure who can speak to the Delphian community from a platform of singular independent authority, but can also, as an 'adopted son of Pytho,' serve as a kind of intermediary or 'proxenos' for citizens of other communities visiting Delphi" (2005:106–107).

Whereas Bakhtin (1981:15–16) describes the epic past, and by implication the epinician past, as "walled off absolutely from all subsequent times, and above all from those times in which the singer and his listeners are located," Pindar's compositions entail a dynamic process of fluid interchange with the past of tradition, the present of original performance, and the future of subsequent reperformance. Again, when we consider the orientation of an original composition toward future reperformance of that work, the dialogical relationship between an original epinician performance and subsequent reperformance is as significantly constitutive of the composition of epinician song as the dialogical relationship between original performance and past tradition. Illustrating this fluid interchange through past, present, and future performance, Martin (2004:344) describes how Pindar's *Pythian* 8

> has managed to move through time, revealing itself to varied audiences, up to our own day, while pointing backwards to, and even imitating, an originating celebration. This dynamic, anaphoric movement reiterates the original communicative act of the ode, which centered on making vivid to a local community the place that its athletic hero's victory occupied along a sunlit pathway stretching back to the heroic age.

The epinician composer's display of competence through strategies of traditionalization bears upon the socio-historical factor of knowledge (versus memory) as a precondition for the emergence of novelistic discourse. Pindar's works are prime examples of how *alêtheia* 'truth' becomes, according to

Nagy, "the criterion of Panhellenism" (1990:63). To illustrate, Nagy cites the following passage of *Olympian* 1:

> ἦ θαυματὰ πολλά, καί πού τι καὶ βροτῶν
> φάτις ὑπὲρ τὸν ἀλαθῆ λόγον
> δεδαιδαλμένοι ψεύδεσι ποικίλοις ἐξαπατῶντι μῦθοι·
> Χάρις δ', ἅπερ ἅπαντα τεύχει τὰ μείλιχα θνατοῖς,
> ἐπιφέροισα τιμὰν καὶ ἄπιστον ἐμήσατο πιστόν
> ἔμμεναι τὸ πολλάκις.
>
> *Olympian* 1.28–32

> Truly wondrous are many things, and, as it seems, mortals'
> speech in excess of a true account,
> stories crafted with ornate lies, are utterly deceptive.
> But grace, which provides all mild things for mortals,
> bringing honor, it makes the unbelievable believable,
> often.

Nagy's analysis (1990:66) of this passage illustrates how *alêtheia* 'truth' becomes a Panhellenic criterion:

> Here we see the juxtaposition of what purports to be a unique and true Panhellenic version with a plethora of false versions, described as *mûthoi* 'myths'. The *mûthoi* 'myths' are the outer core, containing traditions that are *apista* 'untrustworthy' ['unbelievable' in my translation], while *alêtheia* 'truth' is the inner core, containing traditions that are *pista* 'trustworthy' ['believable' in my translation]. In referring to itself, the *alêtheia* of Panhellenic poetics represents *mûthoi* as if they were additions to the kernel of truth as formulated by *alêtheia*. I would argue, however, that *mûthoi* 'myths' stand for an undifferentiated outer core consisting of local myths, where various versions from various locales may potentially contradict each other, while *alêtheia* 'truth' stands for a differentiated inner core of exclusive Panhellenic myths that tend to avoid the conflicts of local versions.[23]

I suggest that, in this context of describing Pindar's art as a novelistic form of discourse, *alêtheia* functions in *epinikion* as the criterion for selection from

[23] Referring to *Olympian* 1.35 and 52–53, and anticipating Nagy 1990:66, Hubbard 1985:103–104 argues that Pindar's concern with a "true" version of the Pelops myth is a matter of "poetic truth, not an historical truth." Aloni 1998:36 explains truth as a stamp of authentication conferred by the audience's perception that the language of a given work is to be identified with the language of the Muses.

among the traditional possibilities for conventional speech acts, song and poetry styles, stories, genre, and media of composition (e.g. *ainos* or *humnos* or *hupothêkai*).[24] It is important to stress that a process of selection is actually endemic to tradition and its power as a dimension of culture. So it is not that selection itself is new in the process of Panhellenism, but that the criteria for selection change.[25] We can also detect Pindar's display of his mastery of the criterion of *alêtheia* in his use of disclaimers of performance (break-off formulas), gnomic statements, and frequently expressed stress upon the right or best story or upon the most effective ways to do epinician song. Such applications of *alêtheia* involve Pindar's strategies for negotiating with his audience for a positive evaluation both by regulating audience expectations and by persuading them of the criteria to apply when making *their* assessments.[26] These strategic dynamics actually point up the relative *absence* of a traditional model to which the audience could refer when evaluating Pindar's competence and highlight the open-endedness constitutive of an original epinician performance. In a sense, these observations only reformulate, in terms of performance tradition, the significance of the fact that *epinikion* was a new genre, whose invention coincided with the emergence of the trend for athletes to commission victory memorials "as a response to social and political developments that threatened the meaning of aristocratic participation in competitive athletics in the late archaic period," as Nicholson writes (2005:15).[27]

24 Such a view of epinician epistemology contrasts markedly with Boeke 2007, who attempts to identify the "cosmological assumptions underlying Pindar's poetry as they are expressed in gnomai" (29); see, for example, her exegesis of *Pythian* 3.80–83 (27), which I would interpret not in the first instance as an expression of cosmology (because such an interpretation depends upon some conjecture, as Boeke acknowledges [2007:28]), but as a passage inviting the addressee, Hieron, to recognize (we could say, apply his *noos*) that Pindar adopts in the song the role of an Instructor of Princes, a move that implicitly praises Hieron as an authoritative addressee vis-à-vis that communicative medium. See Hubbard 1985:100–106 for a discussion of what he identifies as the *alêtheia/pseudos* polarity and Scodel 2001:123–137 for another view of how Pindar establishes his poetic authority.

25 Cf. Mackie's discussion of how in Pindar's art "myths or versions of myths are accepted or rejected by the poet on the grounds that they are 'fitting' or not 'fitting'" (2003:73–75).

26 Aloni 1998:25 identifies performance function, performance occasion, audience role, performer-audience relationship, and commission as criteria for assessing performance.

27 Thus Rose argues that "it is plausible if unprovable that the origin of the genre represented an aristocratic escalation in ideological warfare responding to the more threatening aspects of the relatively 'democratic' tyrannies" (1982:55). While Thomas 2007 is in agreement with Nicholson that the development of *epinikion* should be understood "in conjunction with the other methods of celebrating victory, by monument, epigram, memorial," she disputes the view that tensions between aristocratic and democratic ideologies occasioned the emergence and popularity of the genre.

Here it becomes clearer how the original performance of *epinikion* was constituted as much by subsequent tradition and future reperformance as by prior tradition: original performance of an epinician composition was not reenactment of a particular model, but of various models variously selected by the composer on the basis of the criterion of *alêtheia*; yet reperformance of *epinikion is* reenactment of the model of original performance, whose author is the historical Pindar. While dialogue with the past is partially constitutive of original epinician performance, that dialogue is engaged constitutively, not in terms of memory, but in terms of the Panhellenic criterion of *alêtheia*, which itself is conditioned by the traditional requisites for a composition to become material for mimesis. While it is important to be cautious to avoid anachronism, this discussion of epinician epistemology is apropos of one of Bakhtin's socio-historical preconditions for the emergence of the novel: "[w]hen the novel becomes the dominant genre, epistemology becomes the dominant discipline" (1981:15).

Underlying epinician epistemology is the recognition of the open-endedness of the present. Original performance, in the context of tradition influenced by Panhellenism, is a matter of risk because implicit in the intense negotiation for positive evaluation by an audience is the possibility that performance could be unsuccessful. I would characterize this potential for performance to fail as a matter of failing to establish a composition as a model for reperformance.[28] A crucial element of the performance method is to account for how the aesthetic and entertainment dimensions of verbal artistic performances influence the shape of social interaction between performer and audience; Bauman writes (1977:11):

> Performance involves on the part of the performer an assumption of accountability to an audience for the way in which communication is carried out, above and beyond its referential content. From the point of view of the audience, the act of expression on the part of the performer is marked as subject to evaluation for the way it is done, for the relative skill and effectiveness of the performer's display of competence.[29]

Pindar's compositions can be more fully appreciated by tracking the composer's strategies for negotiating for a positive evaluation from the audience of

[28] See Mackie 2003:39–76 on Pindar's strategies for avoiding provoking the envy or disapproval of the epinician audience, the gods, and the athletic victor.

[29] Cf. Hanks's discussion of "evaluation as a requisite to meaning" from the point of view of Bakhtin's concept of dialogism (1987:679).

the performance of an individual song. The entextualized state of the record for epinician performance obscures exactly this consideration, that performance entails an open-endedness with respect to the outcome (i.e. the audience's evaluation) of performance. It is necessary to think away the boundaries of the material text and to see each victory song as an emergent communicative event in order to grasp that at the moment of performance the composer would have been in the process of demonstrating his artistic skill and vying for a positive evaluation of his work from the audience.[30] This dynamic and dialogical dimension of the composer-audience interaction is what constitutes Pindar's texts as open-ended.[31] Here too we see how the dialogue between original performance and subsequent reperformance is constitutive of the interaction between performer and audience in original performance: the audience's positive evaluation of *epinikion* in an original epinician performance enables the process of establishing that composition as a model for reenactment in subsequent performances.

In terms of my analysis of epinician speech and performance so far, "the performer's display of competence" in *epinikion* includes the composer's practical knowledge of epinician performance keys, simple speech genres, and the competent mimesis of models selected in a given epinician composition through strategies of traditionalization. Beyond this crucial factor's contribution to the open-endedness of an original performance, that the epinician composer is subject to an audience's evaluation of his display of competence in the epinician way of speaking, we have already identified important ways in which contemporaneity and the open-ended present inform Pindar's art:

From the point of view of *epinikion*, performance is a matter of composition in performance.

Epinikion understood as a speech event locates Pindar's art in the here and now of face-to-face, live interaction among composer, chorus, and audience.

The present of original performance is immanent to the chronotopic shape of each speech genre, which depends upon its spatio-temporal relationship, inclusive or exclusive, relative to the performance event.

30 Capturing such *in situ* contestation for audience approval, Mackie attributes Pindar's break-offs to "an oral performer's anxiety about how his audience will react, from moment to moment, to what he is saying" (2003:12).

31 Cf. Hanks 1987:688 on how the processes of reception and evaluation of discourse are sources of open-endedness.

In addition to these ways in which Pindar's art is anchored in an open-ended present, a basic feature of the genre of *epinikion*, it also commemorates the achievements of Pindar's contemporaries. Pindar's songs are important documents of real-world, real-time social relations and cultural practices. In this respect as well, Pindar anchors his art in his present.[32] The open-endedness of this present is a feature of epinician performance that an ethnographically grounded stylistics particularly brings to the fore.

A final and crucial point concerning contemporaneity and novelistic style is that, for Bakhtin, parody is the hallmark of the connection between a work of verbal art and the present. The occurrence of parody can also be identified, if it exists at all in a work of art, by applying an ethnographic stylistics. But this does not always mean that it is possible to grasp the humor or tones of play or satire that may be involved in parody. At the descriptive level, parody may occur when speech genres or styles blend or productively interfere with each other (Bakhtin 1981:75–76). The concept of register is an especially useful tool for exploring such blending or interference. Speech styles register in particular ways, and an ethnographic stylistics parses out how styles come together as communicative means, even if it is not always possible, especially in the case of a text-artifact, to identify the tone or mood of such dialogic effects. Given that stylistic inflections thoroughly saturate Pindar's *epinikia*, I am certain that through a close-grained analysis of the novelistic quality of Pindar's style it is possible to acquire an ear for at least some parodic threads in his songs. I also hope to show that Pindar's art evidences dimensions of parody as more conventionally understood. A description of parodic aspects of *Olympian* 1 goes hand in hand with my description of novelistic features of epinician style.

Polyglossia, epinician epistemology, and the open-ended present of original performance, which constitute the socio-historical backdrop that gives rise to the stylistic features of *epinikion*, render the art form a novelistic mode of discourse. When we consider the dialogical relationship between performance and reperformance in light of these factors, it is possible to qualify what it means for *epinikion* to be a new art form in late Archaic and early Classical Greece.[33] Here *epinikion* is "new" in the sense that it does not have a generic

32 Cf. Bakhtin's identification of the "novelistic spirit" of works such as Menippean satire, ancient Greek romance, Socratic dialogues, and the *Satyricon* of Petronius: "contemporary reality serves as their subject, and—even more important—it is the starting point for understanding, evaluating and formulating such genres" (1981:22).

33 Nicholson connects the invention of *epinikion* with the emergence of the practice of establishing victory memorials (2005:14). Cf. Thomas 2007.

predecessor in the form of an eponymous legendary composer or in the form of an archetypal context of situation.[34] Instead, the art form's link with tradition comes by way of the selection by Pindar, a historical composer, of strategies of traditionalization, used in his work to authenticate his compositions by demonstrating his competence at tapping into traditional schemes for the performance of verbal art in ancient Greek society.[35] Artful selection and competent display of such traditional schemes establish an authoritative link between a composition and its composer. Original performance is the enabling event for effecting such a linkage, so the evaluative position of the audience to performance becomes crucially constitutive of the process of authorship. Under the influence of Panhellenism, the range of possible contexts for the reperformance of *epinikion* as described by Currie (2004) suggests a parallel between the reception end (reperformance) and the production end (original performance) of the process of tradition: without an archetypal model to go on, potential reperformers of *epinikion* would have looked, in part, to a work's author as a model and, in part, considered whether such a model was appropriate to the variety of contexts of situation in which reperformance might have occurred. A dialogical relationship between original performance and reperformance suggests that an epinician composer anticipates the evaluation of potential target audiences in future venues of performance and negotiates for their approval as expressed by the selection of his works for reperformance. It is in this sense that we might say that such potential target audiences are the superaddressees of Pindar's songs and, like any other addressees in a dialogue, they influence the speech subject's choices in communicative

34 Cf. Hanks's study of colonial Mayan texts composed by native Mayan officials: "In their formal and functional details, the texts reflect a process of local innovation, blending Maya and Spanish discourse forms into novel types. They document the rapid emergence of new genres of language use, new types of action in colonial society. In describing such discourse, one is led to treat genres as historically specific elements of social practice, whose defining features link them to situated communicative acts" (1987:668). If we consider the relationship between original performance and reperformance as an intertextual dynamic, then by drawing from Briggs and Bauman it becomes possible to understand the dynamics of tradition in terms of minimizing and maximizing intertextual gaps (1992:149).

35 This can also be conceived of as a strategy for minimizing intertextual gaps (Briggs and Bauman 1992:149). See also Hanks 1987:678, where he describes strategies that native Mayans of the Colonial Period used to authenticate their reports to the Spanish crown. Cf. Bakhtin's concession that "every great and serious contemporaneity requires an authentic profile of the past, an authentic other language from another time" (1981:30). Specifically with respect to Pindar's *epinikia*, Kurke writes: "Paradoxically, Pindar's greatest innovation is his self-conscious traditionality. His confident deployment of traditional patterns in the service of a new genre makes him a master practitioner of this type of poetry" (1991:259).

strategies.[36] What I identify as novelistic features of *epinikion* are products of this communicative process. The centrifugal quality of Pindar's art reflects the centrifugal quality of the relationship between original performance and reperformance, and such generic pliability gives rise to the diverse—indeed, ever novel—ways that Pindar composes his epinician songs. As Bakhtin says of the literary genre of the novel, *epinikion* "has no canon of its own" (1981:3).[37]

With these considerations in mind I now turn to a description of those stylistic features by exploring how Pindar uses devices for creating an image of language, which in turn enables us to further describe the novelistic features of epinician style. Bakhtin gives three categories of means for creating an image of language: "(1) hybridizations, (2) the dialogized interrelation of languages and (3) pure dialogues" (1981:358). A stylistic hybrid involves the co-occurrence of ethnographic features of two or more speech genres in a single utterance. By comparison, the dialogized interrelation of speech genres involves the ways in which an artist orchestrates relationships among speech genres in the emergent process of communication. Hybridization and the dialogical interrelation of simple speech genres depend upon a conventional recognition among participants in the speech event of epinician performance that simple speech genres are genres of style that are sufficiently autonomous to be meaningful in their own right, by virtue of being, in a sense, signifiers without being irreducible structural signs, in a phonological, morphological, or syntactic sense. The same applies to direct discourse, a form of pure dialogue, in Pindar's *epinikia*: as a relatively autonomous utterance, an instance of reported speech is a stretch of communication that can be described in its own right and in relationship with other utterances. "Pure dialogues" in Pindar's *epinikia* involve ways of representing speech so that language itself, its style and its situated use, becomes an image.

[36] I adopt the concept of superaddressee from Bakhtin: "[T]he author of the utterance with a greater or lesser awareness, presupposes a higher *superaddressee* (third) [i.e. third in line after an addressee, a second party in addition to the first, the addresser], whose absolutely just responsive understanding is presumed, either in some metaphysical distance or in distant historical time (the loophole addressee). In various ages and with various understandings of the world, this superaddressee and his ideally true responsive understanding assume various ideological expressions (God, the absolute truth, the court of dispassionate human conscience, the people, the court of history, science, and so forth)" (1986:126, emphasis in original).

[37] In his study of epinician eidography, Lowe's conclusion "that for the third-century editors the *epinikian* existed primarily, and perhaps was originally coined, as a book-title" suggests that even the generic rubric *epinikion* is a non-local, non-native designation for the victory song, applied by convention outside-in by scholars, including the author of the present study (2007:175). See Kurke 2000 for a context-based taxonomy of genres of Greek lyric poetry.

Bakhtin's concept of an image of language, then, offers a theoretical vantage point for addressing the problem of how to describe the ways in which language itself becomes a major thread in the fabric of novelistic forms of art (for him, the novel per se). In what follows I will first describe the dialogue of registers in lines 1–27 of *Olympian* 1, which exemplifies how Pindar generates images of language through hybridization and the dialogized interrelation of speech genres. I will then illustrate how Pindar's gnomic statements are a prominent example of heteroglossia in his epinician compositions. From there, I will turn to a consideration of how direct discourse in Pindar's mythological narratives is an image of language. Finally, I will describe parodic effects in Pindar's treatment of the Pelops myth in *Olympian* 1.

The Dialogue of Registers

In addition to hybridization, Pindar produces images of language by creating dialogized interrelations among simple speech genres through dynamics of embedding one or more speech genres within a (locally) dominant speech genre. This differs from hybridization in that such dynamics of embedding do not obscure the boundaries of relatively discrete utterances to the extent that hybridization does. To illustrate how Pindar produces dialogized interrelations among the ways of epinician speaking I will discuss the following example passage:

> Ἄριστον μὲν ὕδωρ, ὁ δὲ χρυσὸς αἰθόμενον πῦρ
> ἅτε διαπρέπει νυκτὶ μεγάνορος ἔξοχα πλούτου·
> εἰ δ' ἄεθλα γαρύεν
> ἔλδεαι, φίλον ἦτορ,
> μηκέτ' ἀελίου σκόπει
> ἄλλο θαλπνότερον ἐν ἁμέρᾳ φαεννὸν ἄστρον ἐρήμας δι' αἰθέρος,
> μηδ' Ὀλυμπίας ἀγῶνα φέρτερον αὐδάσομεν·
> ὅθεν ὁ πολύφατος ὕμνος ἀμφιβάλλεται
> σοφῶν μητίεσσι, κελαδεῖν
> Κρόνου παῖδ' ἐς ἀφνεὰν ἱκομένους
> μάκαιραν Ἱέρωνος ἑστίαν,
> θεμιστεῖον ὃς ἀμφέπει σκᾶπτον ἐν πολυμήλῳ
> Σικελίᾳ δρέπων μὲν κορυφὰς ἀρετᾶν ἄπο πασᾶν,
> ἀγλαΐζεται δὲ καί
> μουσικᾶς ἐν ἀώτῳ,
> οἷα παίζομεν φίλαν

ἄνδρες ἀμφὶ θαμὰ τράπεζαν. ἀλλὰ Δωρίαν ἀπὸ φόρμιγγα
πασσάλου
λάμβαν', εἴ τί τοι Πίσας τε καὶ Φερενίκου χάρις
νόον ὑπὸ γλυκυτάταις ἔθηκε φροντίσιν,
ὅτε παρ' Ἀλφεῷ σύτο δέμας
ἀκέντητον ἐν δρόμοισι παρέχων,
κράτει δὲ προσέμειξε δεσπόταν,
Συρακόσιον ἱπποχάρμαν βασιλῆα· λάμπει δέ οἱ κλέος
ἐν εὐάνορι Λυδοῦ Πέλοπος ἀποικίᾳ·
τοῦ μεγασθενὴς ἐράσσατο Γαιάοχος
Ποσειδάν, ἐπεί νιν καθαροῦ λέβητος ἔξελε Κλωθώ,
ἐλέφαντι φαίδιμον ὦμον κεκαδμένον.

Olympian 1.1–27

Best is water, but then gold is a burning fire,
just as the preeminence of wealth that makes a man great is
conspicuous at night.
But if you wish to sing of victory prizes,
my heart,
no longer look
to another star in the empty ether, shining by day, warmer than
the sun,
and we will not sing of a competition tougher than Olympia,
from where the often uttered hymn is ornamented
with the inventiveness of the wise: to resound in praise
of the son of Kronos while going
to the rich, blessed hearth of Hieron,
who tends the traditional scepter in Sicily, full of flocks,
who, while he plucks the flower of every virtue,
is also adorned
with the peak of musical craft.
Such is the playing
we men often do around the lovely table. But take the Dorian lyre
from its peg,
if at all the grace of Pisa and Pherenikos
put your mind under the influence of the sweetest thoughts,
when beside the Alpheos River the horse drove,
extending its ungoaded body in the race,
and united its master with dominance,

the Syracusan king and horse rider. His renown shines bright
in the colony with noble people, the colony of Lydian Pelops,
whom the earth-embracing, mighty Poseidon desired,
after Klotho removed him from the purified cauldron.
And Pelops was well furnished with a shoulder bright with ivory.

We can identify the nuanced dynamics of dialogism in this passage on the basis of the patterns of stylistic features characteristic of the ways of epinician speaking. Each of the speech genres occurring at *Olympian* 1.1–27 is discursively ordered in relationship to the others through dynamics of embedding. In terms of the difference between frame and framework, I identify a frame as an *embedding* speech genre and a framework as an *embedded* speech genre. The frame is the ground against which the figure of the framework emerges. There can be multiple, but organized, planes of interaction, so that an embedded framework can function as an embedding frame for yet another, emergent framework. Relative to a frame, a framework is the more emergent (against the backdrop of a frame) stylistic situation, with corresponding modifications (re-keying) to the interaction among participants in that stylistic situation.[38] These modifications, or re-keyings, are what Bakhtin describes as inflections, whereby the relationships among utterances create turbulence at the boundaries between speech genres. In the epinician way of speaking, hypotaxis can articulate the junctures of embedding dynamics.[39] The action of embedding

[38] I note here that this observation is the empirical point of departure for describing the phenomena of reported speech (Bauman 1986a, Hanks 1987, 1992, 1993, 1996b, Vološinov 1986, and Urban 1989), frameworks of participation (Goffman 1981, Hanks 1987, 1996b, Urban 1989, and Tarkka 1993), and metapragmatics (Bauman 1977, Hanks 1993, and Silverstein 1993) in *epinikion*, a project I hope to pursue elsewhere.

[39] Lines 8–11 are embedded in lines 1–27 as indicated by subordinating conjunction ὅθεν (line 8), whose referent is Ὀλυμπία (line 7), in the embedding precatory speech genre of lines 1–7. Lines 12–15 are embedded in the lyric speech genre of lines 8–11 as indicated by relative pronoun ὅς (line 12), whose referent is Ἱέρων (line 11), in the embedding speech genre of lines 8–11, and which subordinates grammatically the *angelia* to the lyric passage. Lines 16–17 are embedded in the *angelia* of lines 12–15 as indicated by οἷα (line 16), a relative or indirect adjective, signaling the lyric passage's grammatical subordination to the *angelia* of lines 12–15. Lines 20–24 are embedded in the prayer of lines 17–19 as indicated by ὅτε (line 20), used as a subordinating conjunction. Lines 25–27 are embedded in *angelia* of lines 20–24, as indicated by the relative pronoun τοῦ (line 25), whose referent is Πέλοψ (line 24) in the *angelia*. Des Places 1947:48–50 lists relative pronouns that introduce a mythological narrative. See Slater 1983:118 on the function of the relative pronoun in introducing a flashback type of lyric narrative and 1983:127 on the "characteristic" use of the relative pronoun in lyric and epic poetry to transition to historical or mythological narrative. Bonifazi 2004b has more recently applied linguistic pragmatics to the description of Pindar's uses of relative pronouns, providing an excellent summary of the secondary literature (42–43) and revising Des Places's list (44–48).

creates dialogical relationships among the speech genres and, so, the stylistic three-dimensionality in *epinikion*. In the following diagram, the left-most margin corresponds to the dominantly organizing speech genre in lines 1–27, *eukhesthai*, the utterance embedding the other speech genres occurring in the passage (embedding is indicated by the symbol ↪):

Lines 1–7: *Eukhesthai*

↪Lines 8–11: Lyric

  ↪Lines 12–15: *Angelia*

    ↪Lines 16–17: Lyric

Lines 17–19: *Eukhesthai*

↪Lines 20–24: *Angelia*

  ↪Lines 25–27: Mythological Narrative

In *Olympian* 1.1–27 Pindar deploys the speech genre of prayer in the service of the speech plan of the lyric speech genre. While lines 1–7 and 17–19, which are the embedding utterances for the remaining lines of the passage, have the second-person addressivity particularly characteristic of prayers, they depict the act of composition, a speech object conventional to the lyric speech genre. In addition to the relationship between prayer and lyric speech genres, the dominantly framing prayer also embeds other speech genres appropriate to communicative conventions of *epinikion* as a whole, and does so in a way that builds into the flow of communication reference to features of the immediate context of performance—i.e. just as the embedding prayer in lines 1–27 has reflexive features, so do the embedded speech genres. Thus the effect of the dialogized interrelation of languages in *Olympian* 1.1–27, whereby prayer represents lyric, permeates all strains of discourse in the passage:

> The two occurrences of the speech genre *angelia* in *Olympian* 1.1–27 have speech objects that are immediately relevant to the occasion of *Olympian* 1's performance and, so, possess a lyric quality (i.e. reflexivity); these speech objects are: the athlete, Hieron (lines 12–15 and 22–24), and his athletic victory (lines 20–24).
>
> The lyric speech genre (lines 8–11 and 16–17) characterizes the performance of *Olympian* 1 in terms of *xenia* 'ritualized friendship', which in turn sets up a frame for the interpretation of the poem as a whole.[40]

[40] On the social economics that informs Pindar's characterization of the *laudator-laudandus* relationship in terms of *xenia*, see Kurke 1991:135–159. According to Athanassaki, at the end of

> These lyric passages, then, have a reflexive quality, not only in terms of their immediate context, but also at the level of complex speech genre.
>
> Mythological narrative at lines 25–27 briefly introduces the central mythological story in the poem and does so specifically in terms of the point upon which Pindar claims later in the song to change the traditional account. The brief segment of mythological narrative has a reflexive quality because it refers to the central myth of the song as a whole, as a complex speech genre.

Here then we see how the dialogized interrelation of speech genres at *Olympian* 1.1–27 also involves a kind of hybridization: the dominantly organizing speech genre, the frame, for lines 1–27 is prayer, and this simple speech genre does the work of another speech genre, lyric. To observe that Pindar uses the speech genre of prayer to execute the speech plan of the lyric genre is also to say that the lyric speech genre is represented by prayer, and this fact is consonant with Bakhtin's explanation of how hybridization creates an "artistic image of language": "[t]he artistic image of a language must by its very nature be a linguistic hybrid (an intentional hybrid): it is obligatory for two linguistic consciousnesses to be present, the one being represented and the other doing the representing, with each belonging to a different system of language" (1981:359). Chapters Three and Four presented the evidence for treating each of the ways of epinician speaking as a register, a discrete "system of language." The "linguistic hybrids" that result from blending the discrete ways of epinician speaking are ubiquitous in Pindar's *epinikia*.

To summarize the foregoing discussion, the opening prayer of *Olympian* 1 sets up the image of the composer designing his song in performance. Pindar uses the speech genre of prayer to build this artistic image of language. At one level of analysis, hybridization is implicated from the start: the precatory speech genre has lyric inflections by virtue of the reflexive quality of its speech plan and speech object, which concern song, performance, and the current occasion of performance, Hieron's victory. This hybridization is maintained throughout lines 1–27, even as the speech genres change—or better, *because of* the way that the speech genres, in effect, elaborate on the dominant image of the passage, the composer designing his song in performance. At another level of analysis, the dialogized interrelations among speech genres in the passage are the vehicle for creating the stylistic space (image) in which hybridization and its communicative effects can

---

Olympian 1 the *laudator* revises this characterization of his relationship with the *laudandus* as *xenia* by characterizing it in terms of a closer relationship, *homilia* (line 116) (2004:322–323).

emerge.[41] Lines 1–27 are characterized by stylistic diversity and by a unifying theme that infiltrates every discursive layer of the passage.[42] In these lines, then, we have an epinician example of a "novelistic hybrid...*an artistically organized system for bringing different languages into contact with one another*, a system having as its goal the illumination of one language by means of another, the carving-out of a living image of another language" (Bakhtin 1981:361, emphasis in original).

Gnomic Statements

Pindar's use of gnomic statements is another example of how the epinician way of speaking possesses stylistic three-dimensionality and the propensity to generate artistic images of language. Recall two points that I have already made about gnomic statements. First, in Chapter One I treated gnomic statements as a form of representing communication that Pindar frequently uses to express rules about the appropriate doing of the epinician way of speaking. Second, in my description of the gnomic speech genre in Chapter 3, I demonstrated how the inclusive indefiniteness of gnomic style renders statements couched in that style as relevant to all participants in the speech event of performance. Taken together, these observations enable us to treat gnomic statements as expressions of appropriateness rules for speech and performance (the composition end of the communicative exchange) and of criteria for the audience's evaluation of performance (the reception end of the communicative exchange). In other words, gnomic statements are typically metacommunicative, and the stylistic features of the speech genre of the epinician *gnôma* complement this metalingual function. From a participant-centered point of view, this indefiniteness distances the speech subject from the speech object and speech plan of a gnomic statement, which often concern social conventions for appropriate speech and behavior, in such a way that the composer speaks (via a choral channel) as the animator of values or beliefs shared by all participants in the speech event of epinician performance.[43] At the level of simple speech genre,

[41] As Bakhtin writes: "The linguistic and stylistic profile of a given element (lexical, semantic, syntactic) is shaped by that subordinated unity to which it is most immediately proximate. At the same time this element, together with its most immediate unity, figures into the style of the whole, itself supports the accent of the whole and participates in the process whereby the unified meaning of the whole is structured and revealed" (1981:262).

[42] Cf. Nagy 1996:99, where he observes of Sappho's description of Aphrodite departing from Olympus in *Song* 1 that "the action takes place not in a third-person diegesis but still in the second person, so that the potential diegesis is subsumed by the syntax of prayer."

[43] Goffman (1981:44–145) identifies three types of "production format" for an utterance:

the gnomic statement is uttered by an indefinite third-person speech subject who gives voice to—animates—the "verbal-ideological belief system" (Bakhtin 1981:312) of wisdom traditions and moral *topoi*. In what follows I will describe social functions of gnomic statements by way of a pragmatic gloss on *gnômai* in *Olympian* 1 that identifies their applied message, how they shape artistic images of language in the "zone of maximal contact" (Bakhtin 1981:11) in the communicative exchange between composer and audience—i.e. by communicating criteria for the evaluation of the current performance.

To illustrate this functional interpretation of epinician *gnômai* I cite the following passage:[44]

> ἦ θαυματὰ πολλά, καί πού τι καὶ βροτῶν
> φάτις ὑπὲρ τὸν ἀλαθῆ λόγον
> δεδαιδαλμένοι ψεύδεσι ποικίλοις ἐξαπατῶντι μῦθοι·
> Χάρις δ', ἅπερ ἅπαντα τεύχει τὰ μείλιχα θνατοῖς,
> ἐπιφέροισα τιμὰν καὶ ἄπιστον ἐμήσατο πιστόν
> ἔμμεναι τὸ πολλάκις·
> ἁμέραι δ' ἐπίλοιποι
> μάρτυρες σοφώτατοι.
> ἔστι δ' ἀνδρὶ φάμεν ἐοικὸς ἀμφὶ δαιμόνων καλά· μείων γὰρ
> αἰτία.
>
> *Olympian* 1.28–35

"animator," "author," and "principal": an animator is "the sounding box in use," "the talking machine"; the author is "someone who has selected the sentiments that are being expressed and the words in which they are encoded"; the principal is "someone whose position is established by the words that are spoken, someone whose beliefs have been told, someone who is committed to what the words say." I describe the speech subject of gnomic statements as an animator at the local level of discourse, at the level of simple speech genre. At the level of the complex genre of *epinikion*, my provisional position is that the epinician composer (e.g. indicated deictically by first-person singular forms) is both author and principal; that a chorus, by convention or in practice, speaking in the voice of the epinician composer are the animators (e.g. as the "sounding box" of first-person singular utterances); other dynamics occur in which the epinician speaker is the author by virtue of his composer role, but the chorus speaks as principal, particularly in gestures of traditionalization. I plan a future study of epinician authorship that draws from Urban's (1989) still more dynamic model of first-person referentiality. On Pindar's first person see Lefkowitz 1963, 1988, 1991, 1995, Floyd 1965 (who interprets first person references on the basis of a division of speaking parts between chorus leader and chorus), Felson 1984, Bremer 1990, Griffith 1991, and Anzai 1994. See Kurke 2007 on poetic voice in Greek lyric poetry generally.

44 This passage is an example of what Slater 1984:255–256 identifies as a "gnomic progression" and Hamilton 1974:4 calls a "Gnomic Cluster," which he defines as a cluster of "three or more" gnomic statements that "occurs only at the beginning or end of the Myth and of the ode." See also Hamilton 1974:115–116 on the form of "Gnomic Clusters."

> Truly wondrous are many things, and, as it seems mortals'
> speech in excess of a true account,
> stories crafted with ornate lies, are utterly deceptive.
> But grace, which provides all mild things for mortals,
> bringing honor, it makes the unbelievable believable,
> often;
> but the remaining days
> are the wisest witnesses.
> It is appropriate for a man to say upright things about the gods;
> for fault is less.

To gloss these lines pragmatically (i.e. in terms of their communicative functions in the praxis of performance), Pindar communicates that deceptive speech occurs among humans (lines 28–29); that *kharis* can contradict truth as well as ratify it (30–32); that time is the ultimate test for the appropriateness or efficacy of speech (lines 33–34); and that one measure of appropriate speech is to say upright things about the gods (line 35). This sequence of thoughts is metacommunicative because it qualifies how the audience is to evaluate the composer's communication—the mythological narrative, in particular, the composition and performance of *Olympian* 1, in general.

Pindar's use of gnomic statements to communicate criteria for evaluating his composition is a form of heteroglossia and, so, is double-voiced in the particular sense formulated by Bakhtin: "It serves two speakers at the same time and expresses simultaneously two different intentions: the direct intention of the character who is speaking, and the refracted intention of the author" (1981:324). The two voices present in the gnomic statements at *Olympian* 1.28–35 include (1) the authenticating voice of the verbal-ideological belief system represented by the gnomic style (i.e. traditional wisdom) and (2) the composer's voice, which appropriates the gnomic style to regiment the audience's evaluation of his composition. The first voice conveys a structural message; the second voice, an applied message. When uttering a gnomic statement, the composer immerses his voice into the third-person speech subject of the gnomic statement. But this immersion does not conflate the two voices; they stand in a dialogical figure-ground relationship: the ground is the relatively immanent status of wisdom traditions and moral *topoi* as represented by the gnomic style itself, and the figure is the emergent context of *Olympian* 1 as a speech event. The two voices present in the gnomic passage at *Olympian* 1.28–35, in Bakhtin's terms, "are dialogically interrelated, they—as it were—know about each other (just as two exchanges in a dialogue know of each other and are structured in this mutual knowledge of each other); it is as if they actually hold a conversation with each other" (1981:324).

In the context of *Olympian* 1 as a whole, lines 28–35 set up a frame for interpreting Pindar's revision of the Pelops myth and initiate a sequence of messages about *kharis* that establish *kharis* as a principal of reciprocity[45]—and, as we will see, as the focus of a bawdy form of paronomasia (cf. Bauman 1996:314–322). The principle of reciprocity is the common thread between parallels built into *Olympian* 1:

> Just as hosting a feast entails the reciprocity of *xenia*, performance is a gesture of reciprocity (i.e. the commemorative song is an appropriate gesture of reciprocity for the achievement of athletic victory).[46]
>
> On the model of *xenia*, the composer and *laudandus* have a relationship based upon reciprocity.
>
> Whereas Tantalos is an abuser of reciprocity, Pelops is an exemplar of reciprocity.
>
> The principle of reciprocity informs the erotic relationship between *erômenos* and *erastês*.[47]
>
> By observing the standards for appropriate speech about the gods (line 35) Pindar practices *kharis*, understood as a principle of reciprocity, by telling a trustworthy account (recall lines 30–32) of the story about how Pelops got his ivory shoulder, and, in turn, the audience can evaluate Pindar's "revision" of the Pelops myth, and the composition as a whole, as a fulfillment of the principal of reciprocity entailed in *kharis*.

Pindar sets up a frame for the interpretation of his composition through his use of metacommunication in the gnomic statements of lines 28–35 and thus engages in "the process of coming to know one's own language as it is

45 See also Mackie 2003:102 on the idea of *kharis* as "reciprocal exchange." Bowra 19642:9 identifies *kharis* as a personification, "the spirit of grace and beauty," and interprets *Olympian* 1.28–34 as Pindar's evaluation of *kharis* as "the source of the falsity of poets." Mullen describes *kharis* as the divine favor "that blazes into appearance for the hero" and identifies a structural correspondence for such effects, whereby manifestations of *kharis* occur predominantly in epodes, a phenomenon suggesting that dance articulates meaning in epinician performance (1982:100–117).

46 On *xenia* in Pindar's *epinikia*, see Hubbard 1985:156–158 and Kurke 1991:135–159.

47 See Gerber 1982:xiv–xv and Young 1971:37–38 for a comparable discussion of thematic parallels in *Olympian* 1.

perceived in someone else's language, coming to know one's own horizon within someone else's horizon" (Bakhtin 1981:365).[48] There is a dialogical dynamic involved here: Pindar's communication of criteria for evaluating his artistic competence is an implicit acknowledgement of the audience's participation in the creation of his song. In part this means that the audience's approval of the song is to be negotiated and secured in the here and now of performance, with the implication that Pindar's art moves in "the zone of maximal contact with the present (with contemporary reality) in all its openendedness." (Bakhtin 1981:11). Again, and as I will show below, the gnomic passage at *Olympian* 1.28–35 is also crucial for creating the parodic overtones in *Olympian* 1.

Direct Discourse as an Image of Language

Direct discourse in mythological narrative involves a dialogue between two contexts: the context of narration in performance and the context of narrated events. In epinician art myth is not completely walled off in a valorized past, but comes to bear in the emergent, here-and-now context of performance in the following three ways. First, through mythological narrative the epinician composer can display to the audience his competence at drawing from the repertoire of traditional stories through strategies of traditionalization. Second, factors particular to an individual performance drive the selection of material for mythological narrative, so that in many of Pindar's *epinikia* narrated events provide a point of view upon events commemorated in epinician performance. Third, the direct discourse of actors in mythological narrative is regularly constituted by rules for epinician speaking—so much so, that a figure's misuse of the epinician register in narrated events serves to negatively characterize her or him.[49] "Insofar as acts of speaking are of focal interest in certain kinds of narrative," as Bauman has insightfully observed,

48 Because it is apropos of the novelistic characteristics of epinician style, I cite here the context for the quotation, which concerns the novelistic plot: "The plot itself is subordinated to the task of coordinating and exposing languages to each other. The novelistic plot must organize the exposure of social languages and ideologies, the exhibiting and experiencing of such languages... In a word, the novelistic plot serves to represent speaking persons and their ideological worlds."

49 A good example of this is the direct discourse attributed to Pelias in Pindar's *Pythian* 4. It may be that Pelias is an effective speaker, as Nicholson 2000:196 observes, but if so Pindar is representing him as a good performer of the wrong discourse for the epinician context in which he speaks. Cf. Bakhtin: "The image of another's language and outlook on the world, simultaneously represented *and* representing is extremely typical of the novel" (1981:45, emphasis in original). See also Bakhtin 1981:46 on "internally dialogized images."

"an understanding of the ways that these speech acts are contextualized within the narrative can enhance our understanding both of how speaking operates and is understood to operate in social life *and* of how narratives are constructed" (1986a:54, emphasis in original). I accordingly argue that Pelops' direct discourse in *Olympian* 1 illustrates the reflexive relationship between speech practices represented in narrated events and the speech practices of epinician performance and, so, is also an example of how Pindar uses the epinician way of speaking as an image of language.[50] Martin has demonstrated that in Homer's language, "muthos denotes an authoritative speech act," going on to show that of three premier forms of *muthos* discourse—commands, flyting, and performances of memory (also called "the recitation of remembered events")—performances of memory stand out as the nexus between what I have been referring to as representing and represented communication: "all important verbal art within the poem [i.e. the *Iliad*], as done by the poem's speakers, depends upon the creative manipulation of this ultimate genre, which matches the poet's medium" (1989:46–47).[51] I am similarly arguing here that Pindar's speakers use the ways of epinician speaking and that the speeches of figures of mythological narratives in Pindar's *epinikia* are images of language insofar as those speeches represent mythological speakers as performers of those conventional ways of speaking.

To begin with, I cite Pelops' speech, a prayer addressed to Poseidon:

> τῷ μὲν εἶπε· "Φίλια δῶρα Κυπρίας ἄγ' εἴ τι, Ποσείδαον, ἐς χάριν
> τέλλεται, πέδασον ἔγχος Οἰνομάου χάλκεον,
> ἐμὲ δ' ἐπὶ ταχυτάτων πόρευσον ἁρμάτων
> ἐς Ἆλιν, κράτει δὲ πέλασον.
> ἐπεὶ τρεῖς τε καὶ δέκ' ἄνδρας ὀλέσαις
> μναστῆρας ἀναβάλλεται γάμον
> θυγατρός. ὁ μέγας δὲ κίνδυνος ἄναλκιν οὐ φῶτα λαμβάνει.
> θανεῖν δ' οἷσιν ἀνάγκα, τά κέ τις ἀνώνυμον
> γῆρας ἐν σκότῳ καθήμενος ἕψοι μάταν,
> ἁπάντων καλῶν ἄμμορος; ἀλλ' ἐμοὶ μὲν οὗτος ἄεθλος
> ὑποκείσεται· τὺ δὲ πρᾶξιν φίλαν δίδοι."
>
> *Olympian* 1.75–85

50 Athanassaki observes the reflexive relationship between representing and represented communication in *Olympian* 1, writing that Pelops' speech is "almost as long as the one the epinician speaker delivered to him a little earlier" in the poem (2004:332).

51 See Martin 1989:43–88 for a description of the speech genres of heroes in the *Iliad* and 89–145 for a treatment of heroes as performers of those speech genres.

> Pelops addressed him: "Come on, Poseidon, if at all the cherished
> gifts of Kypria result in grace,
> restrain the bronze spear of Oinomaos,
> bear me on the swiftest chariot
> to Elis, and bring me to dominance.
> After killing thirteen men,
> suitors, he delays the marriage
> of his daughter. Great risk does not fall to a mortal who lacks
> strength.
> Among those for whom it is necessary to die, why would anyone
> sit in darkness and foolishly boil down a nameless old age
> and be without a share in all upright things? But this contest
> lies before me. May you grant the desired deed."

In this passage of direct discourse, Pelops uses the ways of epinician speaking that constitute the epinician way of speaking. I summarize here the relevant details, noting aspects of formal patterning, which I explain below:

Pattern	*Lines*	*Speech Genre*	*Crucial Features*
A	75–78	*Eukhesthai*	Second-person singular imperatives addressed to Poseidon: ἄγ' (line 75), πέδασον (line 76), πόρευσον (line 77), and πέλασον (line 78). Vocative addressed to Poseidon (line 75).
B	79–81	Mythological Narrative	Pelops briefly relates the story about Oinomaos' fatal contest for suitors.
C	81–84	*Gnôma*	Features of indefiniteness: φῶτα (line 81), οἷσιν (indefinite antecedent, line 82), τις (line 82), and ἀπάντων καλῶν (genitive plural neuter adjectives used substantively, line 84).
b	84–85	Lyric	Reflexive features: ἐμοί (line 84) and οὗτος ἄεθλος (the deictic refers to Pelops' immediate undertaking, line 84).
a	85	*Eukhesthai*	Optative of wish with second-person address to Poseidon.

In the context of the composer's telling of the Pelops story—we can call this the diegetical context—the simple speech genre of mythological narrative is dominant. Here the reported speech, which is embedded in an act of narration, has the same stylistic diversity as the complex genre of *epinikion*, so that there is a reflexive relationship between Pelops' direct discourse and Pindar's composition of *Olympian* 1.[52] Given parallel content between *houtos aethlos* 'this contest' (line 84) and Pelops' description of the contest in the brief mythological narrative at lines 79–81, Pelops' entire speech has a ring structure, A-B-C-b-a, where A and a are *eukhesthai* passages, B and b are thematically parallel,[53] and C is a gnomic statement at the discursive core of the direct discourse. As I will show below, this ring composition of Pelops' speech mirrors the ring composition of *Olympian* 1 as a whole, which also has a gnomic statement at its discursive core. There is another remarkable parallel between the discursive structures of Pelops' speech and *Olympian* 1: just as Pelops' *eukhesthai* at lines 75–78 is the second-person imperative type, so is Pindar's *eukhesthai* at lines 1–6; just as Pelops' *eukhesthai* at line 85 is in the form of an optative of wish, so is Pindar's *eukhesthai* at lines 115–116. I am going to say more below about the reflexive relationship between Pelops' speech and the composition in which it is embedded in light of Pindaric parody, but for the moment this discussion serves to show how direct discourse is an image of language; in this case Pelops' speech is an image of the epinician way of speaking as represented by *Olympian* 1 as a whole.

Given the reflexive relationship between representing communication and represented communication, Pelops' speech is an example of what Bauman has described, in the context of studying the role of reported speech in the relationship between narrated events and the act of narration, as "a shift along the continuum from diegesis to mimesis, from telling to showing" (1986a:65). As an idealized speaker, Pelops is a model performer of Pindar's artistic medium: "[f]orm and content in the speech of Pelops are artfully chosen so as to corroborate the truthfulness of the Pindaric version and establish its authority" (Athanassaki 2004:333). Given the reflexive relationship between narration and narrated speech articulated by the stylistic and structural parallels between Pelops' speech and Pindar's composition, Poseidon is, by extension, a model

52 Cf. Bakhtin: "The context embracing another's word is responsible for its dialogizing background, whose influence can be very great" (1981:340).

53 Demonstrating the descriptive utility of an ethnographic approach to style, while lines 84–85 are dominantly in the lyric style, the fact that Pelops is a figure in a mythological narrative indicates that the lines are more accurately a lyric-mythological narrative stylistic hybrid—and this hybridization makes clearer the relationship between terms B and b in the ring pattern.

addressee: by granting Pelops' request, Poseidon models for the audience to the original performance of *Olympian* 1 an idealized response to *Olympian* 1's performance. Note that the ring composition of Pelops' speech is further articulated by lines 75 and 86, where the narrator sets, as it were, quotation marks around Pelops' display of the epinician way of speaking.[54] The line-initial locations of *tô men eipe* "[Pelops] addressed him [Poseidon]" (75), *hôs ennepen* "thus he spoke" (86), and *epesi* "with words" (86) stress the speech-act quality of Pelops' prayer because these forms of metalanguage are related to the word *epos*, which Pindar often uses to name speech acts such as figures in mythological narratives perform. The phrase οὐδ' ἀκράντοις ἐφάψατο ἔπεσι "and did not use unfulfilled words" (line 87) associates the fulfillment of Pelops' request with his effective use of the epinician way of speaking and Poseidon's positive evaluation of it. Here, then, we have an epinician example of what Martin has shown about the language of heroes in Homer's *Iliad*, that "heroic performance gains approval when it is persuasive... And the sign of persuasion is that speech moves others to act in sympathy with the speaker" (1989:100). The quotative frame discursively articulates this reflexive relationship: *tô men eipe* "[Pelops] addressed him [Poseidon]" (line 75) and *hôs ennepen* "thus he spoke" (86) frame the reported speech of Pelops using *verba dicendi*.[55] This quotative frame transitions from the present of the act of narration and the interaction between the composer and audience to the "present" of the framework of interaction between Pelops and Poseidon (the narrated events) and back again (cf. Bauman 1986a:100). In other words, *tô men eipe* "[Pelops] addressed him" at line 75 effects a transition from diegesis to mimesis and *hôs ennepen* "thus he spoke" at line 86 effects a transition in the opposite direction, from mimesis to diegesis.

Here we see what Bakhtin identifies as another device for including and patterning heteroglossia within a novelistic work of art. The reported speech of characters in Pindar's mythological narratives is "verbally and semantically autonomous," but "may also refract authorial intentions and consequently may to a certain degree constitute a second language for the author" (1981:315).[56] The narrated events and reported speech of Pelops are a second

54 Cf. Bakhtin 1981:340–348 on the framing of reported speech.

55 See Bauman 1986a:66 on quotative frames in reported speech and the *verbum dicendi*.

56 See also Bakhtin's observation that, with respect to the author's appearance "within his own field of representation—important here is the fact that the underlying, original formal author (the author of the authorial image) appears in a new relationship with the represented world. Both find themselves now subject to the same temporally valorized measurements, for the 'depicting' authorial language now lies on the same plane as the 'depicted' language of the hero, and may enter into dialogic relations and hybrid combinations with it (indeed, it cannot help but enter into such relations)" (1981:27–28). Cf. Hanks 1987:671.

voice for Pindar by virtue of their capacity to model, in the figure of Poseidon, how the audience is to evaluate positively the composition and performance of *Olympian* 1.[57] In light of the parodic overtones of *Olympian* 1, which I describe below, Poseidon's positive evaluation of Pelops' speech indicates that parody and the doing of appropriate speech are not incompatible.

Parody in *Olympian* 1

Considered more closely, the gnomic statements at lines 28–35, not only establish *kharis* as a basis for the audience's evaluation of *Olympian* 1, but also give rise to parodic contours in the song. When we understand *kharis* both as a principle of reciprocity and, not unrelated, as the nominal correlate for the verb *kharizesthai* 'to gratify', which in the context of a pederastic relationship can name the sexual gratification of the *erastês* 'lover' by the *erômenos* 'beloved', then it turns out that *Olympian* 1 involves a bawdy treatment of sexuality that introduces parody into the song's artistic scope, a hallmark of novelistic discourse for Bakhtin.[58] *Kharis* in *Olympian* 1 entails a nuanced form of parono-

57 See Hanks 1987:680 for an illustration of how, in the case of colonial Mayan texts composed by native Mayans, "the incorporation of quoted speech also brings with it the authority of its original utterance, and so works to officialize the discourse in which it is embedded." Mackie interprets Pelops' prayer to Poseidon as "an ideal model for the athlete who would successfully manage his exchanges with the gods" and as a model for the poet, who "acknowledges his own dependence upon the gods" (2003:104–105). Here Mackie is concerned with the connotations of *kharis* understood as "reciprocal exchange" in the context of an aristocratic practice of gift-exchange, which the relationship between Pelops and Poseidon exemplifies.

58 As Dover writes: "The word *kharizesthai* is used frequently in the speech of Pausanias in Pl. *Smp.* (e.g. 182a) to denote a boy's 'surrender to' or 'gratification of' an erastes (cf. *Smp.* 217a, 218d)" (1989:44). Cairns 1977 also connects the erotic application of *kharizesthai* with Pindar's use of *kharis* in *Olympian* 1, but identifies a parallel between Pelops and Hieron, with the implication that Hieron is the beloved of a god. Krummen identifies *erôs* as "[d]as beherrschende Thema der mythischen Erzählung in *Olympie* 1"; in the face of a perceived absence of literary precedent for the Pelops myth in the poem, she draws from (1) vase painting, (2) the story pattern of abduction for sexual purposes, exemplified by the myth of Zeus' abduction of Ganymede, (3) homoerotic initiation ritual, (4) the evidence of pederastic practice as evidenced in sympotic and gymnastic contexts, and (5) the didactic function of pederasty to reconstruct the "mythical-ritual 'Expectation'" that would have informed Pindar's audience's reception of his narration (1990:184–204). The ancient source for the homoerotic initiation ritual is a passage from Ephoros (F. Jacoby, *Fragmente der griechischen Historiker* 70); cf. Koehl 1986 and Hubbard 1987:5–7. See further Skinner 2005:62–71 for a discussion of Greek homoerotic initiation and related bibliography and Hubbard 2002:263 on "the initiatory model of the Greek banquet." The question of the newness of Pindar's version of the Pelops myth (thus Krummen's motivation for reconstructing the "mythical-ritual 'Expectation'" that would have informed Pindar's audience's reception of his narration) has received much attention. Köhnken 1974 discusses the then "*communis opinio*" that Pindar "alter[s] traditional features of

masia through which Pindar uses the gnomic style to characterize questionable sexual behavior in terms of the language of wisdom traditions and moral *topoi*.[59] I am accordingly proposing that *epinikion* possesses yet another quality that Bakhtin attributes to the novel: "The novel parodies other genres (precisely in their role as genres); it exposes the conventionality of their forms and their language; it squeezes out some genres and incorporates others into its own peculiar structure, reformulating and re-accentuating them" (1981:5). In the context of this discussion of ancient Greek sexual practices, it is worth noting that ancient sources regularly acknowledge "links between erotic intrigues and athletic activity," as Steiner observes.[60]

In this section of my description of novelistic features of epinician style, I will first describe how Pindar demonstrates his observance of *kharis* understood as a principle of reciprocity by way of displaying his competence in rules for appropriate speech as communicated by gnomic utterances in *Olympian* 1. Then, I will show that Pindar blurs the line between propriety and impropriety by representing the relationship between Pelops and Poseidon as a model of *kharis* in the sense of a principle of reciprocity and also as a case of a socially inappropriate erotic relationship (according to ancient Greek norms for sexuality) that involves a problematic application of the term *kharis*. Finally, and crucially, I will demonstrate that Pindar represents his relationship with Hieron, the *laudandus* of *Olympian* 1, in terms of *kharis* understood in both

a story from religious considerations only" (for a reiteration of this view see Scodel 2001:134) and describes poetic motivations for the poet's revision of the Pelops myth. Nagy 1990:116–135 argues that Pindar's expressed preference for one version of the myth over another "is in fact a poetic expression of a preexisting fusion of two myths, where the earlier myth is officially subordinated to but acknowledged by the later myth." Hansen 2000 identifies Pindar's Pelops myth in *Olympian* 1 as a version of the international tale *Bride Won in a Tournament* (cf. Hansen 2002:56–62), linking the Pelops myth, if not with a literary (radically understood) precedent, then certainly firmly with folk tradition. On folklore motifs in Pindar generally see Grant 1967.

59 Martin includes paronomasia among formal features of proverbs: "Proverbs have their own poetic markings—internal rhymes, assonance, alliteration, binary structure, paronomasia" (1992:25).

60 Steiner 1998:126, who cites Theognis 1335–1336, Aristophanes *Wasps* 1023–1025 and *Peace* 762–763, Aeschines 1.138–189, "Lucian" *Erotes* 9, Plato *Charmides* 154a–154c, *Euthydemos* 237a, *Lysis* 206e, *Symposium* 217c, and *Laws* 636c. These sources document, in particular, homoerotic aspects of the gymnasium and palaestra, on which see Dover 1989:54. In her study of the sexual allure of athletes as represented in visual and literary art, Steiner 1998 anticipates Smith 2007 in attributing to victory statues a lifelike quality. Note that, while Steiner sees an affirmative parallel between *epinikion* and victory statues (see especially 1998:139; cf. Thomas 2007:150), Smith cites *Nemean* 5.1, *Isthmian* 2.46, and *Pythian* 6.114 as evidence of Pindar's hostility toward a form of victory commemoration that competes with his own (2007:92). Ford interprets *Nemean* 5.1–3 and *Isthmian* 2.44–48 as "critiques of monumental silence and stillness" (2002:119–120).

senses, as a principle of reciprocity and as a by-word for questionable sexual practices. We will discover that in these dynamics Pindar uses the reverent quotation marks of the gnomic style to frame the irreverent sexual practices represented in *Olympian* 1.

One passage in the song stands out as a remarkable display of the composer's observance of the rules for appropriate speech expressed by the gnomic statements at lines 28–35. Pindar represents himself as committed to observing the parameters of propriety: "For me it is impossible to say that any of the blessed ones is gluttonous; I stay away from that" (ἐμοὶ δ' ἄπορα γαστρίμαργον μακάρων τιν' εἰπεῖν· ἀφίσταμαι, line 52). Although the first-person forms and the speech object, speech itself, mark it as dominantly lyric, the utterance also has gnomic features:

The construction ἄπορα with infinitive and understood ἐστί is typically impersonal.

The use of the indefinite pronoun τινα.

The substantive use of the adjective μακάρων.

The aphoristic force of the single word sentence ἀφίσταμαι "I stay away from that."

This lyric utterance has the "intonational quotation marks" (Bakhtin 1981:44) of the gnomic style, inflecting the dominantly reflexive quality of the lyric passage with the inclusive indefiniteness characteristic of *gnômai*. The hybridization of gnomic and lyric styles presents the self-characterization of the lyric utterance as a common belief or point of view—a self-characterization presumably to be shared by the audience (again, by virtue of the very inflections of the lyric speech genre with the gnomic speech genre): line 52 demonstrates *stylistically* that Pindar, as a general rule, does not violate the criteria for appropriate speech established in lines 28–35.[61] Specifically, one criterion for the trustworthiness of speech is that one "say upright things about the gods" (line 35). To display his observance of this criterion, in line 52 Pindar represents himself as a composer who proverbially (again, from the point of view established by the gnomic inflection of the lyric utterance) refuses to say that any of the gods is a glutton.[62]

When we explore the way that Pindar represents sexual practices in *Olympian* 1, we find that Pindar is not saying entirely upright things about Poseidon, from the point of view of our current understanding of ancient

61 Cf. Gerber 1982:89, who also notes the connection between lines 35 and 52.

62 Cf. Hanks: "Thus, even within the organization of individual works, shifts in the speech acts being performed are realized through shifts in linguistic style. This reflects the fact that the two are different aspects of the same utterance" (1987:681).

Greek social norms for sexual conduct. In *Olympian* 1 there is a demarcation between food-related practices and sexual practices, such that gluttony—as represented by the false story about Pelops' shoulder told by a jealous neighbor, Tantalos' crime, and Pindar's statement at line 52 that he will not call the gods gluttonous—is subject to censure in a way that the violation of sexual norms is not. While Pindar refuses to say that the gods are gluttons, he does not refuse to describe them—or at least one of them, Poseidon—engaging in gray-area sexual behavior. When we see that this is the case, Pindar's gnomic concern for appropriate speech turns out to be a foil for epinician parody. We could say that some of Pindar's gnomic statements in *Olympian* 1 are not so much gnomic statements per se as they are images of gnomic statements.[63] This becomes evident when we examine how Pindar works on both sides of the divide between propriety and impropriety, representing the relationship between Pelops and Poseidon as a model of *kharis* in the sense of a principle of reciprocity and also as a non-normative erotic relationship.[64]

There are two passages in which Pindar makes explicit the erotic nature of the relationship between Pelops and Poseidon. The very first reference to the Pelops story in *Olympian* 1 foregrounds Poseidon's erotic desire for the hero as a central point of Pindar's "revision" of the "usual" story that Tantalus serves up his son to the gods:[65]

> ...τοῦ μεγασθενὴς ἐράσσατο Γαιάοχος
> Ποσειδάν
>
> *Olympian* 1.25–26
>
> ...whom [Pelops] the earth-embracing, mighty
> Poseidon desired.

[63] Cf. Bakhtin 1981:51–52 on Cervantes's use of sonnets in *Don Quixote*, among other examples of images of style that are parodic.

[64] Cf. Bauman's study of the *coloquio* tradition, a folk drama in Tierra Blanca de Abajo, Mexico, which includes a character, the Hermitaño, "an aged holy man who is at the same time a blatantly burlesque character," whose performance in the *coloquio* involves "a marked disjunction between the scripted role of the Hermitaño as a pious figure and the realization of the role as parodic burlesque" (1996:314–315).

[65] Thus I share Gerber's view: "From the reference to Pelops in the first half of the ring [composition of lines 23–24 and 93–95], Pindar moves directly into the myth with the statement that it was Pelops with whom Poseidon fell in love. This takes pride of place at the very beginning because the love of Poseidon figures prominently throughout the myth and because the analogy will be drawn later between the divine favour and assistance received by Pelops and by Hieron." Note, however, that in Gerber's view Pindar's revision of the Pelops story "pertains to the time and circumstances of Poseidon's love rather than to the love itself" (1982:xii), a position that Köhnken (1983:72) disputes.

In the second passage that refers to the erotic nature of the relationship between god and hero, Pindar describes Poseidon's abduction of Pelops in terms of Zeus' abduction of Ganymede:[66]

> ἔνθα δευτέρῳ χρόνῳ
> ἦλθε καὶ Γανυμήδης
> Ζηνὶ τωὔτ' ἐπὶ χρέος.
>
> *Olympian* 1.43–45

> At a later time
> Ganymede also went there,
> to Zeus, for the same obligation.

With this emphasis upon the erotic nature of the relationship between Pelops and Poseidon in mind, we can next take a look at how Pindar carefully distinguishes between gluttony and sex in terms of whether excess is subject to censure.

There are two contiguous discursive patterns that inform the emergent development of the theme of *kharis* in *Olympian* 1 and justify both the censure of gluttony in the song and the more permissive attitude toward sexual practices: (1) the gnomic passage at 28–35 and the gnomic statement at line 53 frame the composer's prayer to Pelops, lines 36–51 and the lyric-gnomic hybrid at line 52; (2) in turn, the gnomic statements at lines 53 and 64 frame the mythological narrative about Tantalos' offense against the gods, lines 54–64. Here I represent schematically these two patterns, noting as well the dynamics of embedding involved in the passages:[67]

Pattern 1:

A: Lines 28–35: *Gnômai*

B: Lines 36–51: *Eukhesthai* Addressed to Pelops

➥Lines 37–51: Mythological Narrative

  ➥Lines 43–45: Mythological Narrative

b: Line 52: Lyric

a: Line 53: *Gnôma*

[66] On this passage see Gerber 1982:xiii and 80–81.

[67] I.e. I here describe local patterns; for the overall pattern of ring composition using the ways of epinician speaking in *Olympian* 1 see below in this chapter and the Appendix. Applying different analytical approaches than mine, Young 1968:122 identifies lines 53 and 64 as transitional *gnômai* and Köhnken 1983:72–73 identifies lines 35 and 52–53 as "framing sentences" for Pindar's address to Pelops and the mythological content embedded in that address.

Pattern 2:
A: Line 53: *Gnôma*
C: Lines 54–64: Mythological Narrative
A: Line 64: *Gnôma*

These discursive structures parse the main passages of *Olympian* 1's mythological narrative into two panels that break out along lines of distinction between how to evaluate gluttony and non-normative sexual practices, respectively. The first panel, which concerns gluttony, includes the two discursive patterns described above. The second, which concerns exceptional sexual practices, includes the mythological narrative about Pelops (lines 65–96). Binding together these various strains of the fabric are messages concerning propriety and examples that illustrate the performance of *kharis* as a principle of reciprocity.

Pattern 1 of the first panel, created by the gnomic passages at lines 28–35 and line 53, is a form of discursive parallelism in which the positions of simple speech genres within a composition involve patterned repetition. The frame created by these passages sets up a comparison that concerns appropriate speech, suggesting that *kakagoroi* 'slanderers' (line 53) are those who use deceptive speech, as described at lines 28–29:

ἀκέρδεια λέλογχεν θαμινὰ κακαγόρους.

Olympian 1.53

Lack of gain is often the lot of slanderers [*kakagoroi*].

Like many gnomic statements in Pindar's *epinikia*, line 53 is metacommunicative, explaining, in a sense, to the audience that they can evaluate the performance of *Olympian* 1 in terms of whether Pindar avoids such a violation of propriety as slanderers' speech. Whereas slanderers earn *akerdeia* 'lack of gain', the gain involved in epinician performance is, at least, the audience's positive evaluation of Pindar and the capital, social and perhaps monetary, that attends the success of a song of praise. If we read his gnomic statements as criteria for evaluating *Olympian* 1, Pindar cannot be a deceptive speaker or slanderer and must observe the principle of *kharis* in order to be successful. This concern to secure a positive evaluation from the audience plays out to the extent that it informs the way in which Pindar chooses to report the rejected story of how Pelops gets his ivory shoulder (cf. Köhnken 1974:200–201). Pindar buries that version of the story in indirect discourse attributed to a speaker he describes, with an indefinite pronoun and in the language of blame poetics, as "some jealous neighbor" who speaks in secret (line 47)—and, as Pattern 1 above illustrates, that reported speech is itself embedded in a speech genre, mythological narrative, embedded in the prayer addressed to Pelops. If we pause to wonder why Pindar reports the story that Tantalos cooks his son and serves him to the gods at all, the answer is that by doing so Pindar (1) is able to set up the opposition between gluttony, which is subject to censure, and non-normative sexual practice, which is not subject to censure and (2) displays his competence by demonstrating his awareness of the version of the Pelops story in which Tantalos stews his son.[68]

In this connection, we see in Pattern 2 of the diagram above how Pindar presents Tantalos as an example of impropriety specifically with respect to the consumption of food and drink. Tantalos' punishment results from a violation of the rules for reciprocity entailed in *kharis* in a context analogous to the characterization of the context for performance in lines 9–11 and 16–17, a festal situation that involves the practice of *xenia*:

> εἰ δὲ δή τιν' ἄνδρα θνατὸν Ὀλύμπου σκοποί
> ἐτίμασαν, ἦν Τάνταλος οὗτος· ἀλλὰ γὰρ καταπέψαι
> μέγαν ὄλβον οὐκ ἐδυνάσθη, κόρῳ δ' ἕλεν
> ἄταν ὑπέροπλον, ἅν τοι πατὴρ ὕπερ
> κρέμασε καρτερὸν αὐτῷ λίθον,
> τὸν αἰεὶ μενοινῶν κεφαλᾶς βαλεῖν εὐφροσύνας ἀλᾶται.
> ἔχει δ' ἀπάλαμον βίον τοῦτον ἐμπεδόμοχθον
> μετὰ τριῶν τέταρτον πόνον, ἀθανάτους ὅτι κλέψαις
> ἁλίκεσσι συμπόταις
> νέκταρ ἀμβροσίαν τε
> δῶκεν, οἷσιν ἄφθιτον
> θέν νιν.
>
> *Olympian* 1.54–64

> Indeed, if the guardians of Olympos honored any mortal man,
> it was this Tantalos. But he was not able to stomach
> this great prosperity, and for his insatiability he took
> monstrous ruin, which was that the Father

68 I note here that implicit in my discussion of Pindar *Olympian* 1 is the view that lines 26–27 do not indicate Pindar's inclusion of the rejected myth about Pelops' dismemberment and subsequent consumption by the gods, but that they are a poetic description of Pelops' birth (cf. Köhnken 1983:70). This is a contested view, as suggested by Gerber's interpretation that "λέβης must be the 'cauldron' in which Pelops was restored to life" after his dismemberment (1982:57). Nagy's study of *Olympian* 1 as an etiology of the Olympic Games (1990:116–135) depends upon the same interpretation of λέβης, but he does not "deny the associations of Klotho with the theme of rebirth" (132n89).

> hung a hard stone over him.
> He always wishes to cast it from his head and is deprived of
> gladness.
> He has this helpless life of endless pain
> as a fourth labor along with the other three, because after
> deceiving the immortals,
> to his drinking companions
> he gave nectar and ambrosia;
> with these things the gods made
> Tantalos immortal.

Tantalos' fault is to violate the trust extended to him by the gods. By deceiving them and providing his friends with nectar and ambrosia, he abuses the divine gift of immortality and abuses *xenia*. Pindar's language for summarizing the nature of Tantalos' crime against the gods stresses gluttony at lines 55–56, where the language thematically echoes Pindar's lyric-gnomic hybrid statement at line 52, in which he stipulates: "For me it is impossible to say that any of the blessed ones is gluttonous."[69]

Just as lines 28–35 and 53 create a frame for the composer's prayer to Pelops (lines 36–52), the gnomic statements at lines 53 and 64 create a frame for the mythological narrative of lines 54–64, cited above. In the gnomic statement at line 64, "If any man while doing anything hopes to escape the notice of a god, he is wrong" (εἰ δὲ θεὸν ἀνήρ τις ἔλπεταί <τι> λαθέμεν ἔρδων, ἁμαρτάνει), the inclusive indefiniteness of the gnomic style makes the thought applicable to Pindar as well as Tantalos. With this passage I suggest that Pindar is invoking a divine order of evaluation for his composition, a gesture that especially nests the parodic aspects of the song in the reverent quotation marks of the gnomic speech genre. In the course of *Olympian* 1, the image of the author observing the rules for propriety expressed by gnomic statements is maintained in a qualified way—when it comes to gluttony, Pindar's speech conforms to social conventions, but when it comes to sex, especially the sexual practices of a god, Poseidon, it does not. But toward the song's conclusion, just at the point where we can reasonably conjecture that the real-time choral performance gives way to a real-time celebratory feast, this qualification is erased in favor of food, as it were: the artistic *kharis* seems to override even the possibility of impropriety (103–108 and 111–112 invoke the themes of *xenia* and

[69] Steiner 2002:297–302 convincingly demonstrates that *gastrimargon* 'gluttonous' (*Olympian* 1.52) taps into the poetics of blame.

food, favorably equating them with song). It is as if the evaluative capacity of the speech of wisdom traditions is internally criticized and gradually subordinated, in terms of aesthetic merit, to parody—and this with some god watching (possibly the Muse at 112), as suggested by line 64. In these dynamics, then, we have a case where the parody "on genres and generic styles ('languages') enter the great and diverse world of verbal forms that ridicule the straightforward, serious world in all its generic uses" (Bakhtin 1981:52; cf. 59–60).

As a consequence of the principle expressed in the gnomic statement of line 64 and of Tantalos' actions, Pelops loses his place among the gods. Τοὔνεκα (*touneka*) 'for that reason' (line 65) splices the mythological narrative at lines 65–96, where Pindar narrates Pelops' deeds and relationship with Poseidon, with both the preceding gnomic statement (line 64) and the mythological narrative about Tantalos' deception of the gods (lines 54–64):

> τοὔνεκα {οἱ} προῆκαν υἱὸν ἀθάνατοί <οἱ> πάλιν
> μετὰ τὸ ταχύποτμον αὖτις ἀνέρων ἔθνος.
>
> *Olympian* 1.65–66
>
> For that reason the immortals sent Tantalos' son back
> again among the quick-fated race of men.

The dismissal of Pelops from his *khreos* (line 45) to Poseidon is clearly punitive. This suggests that Pelops' *khreos* is a privilege, a situation in which he experiences *kharis* as the beloved of Poseidon—not only in the general sense of reciprocity, but also in the specific sense of an *erômenos*' gratification of an *erastês*. Here we should note that if *kharis* in the context of a pederastic relationship is equivalent in a sense to the verb *kharizesthai* 'to gratify', then it is within the parameters of propriety for Pelops as *erômenos* to gratify his *erastês*, Poseidon. The punishment of Pelops for Tantalos' offense does not appear to sever the ties of *kharis* between Pelops and Poseidon. In fact, when Pindar presents his trustworthy and *kharis*-driven account of the story of Pelops, the language in which Pindar depicts the ongoing relationship between hero and god continues to refer to that relationship's erotic nature, though subtly, through the double meaning of *kharis* as principle of reciprocity and as the gratification of an *erastês* by an *erômenos*.

In the context of a pederastic relationship between Poseidon and Pelops, now that Pelops has reached the age of manhood, *kharis*, understood as a principle of reciprocity, may entail a reversal of the *erastês* and *erômenos* roles: *kharis* implies in *Olympian* 1 that Pelops may move from the *erômenos* role to the *erastês* role, with the implication, suggested by the meaning of *kharizesthai*, that Poseidon, now with *erômenos* status, may provide *kharis* in the sense of gratifying Pelops as *erastês*. This possible scenario is problematic in light of social norms for sexual behavior, and it invests *kharis* with the connotative ambivalence that is the source of parody in *Olympian* 1.

Pindar's emphasis on Pelops' appearance signals a change in the hero's status and the sexual roles that he can appropriately adopt or pursue. As Cairns has observed: "Pindar specifically emphasises that Pelops was carried off to serve the same purpose for Poseidon as Ganymede served for Zeus (44f.). When Pelops later prays to Poseidon, he is described in terms frequently (and ruefully) found in homosexual contexts to emphasise that the παῖς καλός [*pais kalos* 'lovely boy'] has passed beyond puberty, and so is no longer an object of male desire but (like Pelops) fit for marriage" (1977:129–130). Pindar's description of Pelops' changed appearance stresses that the hero has moved from the age appropriate to being an *erômenos* to an age when he could become an *erastês*—and this at the same time that Pindar introduces the topic of Pelops' desire for marriage to Hippodameia:

> πρὸς εὐάνθεμον δ' ὅτε φυάν
> λάχναι νιν μέλαν γένειον ἔρεφον,
> ἑτοῖμον ἀνεφρόντισεν γάμον
> Πισάτα παρὰ πατρὸς εὔδοξον Ἱπποδάμειαν
> σχεθέμεν.
>
> *Olympian* 1.67–71

> When at the flowering age
> whiskers covered his chin with dark,
> he turned his thoughts to ready marriage,
> to have from her father, the man from Pisa,
> the widely renowned Hippodameia.

I think that we should read the passage in terms of real-world, contemporary sexual practices.[70] Lines 67–68 bring into play the possibility that Pelops and Poseidon might alternate sexual roles in their relationship in light of Dover's observation that "[o]nce the beard was grown, a young male was supposed to be passing out of the *erômenos* stage" (1989:86). By focusing upon the features of Pelops' appearance, Pindar cues us to read his mythological narrative in

[70] This approach would have the advantage of being consistent with Bakhtin: "Even where the past or myth serves as the subject of representation in these genres [i.e. "serio-comical genres" of antiquity, the first step in the development of the novel for Bakhtin] there is no epic distance, and contemporary reality provides the point of view" (1981:23).

terms of the code of pederastic practices at just the moment when the hero is about to address his prayer to Poseidon. Social norms do not preclude the possibility that Pelops marry Hippodameia and conduct an erotic relationship with another male, and the artistic design of *Olympian* 1 offers this possibility. If we take into account Dover's observations that "[i]t was shocking if an *erastês* was younger than his *erômenos*" and that "[o]ne could be *erastês* and *erômenos* at the same stage of one's life, but not both in relation to the same person" (1989:87), then it is possible to see the exceptional nature of a scenario in which Pelops would become an *erastês* to Poseidon, who would in turn become the hero's *erômenos*, as implied by the erotic extension of *kharis* as a principle of reciprocity. By virtue of the possibility that Pelops could become the *erastês* of Poseidon, as suggested by the physical description of the hero (lines 67–68), Pindar presents a scenario in which extraordinary sexual practices are in play: Pelops would be a younger *erastês* to Poseidon, whose *erômenos* he had once been. Given the implication of the code of *kharis* that Pindar establishes in the poem, reciprocity—that it would be appropriate for Poseidon to reciprocate Pelops' previous *khreos* in kind—Pelops' first words to Poseidon have a highly provocative quality: "Pelops addressed him: 'Come on, Poseidon, if at all the cherished gifts of Kypria result in grace'" (τῷ μὲν εἶπε· "Φίλια δῶρα Κυπρίας ἄγ' εἴ τι, Ποσείδαον, ἐς χάριν / τέλλεται," *Olympian* 1.75–76). Specific references to Φίλια δῶρα Κυπρίας "cherished gifts of Kypria" and *kharis* (line 75) imply the principle of reciprocity in the context of an erotic relationship (cf. Gerber 1982:118).

I would suggest that Pindar represents Pelops as "teasing" Poseidon with the possibility of an erotic encounter and, so, serves as Pindar's image of "the rogue's gay deception [that] parodies high languages" (Bakhtin 1981:405), such as the gnomic register and the language of conventional supplication (i.e. *lita* 'entreaty', lines 76–78, discussed below). Such a reading gives in turn a playful color to Pelops' utterance of the final word in the protasis of his conditional sentence, τέλλεται (*telletai*) 'result in' (line 76), where the parodic contour of the passage reaches its pitch, as Pelops' request for requital (i.e. *kharis*) for his prior *khreos* (line 45) to Poseidon does not entail the god's gratification, but a set of requests:[71]

71 Here it is interesting to consider the stylistic parallel between this Pindaric passage and the style that Skinner attributes to an *erastês*' address to an *erômenos*, as exemplified by Theognis lines 1235–1238: "The elegiac verse of the Theognidean corpus is permeated with the rhetoric of control employed by the lover to dictate to his beloved. Normally the *erastês* addresses his companion like a preceptor, sometimes encouragingly, at other times sternly, always professing to have the boy's best interest in mind" (2005:55). Pelops does not appear to be advising Poseidon; his mode of discourse is more in the mode of *lita* 'entreaty'. However, the

> πέδασον ἔγχος Οἰνομάου χάλκεον,
> ἐμὲ δ' ἐπὶ ταχυτάτων πόρευσον ἁρμάτων
> ἐς Ἆλιν, κράτει δὲ πέλασον.
>
> *Olympian* 1.76–78
>
> Restrain the bronze spear of Oinomaos,
> bear me on the swiftest chariot
> to Elis, and bring me to dominance.

Given the erotic connotations of *kharis* as a principle of reciprocity and the cues about how to read the sexual roles of Poseidon and Pelops, namely that Pelops' age suggests that he is moving into the *erastês* stage, the story holds out the possibility that Poseidon may assume the *erômenos* role, contrary to social norms. Following the line of argument articulated metacommunicatively by statements couched in or heavily inflected by the gnomic style, Pindar would not be violating any conventions for appropriate speech (lines 28–35) to suggest that the god and hero may engage in an exceptional sexual relationship, so long as the composer does not claim that they are gluttonous (line 52) and he does not suffer the lack of gain that is the lot of slanderers (line 54), presumably a form of punishment for those who offend the gods with their speech.[72] Pindar pushes the envelope to hint that Poseidon may assume the *erômenos* role in a pederastic relationship, a possibility that would violate the social norms for the sexual practices of males in ancient Greek society, as Dover indicates: "Since the reciprocal desire of partners belonging to the same age-category is virtually unknown in Greek homosexuality, the distinction between the bodily activity of the one who has fallen in love and the bodily passivity of the one with whom he has fallen in love is of the highest impor-

blend of injunction (imperative forms at lines 75–78), gnomic statement (line 84), and mythological narrative (line 79–81) is formally parainetic. There is productive gray area in the mode of Pelops' speech, but it is safe to say that the erotic relationship between hero and god contextualizes this speech and that such contextualization suggests, drawing from Skinner's observation, that Pelops is speaking more in the mode of *erastês* than *erômenos*. I cite Dover and Skinner as authorities on ancient sexuality, both of whom identify a power differential between *erastês* (dominant, active) and *erômenos* (subordinate, passive) (cf. Parker 1997:4 and passim), but modifying his earlier stance (1987:9) Hubbard disputes this position, arguing "that the traditional phallocentric reading of Greek pederasty, foregrounding the active agency of the adult *erastês* as the privileged term in a relationship of fundamental power asymmetry, is too reductive to provide an adequate understanding of its complexity" (2002:256).

72 Cf. Dover on the depiction of the relationship between Pelops and Poseidon: "This passage is the most daring and spectacular 'homosexualization' of myth that we have; Pindar's gods are too refined to digest anything but ambrosia, but never so insensitive that their genitals cannot be aroused" (1989:198). Some scholars interpret Poseidon's abduction of Pelops as a mythological representation of a one-time existent practice of initiation into adulthood (see note 58 above).

tance" (1989:16). If *kharis* as a principle of reciprocity is to be sustained in the poem and if the imagery of the poem suggests that Pelops has reached the *erastês* stage, then trading on the "gifts of Kypria" (*kharis* both as reciprocity and as sexual gratification) implies in an open-ended way that Poseidon may move into the *erômenos* role. I suggest that this open-endedness concerning Poseidon's questionable sexual behavior makes the by-now intensely ambivalent sense of *kharis* available for rendering the praise of Hieron and the performance of *Olympian* 1 itself with overtones of parody.

This becomes more evident when we consider that the principle of reciprocity as expressed by *kharis*, with its sexual connotations intact, also applies in the relationship between Pindar and Hieron. While there is much to recommend the parallel between hero and athlete,[73] the evidence in *Olympian* 1 suggests that Pelops is very certainly a model for the performance of *Olympian* 1 and, thus, for the *laudator*'s relationship to his *laudandus*. To recap this evidence briefly:

Pelops uses the epinician way of speaking effectively, providing a model for Pindar's own speech.

The structure of Pelops' speech (described above) is a reflex of the ring composition of Pindar's song, *Olympian* 1 (see below).

Just as Pelops' observance of the rules of propriety communicated by *kharis* (with the word's ambivalent connotations intact) warrants the positive response of Poseidon to the hero's speech, so Pindar's observance of the rules of propriety, especially *kharis* understood as a principle of reciprocity, would secure for the composer a positive evaluation of his composition by the audience.

As demonstrated in Chapter One, *Olympian* 1.17–19 describes the composition of *Olympian* 1 in terms of the reception of a traditional song-making strategy and gives *kharis* as the motivation for that act of composition-as-reception.

Just as Tantalos' relationship with the gods, which entails a violation of *kharis* understood as a principle of reciprocity, is a foil for Pelops'

[73] Dougherty, for example, writes that "Pindar's method of praise tends to include the comparison, explicit or implicit, of the victor to an important mythological or heroic figure associated with his city" (1993:95). A central feature of Köhnken's argument that Pindar revises the Pelops myth for poetic purposes, and not due to religious scruples, is the point that Pelops is a positive parallel to which to compare the *laudandus* Hieron (1974). Hubbard's study (1987) of *Olympian* 1 likewise refutes the claim that Pindar's religious scrupulosity motivates his revision of the Pelops myth.

> relationship with Poseidon, Tantalos is also a foil for Pindar's practice of *kharis* as an artistic act of reciprocity that commemorates the deeds of the *laudandus.*

One of the most connotatively charged parallels between Pindar and Pelops involves the role of the theme of *khreos* in *Olympian* 1. Pindar applies language similar to his description of Pelops' erotic relationship with Poseidon, in terms of *khreos* (line 45), to describe his praise of Hieron:

ἐμὲ δὲ στεφανῶσαι
κεῖνον ἱππίῳ νόμῳ
Αἰοληΐδι μολπᾷ
χρή· πέποιθα δὲ ξένον
μή τιν' ἀμφότερα καλῶν τε ἴδριν †ἅμα καὶ δύναμιν κυριώτερον
τῶν γε νῦν κλυταῖσι δαιδαλωσέμεν ὕμνων πτυχαῖς.

Olympian 1.100–105

It is necessary for me to crown
that man with a rider's measure
in Aeolic song.
I am persuaded that there is not any host
both skilled in upright things and at the same time more
sovereign in power
among people today to ornament with famous layers of *humnoi.*

The word *khrê* (line 103) is an echo of *khreos* (line 45). In fact, both words occur in the fifth line of the antistrophe in which they occur, respectively, which provides formal evidence to demonstrate that there is a parallel between Pelops and Pindar with respect to their fulfillment of *khreos* in the context of observing the principle of reciprocity expressed by *kharis.* Taken to its full extent, the analogy between Pelops (i.e. with reference to line 45) and Pindar would suggest that Pindar's act of *kharis* in the form of a song of praise reciprocating Hieron's victory figuratively places Pindar in the position of *erômenos* to Hieron's *erastês.* Such an interpretation of the parallel evocations of the theme of *khreos* gives the second-person address to Hieron at the end of the poem a palpable quality.[74] Athanassaki, for example, has observed that the shift in

[74] This interpretation is highly resonant with the following observation by Bakhtin: "Everything that makes us laugh is close at hand, all comical creativity works in a zone of maximal proximity. Laughter has the remarkable power of making an object come up close, of drawing it into a zone of crude contact where one can finger it familiarly on all sides, turn it upside down, inside out, peer at it from above and below, break open its external shell, look into its center,

the characterization of the *laudator-laudandus* relationship, from *xenia* through most of *Olympian* 1 to *homilia* in lines 106–114, "is decisive in producing the special intimate effect of the speaker speaking in the presence of his addressee" (2004:323). Further, when we consider that in an original performance a chorus of young men, who would have been the age appropriate to the *erômenos* stage, sang Pindar's composition, we can begin to discern the subtly ribald quality of the song.[75] Considering still further that this chorus was a didactic vehicle for passing on and representing the values of a community, we seem to have something quite opposed to the highly conventional Pindar constructed by exegetical philology: popular laughter. In fact, given the parallels between Pelops and Pindar, the image of the author emerges as a rogue figure in light of Pindar's parody of the high language of gnomic style and myth (cf. Bakhtin 1981:405).

I would further note that lines 103–105 apply the principle of reciprocity to the relationship between composer and *laudandus*. While this passage has the first-person singular verb πέποιθα "I am persuaded" (line 103) and refers to song in the phrase κλυταῖσι δαιδαλωσέμεν ὕμνων πτυχαῖς "to ornament with famous layers of *humnoi*" (105), there are a number of gnomic elements: the indefinite pronoun τινα (line 104); the neuter plural adjective καλῶν (line 104), used substantively; and the article with adverb construction τῶν γε νῦν (line 105), used substantively. The force of these gnomic inflections of the lyric passages at lines 103–105 is to express, through the generalizing features of gnomic style, that the poet's song (the reflexive dimension of these passages) fulfills the principle of reciprocity—with the metacommunicative force that, "in general, this poet fulfills the social conventions of propriety defined in terms of reciprocity," and that the composition of *Olympian* 1 should accordingly receive a positive evaluation from the audience. Here we see an example of how "a crucial part of the process of constructing intertextual relations may be undertaken by the audience" (Briggs and Bauman 1992:157). Finally, in light

doubt it, take it apart, dismember it, lay it bare and expose it, examine it freely and experiment with it" (1981:23).

75 Pindar describes chorus members as *neoi* 'youths' at *Pythian* 5.103, *Nemean* 3.66, *Isthmian* 8.1, *Paean* 6.122, and, possibly, at *Fragment* 227.1. Cf. Herington 1985:30. Mackie 2003:42–43 notes that "programmatic references also describe the chorus that performs the ode as a group of νέοι [*neoi*], 'youths.'" Burnett's study of Aiginetan songs "assume[s] performance by troupes of singing male dancers, amateurs who were, like the victors [commemorated by Pindar's Aiginetan odes], not yet 18 years old" (2005:8). She then describes an erotic ambience created by the nudity of these choreuts and an audience "ready to be delighted by the sight of youthful bodies in motion (a version of the pleasure one might take on a visit to the gymnasium)." Carey identifies gender and age (male and young) as the closest we come to "objective evidence for the status of the chorus which sang the victory ode" (2007:207).

of the case I have made so far for the stylistic three-dimensionality of *epinikion*, we can recognize the phrase κλυταῖσι…ὕμνων πτυχαῖς "famous layers of *humnoi*" (line 105) as an expression of the stratification of languages (styles) in Pindar's verbal art.

Above I described how *Olympian* 1 has two panels of mythological narrative—one whose focus is to highlight gluttony and its censure, one that parodically deploys the same rules for appropriate speech, which lead to the censure of gluttony—to license the depiction of the god Poseidon involved in gray-area sexual behavior. If the parodic dimensions of *Olympian* 1 depend upon the tension between tones of reverence and undertones of ribaldry respectively entailed in these two panels of mythological narrative, Pindar seems to undermine this tension productively in two passages near the end of the song:

> θεὸς ἐπίτροπος ἐὼν τεαῖσι μήδεται
> ἔχων τοῦτο κᾶδος, Ἱέρων,
> μερίμναισιν.
>
> *Olympian* 1.106–108
>
> A guardian god thinks of your concerns,
> taking this on for his responsibility, Hieron.

> ἐμοὶ μὲν ὦν
> Μοῖσα καρτερώτατον βέλος ἀλκᾷ τρέφει.
>
> *Olympian* 1.111–112
>
> For me
> the Muse nourishes an arrow mightiest in courage.

Here we might explore how the word τρέφει (*trephei*) 'nourishes' (line 112) resonates with ἐπίτροπος (*epitropos*) 'guardian' (line 106). Poseidon in his relationship with Pelops exemplifies a θεὸς ἐπίτροπος (*theos epitropos*) 'guardian god'; I cautiously suggest that the language of care in these passages, with its association with food and nourishment, erases the tension between censure of gluttony and non-censure of non-normative sexual practices in such a way as to demonstrate that the power of song is the overriding *kharis*. Here it is interesting to juxtapose Pindar's Muse-provided *belos* 'arrow' (line 112) with Ann Bergren's observation that "archaic Greek thought perceived in the bow and lyre the capacity of attaining an exact mark of sound or space, if the string is plucked properly" (1982:91). Perhaps Hieron's *theos epitropos* 'guardian god' (line 106) is Pindar's Muse (line 112); perhaps what makes Pindar's βέλος (*belos*) 'arrow'—that is, his song—καρτερώτατον (*karterôtaton*) 'mightiest' (line 112) is art's charm or beauty, whose accuracy resolves the tensions of sense (as reflected in lines 28–32 of *Olympian* 1) into the form of design.

Before proceeding with my discussion of Pindaric parody, I pause to make a few points concerning the dialogical relationship between the original performance and reperformance of *Olympian* 1. There are a number of passages that anticipate a sympotic context for the reperformance of *Olympian* 1. First, Pindar depicts Pelops as reclining beside the Alpheos River (line 92) in the way that a participant in a symposium would have reclined on a couch (cf. Steiner 2002:209). In lines 100–105 Pindar represents his composition as an act of crowning Hieron, a gesture that would be appropriate to a sympotic context. Finally, the parodic overtones in *Olympian* 1 generated by the distinction between censure of excess appetite for food and drink and a more permissive attitude toward exceptional sexual behavior would have been especially resonant in a sympotic context. Such passages suggest the multilayered ramifications of dialogism in Pindar's epinician way of speaking: Pindar simultaneously composes a work of art that is subject to two dimensions of audience, the audience to the original performance and the potential target audiences, superaddressees who might reperform and rehear this song.

What emerges, then, from an ethnographic "close reading" of *Olympian* 1 is that the practices entailed in praise poetics are modeled on the practices of "low" aspects of human life, the feast gone awry and non-normative sexual practices, and that *kharis* is the embracive strategy for conduct in all of these fields of cultural practice. Interestingly, then, we see an opposition between food and sexuality, where abuses of moderation with respect to consumption of delicacies of the palate violate the code of reciprocity, but immoderate sexual behavior fulfills reciprocity. In light of this playful manipulation of social norms, we can see how the gnomic style serves to put reverent quotation marks around a less reverent depiction of the god Poseidon, the relationship between Pindar and Hieron, and the performance of *Olympian* 1 itself. I would stress that if Pindar's art were merely a matter of projecting present events onto a plane with an absolute heroic past walled off from his contemporary world (Pindar's present), the well developed parodic dimension of Pindar's song could not exist. In light of the fact that it licenses Pindar's art to surmount the risk of conflict with social codes for normative behavior, *kharis* becomes a less lofty, though no less artful, designation for the power of verbal art. While I emphatically acknowledge the problems of stereotyping and the failure to observe cultural specificity, compared to invoking the gleanings of high art, it more closely approximates what we can authentically understand about Pindar's *Olympian* 1 to describe the poet's use of parody as an edgy instance of Archaic Greek camp—or as Athenaios puts it, Pindar is οὐ μετρίως ὢν ἐρωτικος 'immoderately erotic' (13.601c).[76]

Pindaric parody is most often to be observed in dialogues of registers, exemplified above in my discussion of *Olympian* 1.1–27, in the effects of heteroglossia in gnomic statements, and in direct discourse as an image of language. Instances of parody that arise from such discursive dynamics can be discovered on the basis of the kind of ethnography-driven philology that this study proposes.[77] If we approach Pindaric parody strictly with a view toward finding heretofore unidentified humor in his victory songs, we may miss the more important point that Pindaric parody is one among many forms of speech play that Pindar uses to negotiate complex and often competing audience expectations.[78] In the case of *Olympian* 1, it would be too simple to say that Pindar uses "low art" gestures to appeal to a popular audience. Not only too simple, but inaccurate: I am throughout this study claiming that the high-level artistic competence of Pindar's audiences drives the composer's selection of poetic strategies. The paronomasia involving *kharis* in *Olympian* 1 is nothing if not highly artful, and such artfulness is a function of Pindar's anticipation of the criteria that his audience applies in evaluating his songs.

76 Scanlon quotes Athenaeus as an illustration of how "Pindar's reputation for being, in Athenaeus' words, 'immoderately erotic'...is consistent with the important erotic function of athletics" (2002:224). Carne-Ross 1985:25–30 discusses Pindar's tendency to describe victory in erotic terms. Hubbard, also citing Athenaeus (2002:264n25), connects "the widespread eroticization of Greek athletic culture...and Pindar's particular reputation as an enthusiastic encomiast of young athletes" (2002:264).

77 To briefly indicate that the ribaldry of *Olympian* 1 is not entirely unique to Pindar's epinician corpus, *Olympian* 10, composed for Hagesidamos, 476 BCE victor in boys boxing at Olympia, also features paronomasia involving *kharis*: *kharis* expresses the reciprocity between *laudator* and *laudandus* (line 12); *kharis* also has the more particular meaning of reciprocity in the sense of an *erômenos*' sexual gratification (*kharizesthai*) of his *erastês* (line 17); given this erotic valence for *kharis*, song as *kharis* in the sense of 'reciprocity' (in the form of poetic mimesis) and 'beauty' or 'grace' (line 78) emblematizes the *laudandus*'s *kharis* 'beauty' (line 94) as visible manifestation of his *kleos*, which benefits his *polis* (lines 95–104). The last two occurrences of *kharis* connect Hagesidamos' eligibility for the role of *erômenos* and the composer's role: through his song, the composer is at once like a trainer/*erastês*, who can promote the *kleos* (lines 21 and 95) of a naturally talented protégé, and like Aphrodite, who can bestow an undying *kharis* upon a *pais eratos* 'lovely boy' (lines 104–105). What makes *Olympian* 10 playful and, thus, parodic is that Pindar (1) flouts social conventions for discretion (*aidôs*) about a young man's participation in a homoerotic relationship by making the sexual allure of the *laudandus* a feature of his *kleos* and (2) puts himself in the role of facilitator of this violation of discretion.

78 See Jurenka 1986 for study of humor in Pindar's poetry.

The Art of Dialogism: Orchestration

To conclude this chapter of *Pindar's Verbal Art* I first call attention to a stylistic feature of poetry, as opposed to the prose art of the novel, that prohibits, in Bakhtin's view, the promotion of stylistic stratification: rhythm, which serves to unify poetic language and, in effect, muffles any effects of dialogism. Pindar's epinician songs have complex and thoroughly redundant prosodic patterning, which certainly imposes upon other formal and ideological features of his art its centralizing and unifying forces. Here I cite Bakhtin's statement on the issue of rhythm (1981:298, emphasis in original):

> *Rhythm, by creating an unmediated involvement between every aspect of the accentual system of the whole* (via the most immediate rhythmic unities), destroys in embryo those social worlds of speech and persons that are potentially embedded in the word: in any case, rhythm puts definite limits on them, does not let them unfold or materialize. Rhythm serves to strengthen and concentrate even further the unity and hermetic quality of the surface of poetic style, and of the unitary language that this style posits.

I think the question of the relationship between rhythm and novelistic discourse is at the heart of any objection to my application of the stylistics of the novel to *epinikion*. I would urge in the first instance, however, that I am not at all interested in the opposition between poetry and prose, but in the opposition between high and low categories of verbal art, with all the real-world ideological implications that those categories entail. In the second instance, I call attention to the felicity of characterizing Pindar's kind of artistic mastery as orchestration, Bakhtin's expression for the novelist's skill. When it comes to identifying the nature of Pindar's art in a way that goes hand in hand with a philological method for discovering how that art works, orchestration fits both the object of analysis and the method of analysis: "the real task of stylistic analysis consists in uncovering all the available orchestrating languages in the composition of the novel," as Bakhtin himself writes (1981:416).

We have observed aspects of orchestration in the foregoing analysis of how Pindar creates images of language through hybridization, dialogized interrelations among speech genres, and direct discourse in mythological narrative, as well as in the way that he weaves together multiple thematic layers in the parodic dimensions of *Olympian* 1, especially in the complex paronomasia involving *kharis*. As another, more global illustration of why it is appropriate to characterize Pindar's artistic mastery as orchestration, we can observe such orchestration of language styles in the ring composition organizing the relationships among the ways of epinician speaking in *Olympian* 1:[79]

Diagram 2: Ring Composition in *Olympian* 1

Lines 1–27: *Eukhesthai*

↳Lines 8–11: Lyric

  ↳Lines 12–15: *Angelia*

↳Lines 16–17: Lyric

↳Lines 20–24: *Angelia*

  ↳Lines 25–27: Mythological Narrative

Lines 28a–35: *Gnômai*

Lines 36–51: *Eukhesthai*

↳Lines 37–51: Mythological Narrative

  ↳Lines 43–45: Mythological Narrative

Line 52: Lyric

Line 53: *Gnôma*

Lines 54–64: Mythological Narrative

Line 64: *Gnôma*

Lines 65–96: Mythological Narrative

↳75–85: Direct Discourse

  ↳Lines 75–78: *Eukhesthai*

  ↳Lines 79–81: Mythological Narrative

  ↳Lines 81–84: *Gnôma*

  ↳Lines 84–85: Lyric

  ↳Line 85: *Eukhesthai*

Lines 97–100: *Gnômai*

Lines 100–105: Lyric

Lines 106–111: *Eukhesthai*

Lines 111–112: Lyric

Lines 113–114: *Gnôma*

Lines 114–116: *Eukhesthai*

79 Illig's treatment of ring composition influences subsequent scholarship on the phenomenon (1932:55–67 and passim), but his approach focuses upon the structure of mythological narrative, not the structure of a song as a whole, as Young makes clear (1968:33 and 103–104). Young identifies a ring composition pattern in *Olympian* 1 based upon aspects of content, "superlatives, praise of Hieron, his Olympic victory, a myth about Pelops, a myth about Tantalos, another Pelops-myth, Olympic victory, praise of Hieron, and superlatives" and "transitions between these concentrically balanced topics" (1968:121–123). Slater 1979:63–65 discusses two kinds of ring composition in Pindar, one (recalling Illig) on the basis of temporal "conventions of narrative" and the other, "verbal ring composition." In his analysis *Olympian* 1 has the ring composition characteristic of "complex lyric narrative." Ring composition is fundamental to Greengard's (1980) study of the structure of *epinikion*.

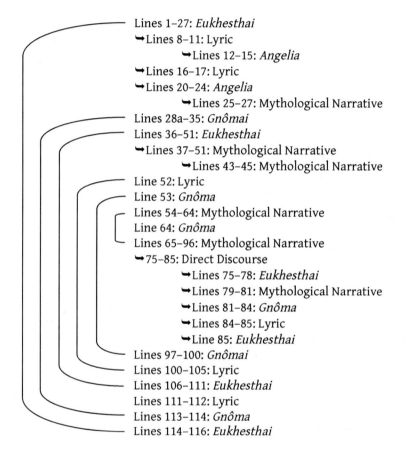

We can note several things communicated pragmatically by this pattern, and these observations will make it possible to interpret the one apparent deviation (lines 111–112) in the overall orchestration of speech genres. First, the ring connecting lines 54–64 and lines 65–96 communicates the antithesis between Tantalos and Pelops whereby Tantalos is a foil to Pelops' exemplary fulfillment of the principle of reciprocity. Second, articulating the parallel between Pindar and Pelops, the overall pattern of ring composition in *Olympian* 1, with a gnomic statement at the discursive center of the ring and *eukhesthai* passages forming the outermost ring, parallels the ring composition of Pelops' speech (lines 75–85), as described above. Third, the centrality of the gnomic statement at line 64 serves to highlight the importance of the message conveyed by that particular *gnôma* and its importance as an instance of metacommunication about social conventions for appropriate speech. Recall as well that line 64 serves to demarcate the two panels containing mythological material, one that concerns the topic of gluttony (lines 36–64), one that concerns the topic of sex (lines 65–94).

The deviation in the pattern of ring composition at lines 111–112 can be understood in terms of the context of that variation:

> θεὸς ἐπίτροπος ἐὼν τεαῖσι μήδεται
> ἔχων τοῦτο κᾶδος, Ἱέρων,
> μερίμναισιν· εἰ δὲ μὴ ταχὺ λίποι,
> ἔτι γλυκυτέραν κεν ἔλπομαι
> σὺν ἅρματι θοῷ κλεΐξειν ἐπίκουρον εὑρὼν ὁδὸν λόγων
> παρ' εὐδείελον ἐλθὼν Κρόνιον. ἐμοὶ μὲν ὦν
> Μοῖσα καρτερώτατον βέλος ἀλκᾷ τρέφει·
> †ἄλλοισι δ' ἄλλοι μεγάλοι· τὸ δ' ἔσχατον κορυφοῦται
> βασιλεῦσι. μηκέτι πάπταινε πόρσιον.
> εἴη σέ τε τοῦτον ὑψοῦ χρόνον πατεῖν,
> ἐμέ τε τοσσάδε νικαφόροις ὁμιλεῖν πρόφαντον σοφίᾳ καθ'
> Ἕλλανας ἐόντα παντᾷ.
>
> *Olympian* 1.106–116

> A guardian god thinks of your concerns,
> taking this on for his responsibility, Hieron.
> Unless he should leave soon,
> I hope a still sweeter victory
> with the swift chariot to celebrate, after finding
> an assisting path of words
> and going by the far-seen mound of Kronos. For me

> the Muse nourishes an arrow mightiest in courage.
> Some men are great at some things, other men are
> great at other things, but the utmost achievement
> reaches its height
> with kings. No longer look further.
> May it be that you walk aloft for this time
> and that I commune just as long with victorious men
> and be distinguished for wisdom among Greeks
> everywhere.

The composer says that the Muse has provided him with the καρτερώτατον βέλος (*karterôtaton belos*) 'mightiest arrow' (line 112), and the root for the adjective is associated with civic power and echoes the occurrences at lines 22 and 78 of the word *kratos* 'power'. This word system unfolds over the course of the poem, surfacing three times: line 22, in reference to Hieron; line 78, where Pelops uses it to describe the kind of *response* he requests of Poseidon; line 112, where the composer uses it to describe the act of composition, which reciprocates Hieron's *kratos* as described in the *angelia* at line 22. I argue that the deviation in the pattern of ring composition in *Olympian* 1 underscores the centrality of *kharis* and reciprocity in the song and foregrounds the fact that *kharis* and reciprocity implicate the audience and its evaluation of Pindar's composition: Pelops requests that Poseidon respond to his prayer with *kratos*; Poseidon grants that request, signaling the god's positive evaluation of Pelops' words; the Muse grants Pindar the *karterôtaton belos* 'mightiest arrow' (line 112) with which to reciprocate for Hieron's achievement; as the song concludes, it now rests with the audience to evaluate whether Pindar has effectively displayed his artistic competence. Poseidon's response, the positive evaluation of the hero's prayer, which is a model of epinician style (composed ultimately by the narrator, not, of course, by the narrated figure of Pelops), provides a model for the audience's response to Pindar's composition, which, recall, Pindar represents in lines 1–27 in terms of a prayer: just as Poseidon's response to Pelops' prayer signals the god's positive evaluation of the hero's use of epinician style, the fulfillment of the composer's concluding prayer (lines 114–116) is a function of the audience's evaluation of the performance, and of *its* competence, expressed in terms of the principle of reciprocity as modeled by Poseidon. So it is in the rupture at lines 111–112 in the otherwise highly patterned ring composition that we witness orchestration in the form of a verbal counterpoint whose practical effect is to highlight the overall design of the song.[80]

80 Currie 2005:75 interprets various verbal echoes in *Olympian* 1, including that involving *kratos*

The Appendix to *Pindar's Verbal Art* documents the organization of speech genres in each of Pindar's *epinikia*, where it will be noted that other poems evidence ring composition among the ways of epinician speaking. There are two consequences of this. First, the fact that a number of Pindar's songs[81] exhibit ring composition involving the ways of epinician speaking serves as a control to my description of each individual speech genre: the fact that the relationships among ways of epinician speaking are patterned in individual songs indicates that these five styles or registers are meaningful to Pindar and are local conventions, perhaps even traditional and constituting a domain of formal features that make it possible to identify *epinikion* as an immanent art (Foley 1991). Second, we can now see in light of this phenomenon of orchestration that, at the levels of medium, event, and composition, rules for speaking thoroughly constitute the epinician way of speaking. As Martin has written with respect to the Homeric texts, we see that in Pindar's epinician texts "cohesion, continuity, and unity *cannot be textually* determined. Instead, they flow from a speech-community's sense of appropriate, genre-bound behaviours" (2000:53, emphasis in original). I would add here that I have studied the dynamics of orchestration only in terms of an ethnographic stylistics that considers how *epinikion* is a complex genre comprised of simple genres. Kurke has shown that Pindar embeds within his *epinikia* other complex genres. In Chapter Four I summarized Kurke's (1990) description of how Pindar's *Pythian* 6 evidences features of *hupothêkai*, which can be connected with the genre of poetry described by Martin as Instruction of Princes. Kurke has also demonstrated that Pindar embeds in his *Isthmian* 1 the poetic genres of "paean, *kallinikos* song, Castoreion, didactic poetry, and homecoming invocation" (1988).[82]

(lines 22 and 78), as setting up a parallel between Hieron and Pelops. For him, this parallel suggests the possibility that Hieron, like Pelops, may enjoy immortality in the form of a hero cult. Bremer 2008:12–17 argues *contra* Currie 2005 that it would have exceeded the bounds of Pindar's sense of religious propriety to suggest that mortal athletes could become immortal.

81 The strongest examples are *Olympian* 1, 2, 6, 8, 9, 11, 12, 13; *Pythian* 1, 5, 9, 11; *Nemean* 4, 7, 8, 9; and *Isthmian* 2, 7, and 8.

82 Kurke adds: "Other examples of generic self-consciousness are *Ol.* 9.1–4 (reference to *kallinikos*), *Ol.* 13.18f (reference to dithyramb), *Pyth.* 6.20–22 (allusion to *Hypothekai*), *Isthm.* 6.66–68 (allusion to Hesiod's *Works and Days*), and the remarkable fragment 128 c S./M., which lists five different genres in the space of ten lines" (1988:112n39). Appealing to the example of choral lyric in drama, Krummen 1990:137 argues in favor of an approach to *Pythian* 5, and *epinikion* generally, that accounts for the ways that a given work can blend together multiple genres. See Race 1990:85–117 on Pindar's incorporation of cultic hymns in his victory songs, a dynamic that can be described and interpreted in terms of intertextuality. Cf. Clay's interpretation of Pindar's description of Athena's invention of the *aulos* and its music (*Pythian* 12.6–12, with particular stress upon the phrase *oulion thrênon diaplexais'* '[Athena] threaded together the pale

In light of the intensely dialogized quality of *epinikion*, the phrase *poikilos humnos* 'elaborate hymn' is a highly resonant Pindaric description of the orchestral quality of his mastery of verbal art. To cite an example:[83]

> ματρομάτωρ ἐμὰ Στυμφαλίς, εὐανθὴς Μετώπα,
> πλάξιππον ἃ Θήβαν ἔτικτεν, τᾶς ἐρατεινὸν ὕδωρ
> πίομαι, ἀνδράσιν αἰχματαῖσι πλέκων
> ποικίλον ὕμνον.
>
> *Olympian* 6.84–87
>
> My mother's mother was Stymphalian, blooming Metopa,
> who bore horse-driving Thebes, whose lovely water
> I drink as I weave
> an elaborate *humnos* for warrior men.

Slater's *Lexicon to Pindar* gives meanings for the word *poikilos* such as 'spotted, dappled', 'embroidered', 'ever changing, crafty', and, in the context of music, 'in varied tones' (1969b:434). These uses indicate that *poikilos* has to do with variegated adornment.[84] Applied to Pindar's compositions, then, a *poikilos humnos* is a song of praise characterized by such variegated adornment, which I have been describing as an intertextual web of stylistic diversity artfully orchestrated.[85] *Olympian* 6.84–87 not only serves as an example of how Pindar

---

dirge', line 8): "Athena does not simply weave a *thrênos* ['lament'], but she *interweaves* two very different sounds: the Gorgon's mournful song of loss and Perseus' triumphal shout of victory" (1992:523, emphasis in original). Carey 1995:97n21 observes that the "tendency to stretch the genre and hybridize is very typical of Pindar." Currie 2005:21–24 sees the "generic indeterminacy" of *epinikion* as a function of both the ambiguity of evidence internal to epinician texts and modern assumptions, such as an assumed distinction between secular and religious functions or contexts of epinician performance. See recently Kurke 2007:156 on *epinikion*'s "anomalous hybrid form."

83 Cf. φόρμιγξ ποικιλόγαρυς (*Olympian* 3.8), ποικιλοφόρμιγξ ἀοιδά (*Olympian* 4.2), ποικίλον κιθαρίζων (*Nemean* 4.14), ποικίλοι ὕμνοι (*Nemean* 5.42), and τειχίζωμεν ἤδη ποικίλον κόσμον (*Fragment* 194.2–3). Nicholson 2000 shows that in *Pythian* 4 Pindar deploys the polysemous word *strômna* 'coverlet' (line 230)—note, a fabric image, albeit not a woven fabric—to integrate multiple narratives.

84 Bundy glosses *poikilia* as *variatio* in the context of describing a lack of verbal repetition in *Isthmian* 1 (1962:47). For Newman and Newman "variety is the essence of the ποικιλία [*poikilia*] to which Pindar lays claim" (1984:39). Evocative of the carnivalesque quality that they attribute to epinician performance, Newman and Newman juxtapose the "harlequin's motley dress" to Pindaric *poikilia* (49).

85 Pindar's style need no longer be described in such terms as "*le malaise de l'instable et de l'erratique*" (Hummel 2001:48) on the basis of this understanding of the artistry of stylistic diversity in Pindar's songs. Given that for Pindar *poikilos humnos* describes the artful patterning of multiple registers and that Pindar's audience would have been fluent in epinician art, I would

describes orchestration as a matter of composing a *poikilos humnos* but also reflects what we have been considering here in detail, the features of intertextuality that give *epinikion* its novelistic quality. Especially because Pindar represents himself as *weaving* a *poikilos humnos*, this phrase is an excellent description of the orchestrated dialogism that is characteristic of *epinikion*, as illustrated by the ring composition involving simple speech genres in *Olympian* 1.[86] Pindar's monumental skill at orchestration, as expressed by his characterization of his art form as *poikilos humnos*, strongly reflects Bakhtin's characterization of the art of the novel: "The novel can be defined as a diversity of social speech types (sometimes even diversity of languages) and a diversity of individual voices, artistically organized" (1981:262).

I conclude this chapter by returning to Martin's point, quoted above, about textual cohesion. If utterances that are not embedded provide the discursive "surface" of each epinician song, it is tempting to interpret embedding dynamics as discursive moves below that "surface" and back again. The same applies to ring composition generally: ring composition suggests a discursive return to some prior discursive position. Such an interpretation of embedding dynamics and ring composition, as Bonifazi points out, is too limiting because it fails to account for what she calls the "forward" of here-and-now communi-

---

not attribute Pindar's perceived obscurity to the quality of *poikilia*, as Pfeijffer 1999a:22–34 and Hamilton 2003:77–96 do. For Hamilton Pindar's reputation for obscurity goes back to the Classical Period. After citing Eupolis Fr. 266 as evidence of Pindar's irrelevance and Euripides *Elektra* 387–388 and Xenophanes *Fragments* 20.20–22 as evidence of derisive attitudes toward athletics, Hamilton interprets parody of Pindaric poetry in Aristophanes *Birds* 907–946 as an indication that, "whether his poems could no longer speak to the world or the world grew incapable of hearing the poet, Pindar's literary afterlife was severely undercut before it ever began" (2003:17–23). Cole 1992:15 expresses a similar view. Parody, however, suggests an inclusive rather than limited appreciation for Pindar: to get the joke—and it would seem that the success, competitive and artistic, of Aristophonic comedy depended upon humor that resonated with, rather than alienated, his audience—the theater-goers must have been familiar with Pindar's poetry. In a similar vein, Hubbard writes: "There is no question that Pindar's odes for the Sicilian potentates were familiar enough to be parodied contemporaneously by Bacchylides (3.85–87) and a generation later by Aristophanes (*Birds* 924–45). In the *Knights* (1264–66, 1329; cf. *Ach.* 637–39) Aristophanes parodies at least two other poems of Pindar. Parody by definition presupposes a broad audience acquainted with the work parodied" (2004:71–72). Diametrically opposing the view of Hamilton, Hubbard even cites Eupolis—but as evidence for Pindar's popularity at Athens (2004:72). Carey has captured well the ideological implications for the variety of audiences for which Simonides, Pindar, and Bakkhulides compose their *epinikia*: "[t]he fact that songs, including epinikians, composed by Pindar and Simonides to honour rulers and toffs could be cited and parodied for a mass audience in democratic Athens suggests that knowledge and enjoyment of praise songs for members of the international elite were not restricted by ideological or social boundaries" (2007:210).

86 Cf. *Nemean* 4.93–94: "Someone who praises such a man as Melesias would ward off a quarrel by weaving his words" (οἷον αἰνέων κε Μελησίαν ἔριδα στρέφοι / ῥήματα πλέκων).

cation in performance: "performance is a linear continuum, there is no ring; the cognitive processes of reception are always in progress, there is no return" (2004b:62–63). Building upon the image of weaving associated with Pindar's *poikilos humnos*, I want to suggest that we think of orchestration as a process of threading the ways of epinician speaking, the weft, into the performance "forward," the warp, the linear movement of composition and reception.[87] In this way I hope to bring out the fact that orchestration, *poikilia*, so conceived points beyond any static formalism that my description of those dynamics may suggest, toward the possibility of greater fluency in the pragmatic and dynamic communicative strategies at the artistic command of Pindar and his audiences.

87 Thus my position is *contra* Hamilton's characterization of Pindaric *poikilia* as "[t]he unity of the [Pindaric] text...constituted by an irreconcilable disunity," a unity achieved by "weaving together two distinct strands, two tendencies at cross-purposes," the light of praise and the darkness of obscurity (2003:81). As Köhnken (2005) has pointed out, a poetics of obscurity can be more properly attributed to receptions of Pindar than to Pindar himself.

Conclusion

> The line outside the bus starts with Iris. Behind her stands the widow of the pastor in Michigan who died after being hit by a car, could Lance write a letter to be read at the funeral? Behind her stand the parents of a twelve-year-old Pennsylvania boy wondering if Armstrong might have a minute to make a phone call. Behind them stand still others, more and more every day, every minute, like the parents in France who wrapped up their sick child in a white blanket and met Armstrong in a field. Could Lance just touch him on the forehead, just once? Please?
>
> Daniel Coyle, *Lance Armstrong's War*

> No less an authority on matters of cool than former Clash road manager Johnny Green describes cycling as the new rock 'n' roll in his book *Push Yourself Just a Little Bit More*, and it is all thanks to Lance Armstrong. Lance's association with Nike, and black and white publicity photos showing just the kind of square jaw line and intense look which play particularly well among the younger demographic have promoted him to A-list celebrity status.
>
> *Cycle Sport Magazine*

High/low, elite/popular, exclusive/inclusive—the figure of Lance Armstrong collapses such binary oppositions. As a person who has not only survived cancer but has also attained the highest achievements in the most prestigious professional cycling event in the world, his presence and, better, his touch evidently convey a healing, talismanic power for many. For many, Armstrong is an inspiration. He is also a media magnet, a high-end spokesperson, and a brand. This is certainly not the place for developing a cultural analysis of Lance Armstrong, but if one were to undertake such a project, to exclude the low, the popular, the inclusive from the Armstrong field of cultural production would betray an analytical bias that further indexes the ideological predisposition(s) of the interpreter.

Returning to the question of what the word *kômos* can tell us about epinician performance, in my Introduction I argued that Malcom Heath's study (1988) of the word is inadequate on methodological grounds for determining whether Pindar refers to the *khoros* when he uses *kômos*. However, as a study of *kômos* per se, Heath's analysis confirms the widely recognized application of the word to "a ritualistic, drunken procession" (Rothwell 2007:7). From the point of view of ideology rather than methodology, what is really at issue in the choral-monody debate is the resistance to linking popular cultural life with epinician art in order to preserve the exclusive, "high art" status of *epinikion*. So the monodists in the choral-monody debate posit a solo mode of performance for *epinikion* rather than associate it with the unbecoming low behavior characterized by our understanding of *kômos*, and the choralists maintain that for Pindar a *kômos* is not *that kind* of *kômos*, but a *khoros*.

I have shown that a similar logic applies to scholarship addressing the question of whether Pindar composed his songs in a written or oral medium. Christopher Carey and Andrew Miller specifically express the view that the real craft of *epinikion* happens backstage, as it were, when a song is written, implying that oral, improvised art is of a low quality.[1] Against the claims of these and other adherents to the "oral subterfuge" hypothesis, I have demonstrated that Pindar always represents his medium in terms of speech. To the evidence for approaching Pindar's language as a spoken medium, presented in Chapter 1, we can add that, by discovering how each epinician song is keyed for performance, it is appropriate to approach the epinician text as a speech event and that, in turn, each epinician speech event is constituted by patterned ways of speaking that the epinician composer orchestrates into a unified communicative act.

The opposition between an oral and written Pindar correlates to the opposition between a popular and elite Pindar. Indeed, Hermann Fränkel,

[1] Pfeijffer sustains this oral/low and *epinikion*/high opposition in his explanation of what he calls the "polyinterpretability" of Pindar's songs, which "ties in with his general tendency to present his odes as if they were *spontaneous, informal* celebration, created at the very spot, rather than the *intricate, well rehearsed* performances that they were" (1999a:25–26, my emphasis). In his "close reading" of *Olympian* 12 Silk asserts the "elevated" quality of Pindar's poetry, arguing that this "elevation is, and is shown to be, the linguistic corollary of its aristocratic ideology" (2007:180).

describing the inclusive and exclusive dimensions of Pindar's art, has argued both that *epinikion* involved "festal public performance" and that "the text became an heirloom in the family" (1973:429). These widely recognized views assume two kinds of audience: popular and exclusive. Kurke has characterized the complexity of Pindar's audience in the following way (1991:260):

> [T]he uneasy balance of different interest groups in the audience—the individual house, the Panhellenic aristocracy, and the city—is itself the result of profound historical developments in this period. Pindar's era was heir to the crisis of the aristocracy, the last flowering of tyranny, the rise of the democratic polis, and the shift from a premonetary to a money economy. Such social turbulence demands sophisticated poetic strategies. Pindar responds with a densely layered text that simultaneously evokes many different, even competing, symbolic systems and ideologies.

While New Historicists such as Kurke, Dougherty, and Nicholson have made impressive contributions to our understanding of the cultural poetics of commemorating athletic victories in ancient Greece, the popular dimensions of *epinikion* remain underserved by students of Pindar. If it is true that "as a newcomer, the victory ode needed to validate itself to its diverse audience in order to be able to perform its social function" (Kurke 1991:259), then it is necessary to discover the inclusive dimensions of Pindar's art in order to develop a well-rounded cultural poetics. Nicholson notes that fluency in the conventions of victory songs "must have restricted their reach to the elites, but it is clear from their content, as well as from the testimony that Pindar's ode to Diagoras of Rhodes [*Olympian* 7] was dedicated to the temple of Lindian Athena, that they were directed to members of the victor's city, not just his friends and clan" (2005:11).[2] The point is well made, but not developed further, since Nicholson's study explores the elite interests served by the public display

2 Kurke 1991:5 also discusses this episode as an indication of the popular dimension of Pindar's audience. Thomas has recently posed a serious challenge to the view that *epinikion* is aligned with aristocratic ideology in opposition to democratic ideology: "It is clear that the Pindaric victory ode is a phenomenon mainly devoted to the aristocratic and wealthy elite of Greece, and celebrates what are essentially aristocratic values, *aretê*, beauty, athletic prowess. But it is worth remembering that the Athenian people applied just the same set of aristocratic ideals to itself, to the democratic *dêmos*. There is also little sign of much self-conscious democratic ideology (though much anti-tyrant feeling), at least in the early stages of the democracy. The idea that these values were deliberately elevated by Pindar in antagonism to the new democratic ideas seems stretched" (2007:142). Kurke 2007:157–158 has recently explored the differing rhetorical strategies of *epinikia* for elite tyrants and those for middling private citizens.

of victory memorials. A similar gap exists in one of Kurke's most productive insights about ancient Greece: the talismanic quality of the victorious athlete and the "economy of *kûdos*," where she defines *kudos* as "magical potency in battle" (1993:133; cf. Currie 2005:128–129). It would seem that the economy of *kudos* entails popular dimensions, since "[t]he city...rewards [the returning athlete] for his victory with a lavish reentry rite, crowns and fillets, the lifelong privilege of eating in the prytaneion, large monetary awards, special front-row seats in the theater, and sometimes a statue set up at public expense in the city or at the site of the games" (1993:141). But Kurke finally argues that "we must ground our cultural poetics in a politics and see the phenomenon of *kudos* as an attempt by the aristocracy to lay claim to special power within the polis" (1993:153).

In *epinikion*, traditional song-making comes into contact with real-world concerns of contemporary life in such a way that there is a collision of functions and purposes associated with epinician performance. On the one hand, the ode as a victory memorial had to address the concern of, in effect, making the representation of aristocratic ideology a popular possession: Pindar's "subject, human accomplishment, is catholic and momentous" (Young 1968:112). On the other hand, the composer's interest in working within a song tradition predicated upon authority in the form of artistic competence potentially conflicted with the functions of memorializing a victory: the composer's competence, which is a crucial denominator of successful performance and subsequent reperformance, and the survival of the epinician word entail a gauge of display that potentially competes with the patron's display of his achievement through the victory memorial of performance.[3] As Pindar's frequent concern with envy suggests, a master praise poet might risk failing in his obligation to a patron by outdoing him. Laughter is one strategy for mitigating the tensions between these two sets of social functions, to commemorate locally in original performance the athlete's victory and to introduce an epinician song into the Panhellenic corpus of verbal art as a model for reperformance.

For example, I have argued that in *Olympian* 1 Pindar represents his praise of Hieron as the fulfillment of *khreos* understood as an act of *kharis*, both in the sense of reciprocity and in the sense of a roguish suggestion that the composer, as an over-the-hill *erômenos*, might sexually gratify his *laudandus-erastês*. In this formulation, *kharis* as Pindar uses the concept in *Olympian* 1 both conveys an

3 In a similar vein Mackie describes how the epinician composer "must also worry about how the victor will react to what he has to say" (2003:27–36).

affirmation of aristocratic ideology through its association with gift-exchange and motivates popular laughter. By masterfully representing himself in a low guise as rogue, Pindar deftly strikes a mutually satisfying contrast between his artistic achievement and Hieron's athletic achievement.[4]

While there are many parallels between my criticism of approaches to the study of epinician performance and Bakhtin's criticisms of scholarship on the novel, I cite here an example that highlights stylistics, which along with speech and performance has been central to *Pindar's Verbal Art* (Bakhtin 1981:263):

> Such a combining of languages and styles into a higher unity is unknown to traditional stylistics; it has no method for approaching the distinctive social dialogue among languages that is present in the novel. Thus stylistic analysis is not oriented toward the novel as a whole, but only toward one or another of its subordinated stylistic unities. The traditional scholar bypasses the basic distinctive feature of the novel as a genre; he substitutes for it another object of study, and instead of novelistic style he actually analyzes something completely different. He transposes a symphonic (orchestrated) theme on to the piano keyboard.

This criticism of "traditional stylistics" occurs in the context of Bakhtin's description of heteroglossia and the dialogical quality of style in the novel.[5] In a similar vein, I have variously argued that conventional exegesis is ill-equipped to describe the polyphonic and multivalent language of Pindar's art: exegesis simply starts from the wrong set of questions, treating *epinikion* as a written form of art rather than a spoken one, privileging the referential func-

4 This double-voicedness of *kharis* serves the "double-project" that victory memorials fulfill; as Nicholson puts it: "the need to justify the continuing political power of the aristocrats to both the aristocrats themselves and the wider community" (2005:16). I would, in addition, call attention to the carnivalesque quality of the parodic representations of athletic victory, as described by Nicholson (2005:15): "The meaning of an athletic victory was neither self-evident nor uncontested: that it was the pinnacle of human achievement, a sign of supreme virtue and divine favor, and a boon to the victor's civic community had to be established, and had to be established against very different versions of its meaning. Some of these versions survive—such as the elegies of Xenophanes of Colophon and Tyrtaeus of Sparta that deny the usefulness of a champion athlete to the good government and military security of his city, or the vases that ridicule the aristocratic ideals of fairness and nobility by depicting pancratiasts gouging their opponents' eyes and boxers punching their genitals—but such evidence only hints at the size of the crisis threatening aristocratic athletics"; see Nicholson 2005:222n84 for testimonia and sources.

5 For recent examples of traditional stylistics see Pfeijffer 1999a:22–54, Hornblower 2004:354–372 (comparing Thucydides and Pindar), and Fearn 2007:219–225 (Bakkhulides).

tion of language over the poetic function of language, siding with historical conjecture over and against historical practice, and, finally, treating an art form with significant popular dimensions strictly as a form of high literature. From the perspective of a practice-centered and ethnographically grounded philology, the text-artifact of Pindar's *epinikia* is a record of communication occurring between the epinician composer-performer Pindar and his audience via the channel of a chorus. The study of Pindar's *epinikia* then begins with the description of epinician language as a special way of speaking dedicated to epinician performance. The purpose of *Pindar's Verbal Art* has been to lay the groundwork for such a performance- and practice-centered description of epinician language. On the basis of this description, I find that *epinikion* is a novelistic form of traditional discourse. As I have already stated, I do not claim that *epinikion* belongs to the genre of the novel, but that it is a mode of communicative practice that is immanently grounded in its ambient present, characterized by flux and open-endedness, and replete with parodic moments and heteroglossia, which are crucially constitutive features of the novel for Bakhtin.

The vantage point that the study of Pindar's poetry offers on the project of classical philology ultimately drives my interest in epinician poetics, so that *Pindar's Verbal Art* is as much about philology as it is about Pindar. My approach to classical philology is that it is the endeavor to describe the social practices recorded in ancient texts. Because ancient texts are records of past cultural contexts, philology always entails history: there are historical factors shaping the evidence and how an analyst encounters it historically; there is temporal distance between the context recorded in ancient texts and the context of encounter with those ancient texts; and the doing of history, understood as a metadiscursive re-presentation of past events to a contemporary audience, is embedded in the process of philological analysis. Classical philology is for me the study concomitantly of history and of culture through the language records produced by communities. From this point of view philology takes in under its analytical purview two overlapping fields of investigation: discourse as historical record and discourse as record of culture. A difference in attitude toward events, discourses, and the relationships between them distinguishes history in an outside-in approach to context from history in a practice approach to the study of culture. History in exegesis considers how events, discourses, and the relationships between them inform the production of a narrative historiography that recounts a chronological sequence of events. The cultural poetics of New Historicism has focused on the exclusive dimensions of *epinikion* as coin in a gift economy or as a vehicle for promoting aristocratic ideology. History from a practice perspective, however, treats events, discourses, and the relationships between them as cultural systems at once socially situated in local contexts and related to other contexts, including the historical context of philological analysis itself.

Appendix

This Appendix documents the analysis described in Chapters 3 and 4 above and applied to all of Pindar's *epinikia*. The primary purpose of this Appendix is to provide supporting evidence for the arguments presented in Chapters 3 and 4, principally that five ways of epinician speaking—*gnôma*, lyric, *angelia*, mythological narrative, and *eukhesthai*—constitute the epinician way of speaking. This Appendix also documents the fact that many of Pindar's *epinikia* exhibit some discernable pattern of orchestration, suggesting that the ways of epinician speaking are compositional devices, discursive formulae. The implication of such orchestration is that Pindar is an oral poet. One direction of future research would be to consider to what extent the ways of epinician speaking are traditional. As discussed in Chapter 5, epinician utterances often exhibit hybridizations, so that a single utterance may have features of more than one way of epinician speaking. I have described above how the criterion of addressivity enables us to identify the dominantly constitutive speech genre of such hybrid utterances. I apply that criterion in the diagrams that follow. The patterns of orchestration suggest that this criterion is meaningful from the point of view of Pindar and his language. There are a few "rules" for the presentation method that I adopt here: (1) an utterance is unembedded in relation to a preceding utterance when it is located at the left-most margin of the list of utterances occurring in a song; (2) one utterance is embedded in another when the embedded utterance stands in a hypotactic relationship to the embedding utterance; (3) embedding is indicated by the symbol ↪. In addition to diagramming the discursive structure of each epinician song, I occasionally address points of interpretation that any patterns suggest. Each individual song comes with its particular burden of interpretive history. If I were to engage with that history, this Appendix would multiply the length of *Pindar's Verbal Art*. For the sake of expediency, then, my treatment of scholarship in this appendix is minimal.

Olympian 1

Lines 1–27: *Eukhesthai*
➥Lines 8–11: Lyric
        ➥Lines 12–15: *Angelia*
➥Lines 16–17: Lyric
➥Lines 20–24: *Angelia*
        ➥Lines 25–27: Mythological Narrative
Lines 28–35: *Gnômai*
Lines 36–51: *Eukhesthai*
➥Lines 37–51: Mythological Narrative
        ➥Lines 43–45: Mythological Narrative
Line 52: Lyric
Line 53: *Gnôma*
Lines 54–64: Mythological Narrative
Line 64: *Gnôma*
Lines 65–96: Mythological Narrative
➥75–85: Direct Discourse
        ➥Lines 75–78: *Eukhesthai*
        ➥Lines 79–81: Mythological Narrative
        ➥Lines 81–84: *Gnôma*
        ➥Lines 84–85: Lyric
        ➥Line 85: *Eukhesthai*
Lines 97–100: *Gnômai*
Lines 100–105: Lyric
Lines 106–111: *Eukhesthai*
Lines 111–112: Lyric
Lines 113–114: *Gnôma*
Lines 114–116: *Eukhesthai*

I discuss *Olympian* 1's discursive structure in detail in Chapter 5, including the deviation from the overall pattern of ring composition at lines 111–112.

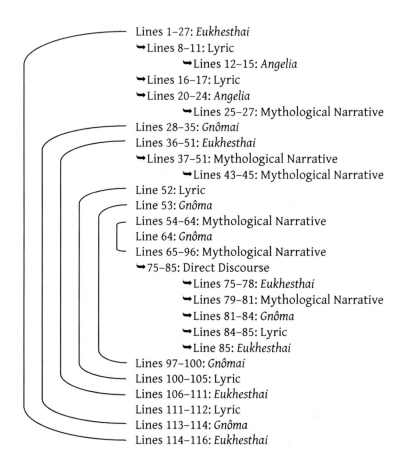

Olympian 2

Lines 1–2: *Eukhesthai*
Lines 3–4: Mythological Narrative
Lines 5–11: *Angelia*
Lines 12–15: *Eukhesthai*
Lines 15–17: *Gnôma*
Line 18: *Gnôma*
Lines 19–22: *Gnôma*
Lines 22–23: Mythological Narrative
Lines 23–24: *Gnôma*
Lines 25–30: Mythological Narrative
Lines 30–33: *Gnôma*
Lines 33–34: *Gnôma*
Lines 35–45: *Angelia*
→Lines 38–45: Mythological Narrative
Lines 46–47: Lyric
Lines 48–51: *Angelia*
Lines 51–52: *Gnôma*
Lines 53–56: *Gnôma*
Lines 56–60: *Gnôma*
Lines 61–65: *Gnôma*
Lines 65–67: *Gnôma*
Lines 68–83: *Gnôma*
→Lines 70–83: Mythological Narrative
Lines 83–86: Lyric
Line 86: *Gnôma*
Lines 86–88: *Gnôma*
Line 89: *Eukhesthai*
Lines 89–90: Lyric
Lines 91–95: *Eukhesthai*
Lines 95–98: *Gnôma*
Lines 98–100: *Gnôma*

There is an interlocking pattern, A-B-A-B, among gnomic and mythological narrative utterances at lines 15–30. A lyric passage (lines 83–86) demarcates two chiastic patterns, A-B-C-B-A (lines 30–83 and 86–100). Given that the content of lines 3–4 parallels the content of the following *angelia*, these items may form terms B of a chiastic pattern with the *eukhesthai* utterances, terms A, of lines 1–2 and 12–15: A-B-B-A.

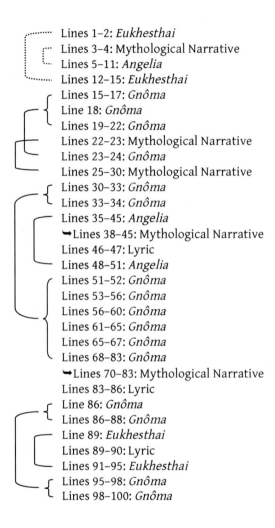

Olympian 3

Lines 1–4: *Eukhesthai*
Lines 4–9: Lyric
➥Lines 9–38: *Gnôma*
    ➥Lines 13–38: Mythological Narrative
Lines 38–41: Lyric
Lines 42–44: *Angelia*
Lines 44–45: *Gnôma*
Line 45: *Eukhesthai*
Line 45: *Eukhesthai*

If the discursive patterning recommends either that we disregard embedding dynamics or that we treat *tas* (line 9) as an article instead of a relative pronoun, then there is an *angelia* (lines 42–44) nested in an interlocking pattern (among lyric and gnomic utterances), which *eukhesthai* utterances ring; thus, A-B-C-B-D-C-A. Item D is inconsistent with an overall pattern; such inconsistency turns out to be patterned across Pindar's epinician corpus as a whole.

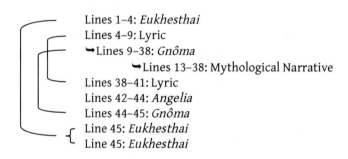

Olympian 4

Lines 1–3: *Eukhesthai*
Lines 4–5: *Gnôma*
Lines 6–10: *Eukhesthai*
Lines 10–12: *Angelia*
Lines 12–13: *Eukhesthai*
Lines 14–16: Lyric
Lines 17–18: *Eukhesthai*
Lines 18–27: *Gnôma*
- ➥Lines 19–27: Mythological Narrative
    - ➥Direct Discourse
        - ➥Line 24: Lyric
        - ➥Line 25: *Gnôma*
        - ➥Lines 25–27: *Gnôma*

The pattern is generally interlocking, but has a chiastic dimension among items B and C: A-B-A-C-A-C-A-B. Because the dominantly lyric passage at lines 14–16 is highly inflected by features of the *angelia* style, I describe them as discursively analogous (terms C).

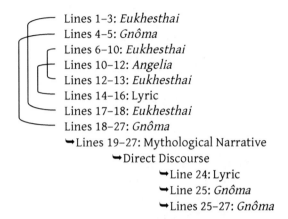

Olympian 5

Lines 1–8: *Eukhesthai*
→Lines 4–8: *Angelia*
Lines 9–14: *Eukhesthai*
Lines 15–16: *Gnôma*
Line 16: *Gnôma*
Lines 17–23: *Eukhesthai*
Lines 23–24: *Gnôma*

There is an interlocking pattern A-B-A-B among *eukhesthai* utterances and *gnômai*. The embedded *angelia* of lines 4–8 is an outstanding example of how epinician styles interact dialogically: although the relative pronoun (line 4) signals the onset of embedding and although there is a change of verbal tense (present to past) and person (second to third), a second-person pronoun *tin* (line 7) occurs in the embedded *angelia*. I interpret the change of addressee from Kamarina (lines 1–8) to Pallas (lines 9–14) as the onset to a new (unembedded) utterance, which is also an *eukhesthai-angelia* hybrid. The stylistic hybridity of lines 9–14 forms an undeniable parallel with lines 1–8, recommending the structural interpretation that I offer. The single-sentence *eukhesthai* of lines 17–23 has two addressees, Zeus and Psaumis, a juxtaposition that the concluding *gnôma* qualifies.

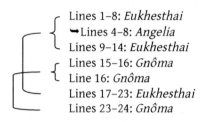

Olympian 6

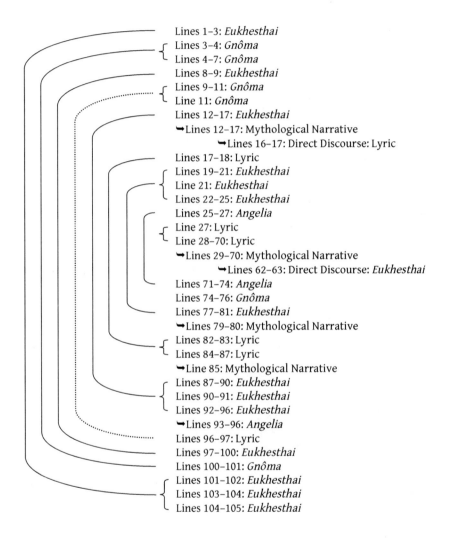

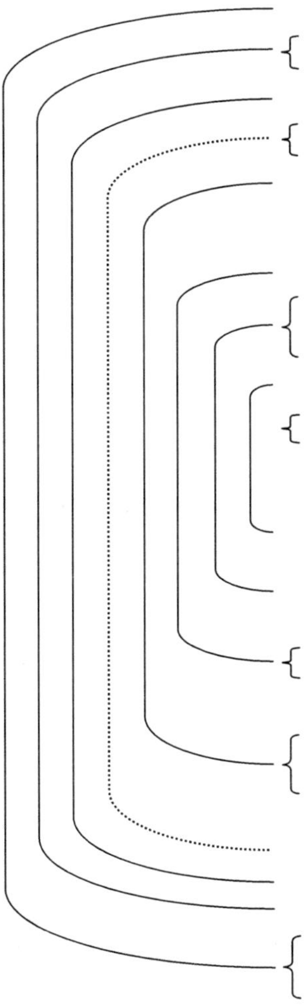

Lines 1–3: *Eukhesthai*
Lines 3–4: *Gnôma*
Lines 4–7: *Gnôma*
Lines 8–9: *Eukhesthai*
Lines 9–11: *Gnôma*
Line 11: *Gnôma*
Lines 12–17: *Eukhesthai*
➥Lines 12–17: Mythological Narrative
➥Lines 16–17: Direct Discourse: Lyric
Lines 17–18: Lyric
Lines 19–21: *Eukhesthai*
Line 21: *Eukhesthai*
Lines 22–25: *Eukhesthai*
Lines 25–27: *Angelia*
Line 27: Lyric
Line 28–70: Lyric
➥Lines 29–70: Mythological Narrative
➥Lines 62–63: Direct Discourse: *Eukhesthai*
Lines 71–74: *Angelia*
Lines 74–76: *Gnôma*
Lines 77–81: *Eukhesthai*
➥Lines 79–80: Mythological Narrative
Lines 82–83: Lyric
Lines 84–87: Lyric
➥Line 85: Mythological Narrative
Lines 87–90: *Eukhesthai*
Lines 90–91: *Eukhesthai*
Lines 92–96: *Eukhesthai*
➥Lines 93–96: *Angelia*
Lines 96–97: Lyric
Lines 97–100: *Eukhesthai*
Lines 100–101: *Gnôma*
Lines 101–102: *Eukhesthai*
Lines 103–104: *Eukhesthai*
Lines 104–105: *Eukhesthai*

This song has an overall ring-composition structure. This pattern suggests some discursive relationship between the gnomic passage at lines 9–11 and the lyric passage at lines 96–97 (indicated by dotted line). Features of *angelia* so heavily inflect the gnomic utterance at lines 74–76 that perhaps it should be taken with lines 71–74.

Olympian 7

	Lines 1–10: Lyric
	Line 10: *Gnôma*
	Lines 11–12: *Gnôma*
	Lines 13–19: Lyric
A	Lines 20–23: *Eukhesthai*
B	Lines 23–24: *Angelia*
C	Lines 24–25: *Gnôma* Lines 25–26: *Gnôma*
D	Lines 27–30: Mythological Narrative (Tlapolemos)
C	Lines 30–31: *Gnôma*
D	Lines 31–38: Mythological Narrative (Tlapolemos) Lines 39–43: Mythological Narrative (Helios and Heliadai)
C	Lines 43–47: *Gnôma*
D	Lines 48–53: Mythological Narrative (Helios and Heliadai)
C	Line 53: *Gnôma*
D	Lines 54–76: Mythological Narrative (Helios and Rhodes)
B	Lines 77–87: *Angelia*
A	Lines 87–90: *Eukhesthai*
B	Lines 90–92: *Angelia*
A	Lines 92–93: *Eukhesthai*
B	Lines 93–94: *Angelia*
	Lines 94–95: *Gnôma*

Given that lines 1–19 have a chiastic structure and that lines 94–95 are a gnomic coda to the song—and if we identify *eukhesthai* utterances as A, *angeliai* as B, gnomic utterances as C, and passages of mythological narrative as D—then the discursive pattern of lines 20–94 is: A-B-C-D-C-D-C-D-C-D-B-A-B-A-B, an elaborated chiastic pattern (terms A and B) embracing an elaborated interlocking pattern (terms C and D).

Olympian 8

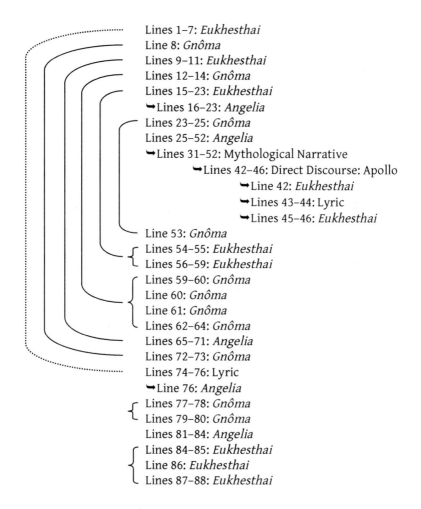

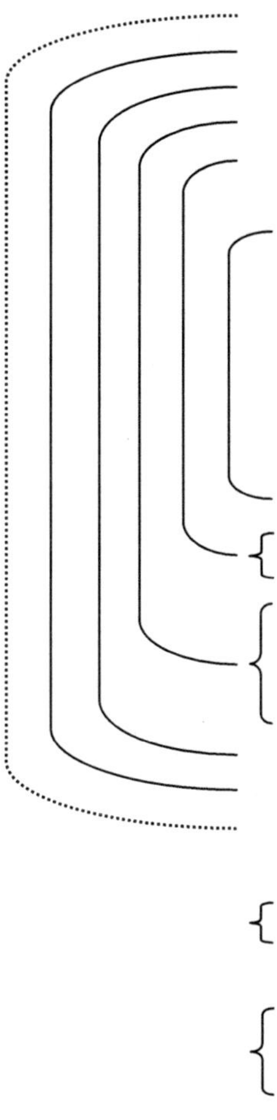

Lines 1–7: *Eukhesthai*
Line 8: *Gnôma*
Lines 9–11: *Eukhesthai*
Lines 12–14: *Gnôma*
Lines 15–23: *Eukhesthai*
↪Lines 16–23: *Angelia*
Lines 23–25: *Gnôma*
Lines 25–52: *Angelia*
↪Lines 31–52: Mythological Narrative
↪Lines 42–46: Direct Discourse: Apollo
↪Line 42: *Eukhesthai*
↪Lines 43–44: Lyric
↪Lines 45–46: *Eukhesthai*
Line 53: *Gnôma*
Lines 54–55: *Eukhesthai*
Lines 56–59: *Eukhesthai*
Lines 59–60: *Gnôma*
Line 60: *Gnôma*
Line 61: *Gnôma*
Lines 62–64: *Gnôma*
Lines 65–71: *Angelia*
Lines 72–73: *Gnôma*
Lines 74–76: Lyric
↪Line 76: *Angelia*
Lines 77–78: *Gnôma*
Lines 79–80: *Gnôma*
Lines 81–84: *Angelia*
Lines 84–85: *Eukhesthai*
Line 86: *Eukhesthai*
Lines 87–88: *Eukhesthai*

Lines 1–76 have a ring-composition structure if we grant that the *angelia* inflections of the *eukhesthai* utterance at lines 9–11 make that passage discursively parallel to lines 65–71 and assume that the *eukhesthai* utterance at lines 1–7 has a reflexive quality that communicates how the epinician composer describes his task at lines 74–76.

Olympian 9

Lines 1–4: *Angelia*
Lines 5–10: *Eukhesthai*
↪Lines 9–10: Mythological Narrative
Lines 11–12: *Eukhesthai*
Lines 12–14: *Eukhesthai*
Lines 14–16: *Eukhesthai*
Lines 16–20: *Eukhesthai*
↪Lines 19–20: *Angelia*
Lines 21–27: *Eukhesthai*
Lines 28: *Gnôma*
Lines 28–29: *Gnôma*
Lines 29–35: Mythological Narrative
Lines 35–36: *Eukhesthai*
Lines 37–39: *Gnôma*
Line 40: *Eukhesthai*
Lines 40–41: *Eukhesthai*
Lines 41–46: *Eukhesthai*
↪Lines 42–46: Mythological Narrative
Line 47: *Eukhesthai*
Lines 48–49: *Eukhesthai*
Lines 49–79: Mythological Narrative
Lines 80–81: *Eukhesthai*
Lines 82–83: *Eukhesthai*
Lines 83–99: Lyric
↪Lines 84–99: *Angelia*
Line 100: *Gnôma*
Lines 100–104: *Gnôma*
Lines 104–105: *Gnôma*
Lines 106–107: *Gnôma*
Lines 107–108: *Gnôma*
Lines 108–112: *Eukhesthai*

There appears to be a general ring-composition pattern with outliers at lines 1–4 and 80–99. Alternatively, there is an interlocking pattern, A-B-C-D-A-B-E-C-D, where A identifies the mythological narrative passages at lines 29–35 and 49–79; B, the *eukhesthai* passages at lines 35–36 and 80–83; C, the gnomic passages at lines 37–39 and 100–108; D, the *eukhesthai* passages at lines 40–49 and 108–112; and E, the lyric passage with embedded *angelia* at lines 83–99, a case of (patterned?) structural inconsistency. Perhaps both patterns apply.

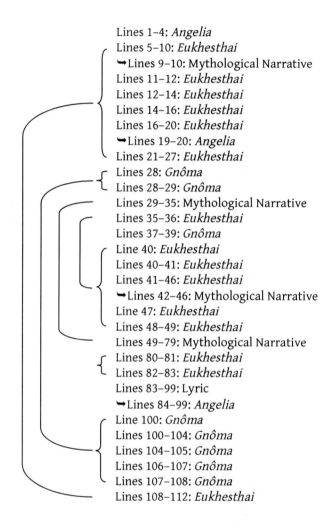

Olympian 10

Lines 1–3: *Eukhesthai*
Line 3: Lyric
Lines 3–6: *Eukhesthai*
Lines 7–8: Lyric
Line 9: *Gnôma*
Lines 9–12: *Eukhesthai*
Lines 13–15: *Angelia*
Lines 15–16: Mythological Narrative
Lines 16–19: *Eukhesthai*
Lines 20–21: *Gnôma*
Lines 22–23: *Gnôma*
Lines 24–38: *Gnôma*
➥Lines 24–38: Mythological Narrative
Lines 39–40: *Gnôma*
Lines 41–77: Mythological Narrative
Lines 78–83: *Eukhesthai*
Lines 84–85: *Eukhesthai*
Lines 86–87: *Gnôma*
Lines 88–90: *Gnôma*
Lines 91–93: *Eukhesthai*
Lines 93–94: *Eukhesthai*
Lines 95–96: Lyric
Lines 97–99: Lyric
Lines 99–105: Lyric
➥Lines 100–105: *Angelia*
➥104–105: Mythological Narrative

Lines 15–90 have an interlocking pattern, A-B-C-A-B-C. Lyric and *eukhesthai* passages dominate the beginning and end of the song. Lines 1–12 could be described structurally as a generally interlocking pattern, A (*eukhesthai*)-B (lyric)-A (*eukhesthai*)-B (lyric)-C (*gnôma*)-A (*eukhesthai*); if so, the *angelia* (lines 13–15) would be a kind of coda to the opening of the song, and that coda would parallel lines 100–105. There is a mythological *angelia* (lines 64–73) embedded in the central mythological narrative (41–77). Lines 73–77 offer a mythological representation of epinician performance.

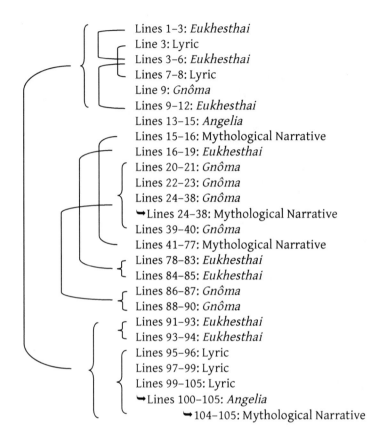

Olympian 11

Lines 1–3: *Gnôma*
Lines 4–6: *Gnôma*
Lines 7–8: Lyric
Lines 8–9: *Eukhesthai*
Line 10: *Gnôma*
Lines 11–15: *Eukhesthai* (Addressee: Hagesidamos)
Lines 16–19: *Eukhesthai* (Addressee: the Muses)
Lines 19–20: *Gnôma*

Olympian 11 has a lyric passage that deviates from an overall ring-composition pattern, another case of inconsistency that appears to be patterned across the epinician corpus. It is possible to interpret the structure of *Olympian* 11 as interlocking (with patterned inconsistency), A (*gnôma*)-C (lyric)-B (*eukhesthai*)-A (*gnôma*)-B (*eukhesthai*)-A (*gnôma*).

Olympian 12

Lines 1–5: *Eukhesthai*
Lines 5–6: *Gnôma*
Lines 7–9: *Gnôma*
Lines 10–12: *Gnôma*
Lines 13–19: *Eukhesthai*

Olympian 12 has a relatively straightforward ring-composition structure. The *eukhesthai* of lines 13–19 has *angelia* inflections and coincides exactly with the song's epode.

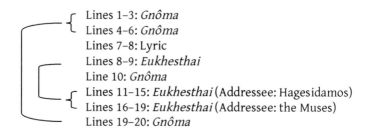

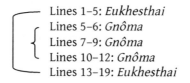

Olympian 13

Lines 1–5: *Eukhesthai*
Lines 6–10: Mythological Narrative
Lines 11–12: Lyric
Line 13: *Gnôma*
Lines 14–17: *Eukhesthai*
Line 17: *Gnôma*
Line 18–23: Mythological Narrative
Lines 24–28: *Eukhesthai*
Lines 29–40: *Eukhesthai*
→Lines 29–40: *Angelia*
Lines 40–42: *Eukhesthai*
Lines 43–45: *Eukhesthai*
Lines 45–46: Lyric
Lines 47–48: *Gnôma*
Line 48: *Gnôma*
Lines 49–54: *Eukhesthai*
Lines 55–82: Mythological Narrative
→Lines 67–69: Direct Discourse: *Eukhesthai*
Line 83: *Gnôma*
Lines 84–90: Mythological Narrative
Line 91: *Eukhesthai*
Line 92: Mythological Narrative
Lines 93–95: Lyric
Lines 96–97: Lyric
Lines 98–100: *Eukhesthai*
Lines 101–102: *Angelia*
Line 103: Lyric
Lines 104–105: Lyric
Lines 105–106: *Eukhesthai*
Lines 106–112: *Angelia*
Lines 112–113: *Eukhesthai*
Line 114: *Eukhesthai*
Line 115: *Eukhesthai*

I present here one way to describe the discursive structure of this song. There are others. A first gray area concerns lines 6–10: maybe the passage is better described as an *angelia*; and it may be embedded in the preceding utterance if *tâ* (line 6) is a relative pronoun, as is likely, and not an article. There is an interlocking pattern woven into the ring-composition pattern of lines 1–91: A (lyric, lines 11–12)-B (*gnôma*, line 13)-A (lyric, lines 45–46)-B (*gnômai*, lines 47–48).

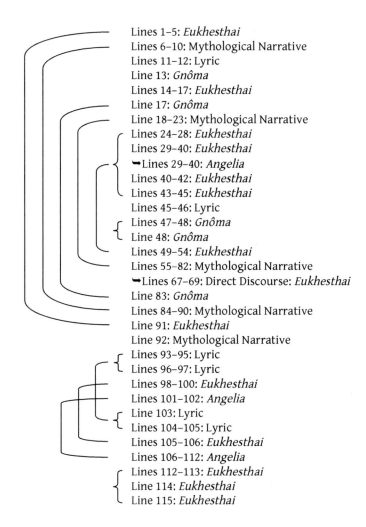

Olympian 14

Lines 1–5: *Eukhesthai* (Addressee: the Graces)
Lines 5–7: *Eukhesthai* (Addressee: the Graces)
Lines 8–9: *Gnôma*
Lines 9–12: Mythological Narrative
Lines 13–15: *Eukhesthai* (Addressee: The Graces)
Lines 15–20: *Eukhesthai* (Addressee: Thalia)
Lines 20–24: *Eukhesthai* (Addressee: Echo)
→Lines 22–24: *Angelia*

Prayers addressed to the Graces are the most salient feature of this song. *Eukhesthai* utterances frame lines 8–12.

Pythian 1

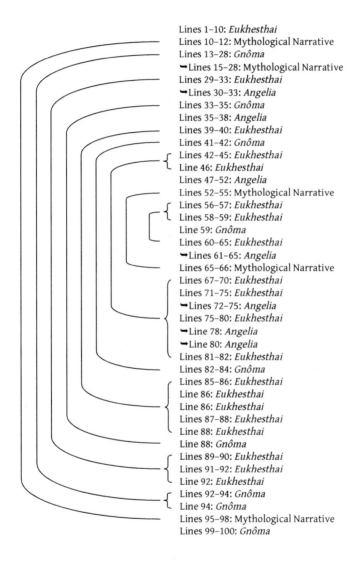

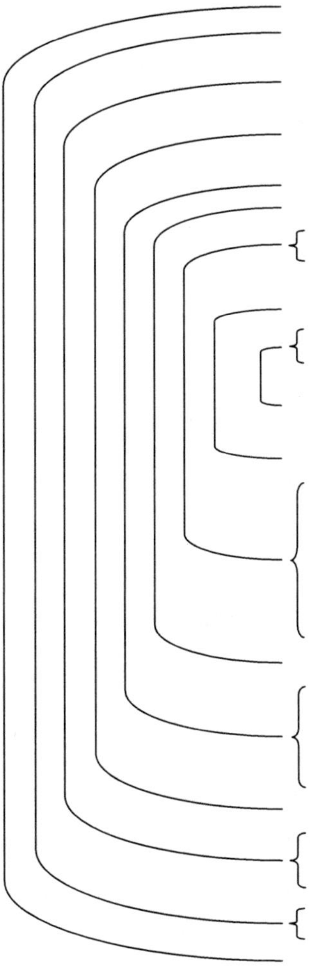

Lines 1–10: *Eukhesthai*
Lines 10–12: Mythological Narrative
Lines 13–28: *Gnôma*
➥Lines 15–28: Mythological Narrative
Lines 29–33: *Eukhesthai*
➥Lines 30–33: *Angelia*
Lines 33–35: *Gnôma*
Lines 35–38: *Angelia*
Lines 39–40: *Eukhesthai*
Lines 41–42: *Gnôma*
Lines 42–45: *Eukhesthai*
Line 46: *Eukhesthai*
Lines 47–52: *Angelia*
Lines 52–55: Mythological Narrative
Lines 56–57: *Eukhesthai*
Lines 58–59: *Eukhesthai*
Line 59: *Gnôma*
Lines 60–65: *Eukhesthai*
➥Lines 61–65: *Angelia*
Lines 65–66: Mythological Narrative
Lines 67–70: *Eukhesthai*
Lines 71–75: *Eukhesthai*
➥Lines 72–75: *Angelia*
Lines 75–80: *Eukhesthai*
➥Line 78: *Angelia*
➥Line 80: *Angelia*
Lines 81–82: *Eukhesthai*
Lines 82–84: *Gnôma*
Lines 85–86: *Eukhesthai*
Line 86: *Eukhesthai*
Line 86: *Eukhesthai*
Lines 87–88: *Eukhesthai*
Line 88: *Eukhesthai*
Line 88: *Gnôma*
Lines 89–90: *Eukhesthai*
Lines 91–92: *Eukhesthai*
Line 92: *Eukhesthai*
Lines 92–94: *Gnôma*
Line 94: *Gnôma*
Lines 95–98: Mythological Narrative
Lines 99–100: *Gnôma*

The beginning and end of *Pythian* 1 do not conform to the overall ring-composition structure of the song. *Angeliai* at lines 35–38 and 47–52 are also outliers, but the latter passage could be taken with the preceding *eukhesthai* utterances (lines 42–46), given that *angeliai* are embedded among the *eukhesthai* utterances of lines 67–82.

Pythian 2

Lines 1–8: *Eukhesthai*
➥Lines 5–12: *Angelia*
Lines 13–14: *Gnôma*
Lines 15–17: Mythological Narrative
Line 17: *Gnôma*
Lines 18–20: *Eukhesthai*
Lines 21–34: Mythological Narrative
Line 34: *Gnôma*
Lines 35–36: *Gnôma*
Lines 36–48: Mythological Narrative
Lines 49–52: *Gnôma*
Lines 52–56: Lyric
A Line 56: *Gnôma*
B Lines 57–58: *Eukhesthai*
A Lines 58–61: *Gnôma*
B Lines 62–63: *Eukhesthai*
A Lines 63–64: *Gnôma*
B Lines 64–65: *Eukhesthai*
Lines 65–67: *Eukhesthai*
Lines 67–68: Lyric
Lines 69–71: *Eukhesthai*
Line 72: *Eukhesthai*
Lines 72–73: *Gnôma*
Lines 73–75: Mythological Narrative
A Lines 76–78: *Gnôma*
B Lines 79–80: Lyric
A Lines 81–82: *Gnôma*
B Line 83: Lyric
Line 83: *Eukhesthai*
Lines 84–85: *Eukhesthai*
Lines 86–88: *Gnôma*
Lines 88–89: *Gnôma*
Lines 89–90: *Gnôma*
Lines 90–92: *Gnôma*
Lines 93–94: *Gnôma*
Lines 94–96: *Gnôma*
Line 96: *Eukhesthai*

Pythian 2 has two sections with a mainly interlocking pattern (lines 21–52 and 52–68), two with a mainly chiastic pattern (lines 1–20 and 69–96). The epinician composer's intentions expressed by *eukhesthai* utterances at lines 83–85 seem to answer to the mythological exemplum of Rhadamanthus (lines 73–75).

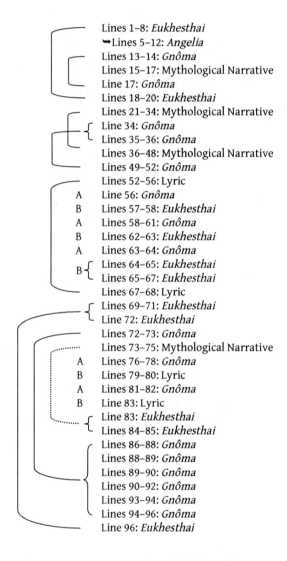

Pythian 3

Lines 1–11: *Eukhesthai*
➥Lines 5–11: Mythological Narrative
A Lines 11–12: *Gnôma*
B Lines 12–20: Mythological Narrative
A { Line 20: *Gnôma*
Lines 21–23: *Gnôma* }
B Lines 24–29: Mythological Narrative
A Lines 29–30: *Gnôma*
B Lines 31–36: Mythological Narrative
A Lines 36–37: *Gnôma*
B Lines 38–53: Mythological Narrative
➥Lines 40–42: Direct Discourse: *Eukhesthai*
A Line 54: *Gnôma*
B Lines 55–58: Mythological Narrative
A Lines 59–60: *Gnôma*
Lines 61–62: *Eukhesthai*
Lines 63–76: Lyric
➥Lines 69–71: *Angelia*
➥Lines 74: *Angelia*
{ Lines 77–79: *Eukhesthai*
Lines 80: *Eukhesthai* }
{ Lines 81–82: *Gnôma*
Lines 82–83: *Gnôma* }
Line 84: *Eukhesthai*
Lines 85–86: *Gnôma*
Lines 86–103: Mythological Narrative
{ Lines 103–104: *Gnôma*
Lines 104–105: *Gnôma*
Lines 105–106: *Gnôma* }
{ Lines 107–109: *Eukhesthai*
Lines 110–111: *Eukhesthai* }
{ Lines 112–114: *Gnôma*
Lines 114–115: *Gnôma* }

Lines 11–60 have an interlocking pattern, possibly nested in *eukhesthai* utterances. There seems to be a simple chiastic arrangement among speech genres in lines 61–80, assuming that the *eukhesthai* of lines 61–62 is doing double structural duty. Lines 81–115 have a ring-composition pattern.

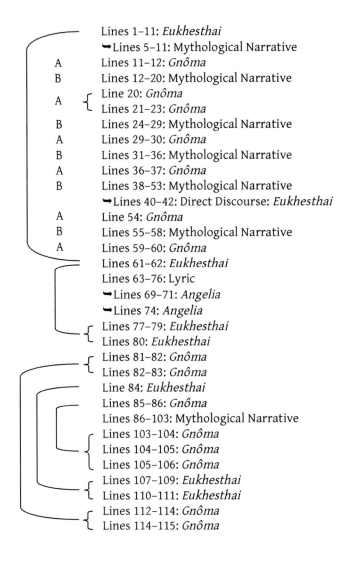

Pythian 4

Lines 1–58: *Eukhesthai*
➥Lines 4–58: Mythological Narrative
➥Lines 13–56: Direct Discourse: *Eukhesthai*
➥Lines 20–56: Mythological Narrative
Lines 59–63: *Eukhesthai*
➥Lines 61–63: Mythological Narrative
Lines 64–67: *Angelia*
Lines 67–68: *Eukhesthai*
Lines 68–246: Mythological Narrative
➥Lines 87–92: Direct Discourse: Mythological Narrative
➥Lines 97–100: Direct Discourse: *Eukhesthai*
➥Lines 102–119: Direct Discourse
➥Lines 102–103: *Eukhesthai*
➥Lines 103–115: Mythological Narrative
➥Lines 116–117: *Eukhesthai*
➥ Line 118: Lyric
➥Lines 119: Mythological Narrative
➥Lines 138–155: Direct Discourse
➥Line 138–142: *Eukhesthai*
➥Lines 142–145: Mythological Narrative
➥Lines 145–146: *Gnôma*
➥Lines 147–155: *Eukhesthai*
➥Lines 152–153: Mythological Narrative
➥Lines 156–167: Direct Discourse: *Eukhesthai*
➥Lines 161–162: Mythological Narrative
➥Lines 229–231: Direct Discourse: *Eukhesthai*
Lines 247–248: Lyric
A Lines 249–262: *Eukhesthai*
Line 263: *Eukhesthai*
B Lines 263–269: *Gnôma*
A Line 270: *Eukhesthai*
B Lines 271–274: *Gnômai*
A Lines 275–278: *Eukhesthai*
Line 279: Lyric
A Lines 279–286: *Angelia*
B Line 286: *Gnôma*
A Line 287: *Angelia*
B Lines 287–289: *Gnôma*
A Lines 289–290: *Angelia*
Line 291: Mythological Narrative
B Lines 291–293: *Gnôma*
A Lines 293–297: *Angelia*
Lines 298–299: *Eukhesthai*
➥Lines 298–299: *Angelia*

For the sake of space I do not provide detailed descriptions of the discursive structure for each instance of direct discourse in this song. There is a simple ring structure in lines 1–68. Lyric passages (lines 247–248 and 279) embrace an interlocking pattern, A-B-A-B, etc., in lines 249–278. A brief passage in the style of mythological narrative (line 291) breaks up the interlocking pattern of lines 279–297. The ring structure of lines 1–68 and the interlocking patterns of lines 247–297 ring the central mythological narrative of lines 68–246.

Pythian 5

Lines 1–4: *Gnôma*
Lines 5–11: *Eukhesthai*
Lines 12–13: *Gnôma*
Line 14: *Eukhesthai*
Lines 15–19: *Eukhesthai*
Lines 20–23: *Eukhesthai*
Lines 23–42: *Eukhesthai*
→Lines 27–42: *Angelia*
Lines 43–44: *Gnôma*
Line 45: *Eukhesthai*
Lines 46–53: *Eukhesthai*
→Lines 49–53: *Angelia*
Line 54: *Gnôma*
Lines 55–57: *Angelia*
Lines 57–59: Mythological Narrative (Battos)
Lines 60–72: Mythological Narrative (Apollo)
Lines 72–76: Lyric
→Lines 74–76: Mythological Narrative
Lines 77–85: *Eukhesthai*
→Lines 82–85: Mythological Narrative
Lines 85–103: *Angelia*
→Lines 87–103:Mythological Narrative
    →Lines 96–103: *Angelia*
Lines 104–107: Lyric
Line 108: *Eukhesthai*
Lines 109–117: *Angelia*
Lines 118–121: *Eukhesthai*
Lines 122–123: *Gnôma*
Line 124: *Eukhesthai*

Two patterned sections, one in the first half of the song, one in the second, ring lines 55–76: in the first half of *Pythian* 5, lines 1–54 have a ring-composition structure; in the second half, lines 77–117 have an interlocking pattern and lines 118–124 have a simple ring pattern. I am assuming that the analogous content of the *angelia* at lines 55–57 (praise for the city of the *laudandus*) and the lyric passage at lines 72–76 (commemoration of the Ageidai, a family descended from one of the autochthonous inhabitants of Thebes, the *laudator*'s city) indicates a formal relationship between the two utterances.

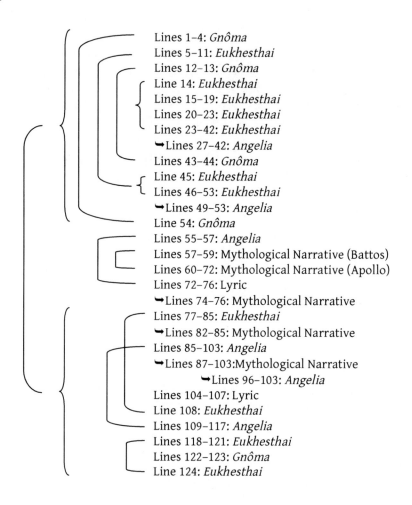

Pythian 6

Line 1: *Eukhesthai*
Lines 1–14: Lyric
Lines 14–18: *Eukhesthai*
Lines 19–43: *Eukhesthai*
→Lines 21–27: Mythological Narrative
→Lines 28–43: Mythological Narrative
Lines 44–49: *Angelia*
Lines 50–51: *Eukhesthai*
Lines 52–54: *Angelia*

The one-word opening prayer, *Akousat'* 'Hear!', is appropriate to this song's emphasis upon *angelia*, as evidenced by the appearance of the verb *apangelei* 'will proclaim' (line 18) and the *angelia* passages at lines 44–49 and lines 52–54. Since the mythological narrative of lines 28–43 shares the same discursive level as the mythological narrative of lines 21–27, which is clearly embedded in the preceding *eukhesthai* utterance, I describe both passages of mythological narrative as embedded in that *eukhesthai* utterance. Although the mythological narrative passages are embedded, they parse two other patterns: (1) *eukhesthai*-lyric-*eukhesthai* (lines 1–43) and (2) *angelia-eukhesthai-angelia* (lines 44–54). In the lyric passage (lines 1–14), the composition builds the "treasury of hymns," whose façade utters the *eukhos*-type of *eukhesthai* at lines 14–18. In other words, the lyric passage, in a sense, anticipates what the following *eukhesthai* utterance enacts. Further, given that the "treasury of hymns" is a metaphor for the song, which proclaims the virtues of Thrasyboulos in the *angeliai* of lines 44–49 and 52–54, the second pattern, *angelia-eukhesthai-angelia* (lines 44–54), performs the function described (notice *apangelei* 'will proclaim', line 18) in the first pattern, *eukhesthai*-lyric-*eukhesthai*, so that the two patterns are more functionally analogous than formally patterned—though there is some formal patterning too: the audience hears (*Akousat'* 'Hear!' [second-person plural], line 1) the treasury-song's (first pattern) victory announcement (second pattern).

Pythian 7

Lines 1–4: Lyric
Lines 5–8: *Eukhesthai* (Addressee: Apollo)
Lines 9–12 *Eukhesthai* (Addressee: Apollo)
Lines 13–18: *Eukhesthai* (Addressee: Megakles)
Line 18: Lyric
Lines 18–19: Lyric
Lines 19–20: *Gnôma*

This brief song has a simple ring-composition structure with a gnomic coda.

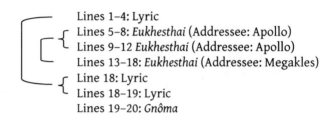

Pythian 8

Lines 1–5: *Eukhesthai*
Lines 6–7: *Eukhesthai*
Lines 8–13: *Eukhesthai*
➥12–13: Mythological Narrative
Lines 13–14: *Gnôma*
Line 15: *Gnôma*
Lines 16–20: Mythological Narrative
➥Lines 18–20: *Angelia*
Lines 21–28: *Angelia*
A Lines 29–32: Lyric
B Lines 32–34: *Eukhesthai*
Lines 35–56: *Eukhesthai*
➥Lines 39–56: Mythological Narrative
➥Lines 44–55: Direct Discourse
➥Lines 44–45: *Gnôma*
➥Lines 45–47: Lyric
➥Lines 47–55: Mythological Narrative
A Lines 56–60: Lyric
B Lines 61–66: *Eukhesthai*
Lines 67–69: *Eukhesthai*
A Lines 70–71: Lyric
B Lines 71–72: *Eukhesthai*
Lines 73–75: *Gnôma*
Lines 76–77: *Gnôma*
Line 78: *Eukhesthai*
Lines 78–80: *Eukhesthai*
Lines 81–86: *Eukhesthai*
Lines 86–87: *Gnôma*
Lines 88–92: *Gnôma*
Lines 92–94: *Gnôma*
Lines 95–96: *Gnôma*
Lines 96–97: *Gnôma*
Lines 98–100: *Eukhesthai*

The features of *angelia* in lines 16–28 suggest the parallel with lines 78–86, which address a report (*angelia*) of the *laudandus*'s achievements to the *laudandus*.

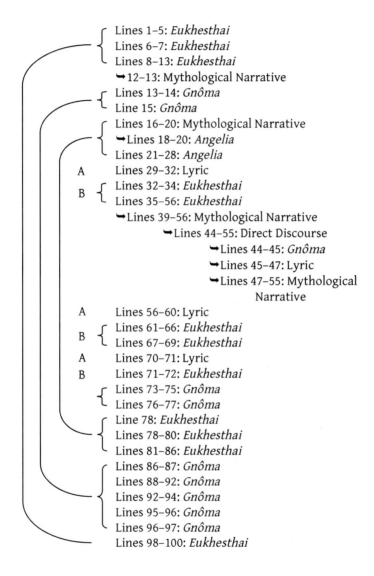

Pythian 9

- Lines 1–66: *Eukhesthai*
  - ↪Lines 5–66: Mythological Narrative
    - ↪Lines 30–37: Direct Discourse
      - ↪Lines 30–37: *Eukhesthai*
        - ↪Lines 31–37: Mythological Narrative
    - ↪Lines 39–65: Direct Discourse
      - ↪Lines 39–41: *Eukhesthai*
      - ↪Lines 42–43: *Eukhesthai*
      - ↪Lines 43–44: *Eukhesthai*
      - ↪Lines 44–45: *Eukhesthai*
      - ↪Lines 46–49: *Eukhesthai*
      - ↪Lines 50–51: *Eukhesthai*
      - ↪Lines 51–53: *Eukhesthai*
      - ↪Lines 54–65: Mythological Narrative
- Lines 67–68: *Gnôma*
- Lines 68–70: Mythological Narrative
- Lines 71–75: *Angelia*
- Line 76: *Gnôma*
- Lines 77–78: *Gnôma*
- Lines 78–79: *Gnôma*
- Lines 79–86: *Angelia*
- ↪Lines 80–86: Mythological Narrative
- Lines 87–88: *Gnôma*
- Line 89: *Eukhesthai*
- Lines 89–90: *Eukhesthai*
- Lines 90–92: Lyric
- Lines 93–94: *Eukhesthai*
- Lines 95–96: Mythological Narrative
- Lines 97–103: *Eukhesthai*
- Lines 104–125: Lyric
- ↪105–125: Mythological Narrative

Note that in the *angelia* of 71–75 the tense moves from past to future, mirroring perhaps the future tense of Kheiron's mythological narrative at 54–65. Although a relative pronoun at line 80 indicates embedding, the discursive structure of the song recommends treating 80–86 as corresponding to lines 68–70.

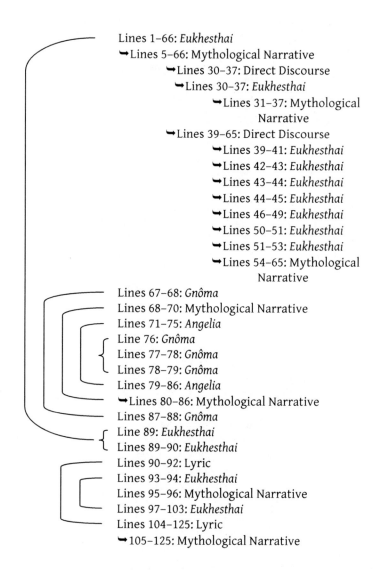

Pythian 10

Lines 1–2: *Angelia*
Lines 2–3: *Angelia*
Line 4: Lyric
Lines 4–6: Lyric
Line 7: *Angelia*
Lines 8–9: *Angelia*
Line 10: *Eukhesthai*
Line 11: *Eukhesthai*
Lines 11–16: *Angelia*
Lines 17–18: *Eukhesthai*
Lines 19–21: *Eukhesthai*
Lines 21–22: *Eukhesthai*
Lines 22–26: *Gnômai*
Lines 27–29: *Gnômai*
A Lines 29–48: *Eukhesthai*
➥Lines 31–48: Mythological Narrative
B Lines 48–50: Lyric
A Lines 51–52: *Eukhesthai*
B Lines 53–54: Lyric
Lines 55–59: *Eukhesthai*
Lines 59–63: *Gnôma*
Lines 64–66: Lyric
Lines 67–68: *Gnôma*
Lines 69–71: *Eukhesthai*
Lines 71–72: *Gnôma*

Two simple ring structures (lines 1–9 and 10–22) followed by a gnomic coda (lines 22–29) organize the first part of the ode. A second part has an interlocking pattern (lines 29–54) and a ring-composition pattern (lines 55–71), followed by a gnomic coda.

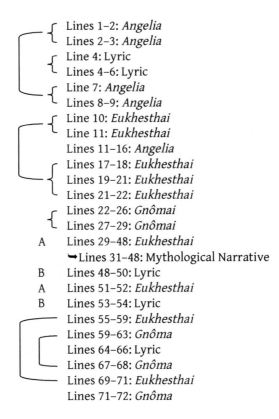

Pythian 11

Lines 1–16: *Eukhesthai*
➥Lines 13–16: *Angelia*
    ➥Lines 17–25: Mythological Narrative
Lines 25–27: *Gnôma*
Line 28: *Gnôma*
Line 29: *Gnôma*
Line 30: *Gnôma*
Lines 31–37: Mythological Narrative
Lines 38–40: Lyric
Lines 41–45: *Eukhesthai*
Lines 46–50: *Angelia*
Lines 50–51: *Eukhesthai*
Lines 52–53: Lyric
Line 54: Lyric
Line 54: *Gnôma*
Lines 55–58: *Gnôma*
Lines 59–64: Mythological Narrative

The patterning of this song suggests that the vocative *ô philoi* 'oh friends' (line 38) should be interpreted as an apostrophe in contrast with a second-person address, which is constitutive of the *eukhesthai* speech genre. The same applies to the vocative in line 62.

Pythian 12

Lines 1–27: *Eukhesthai*
➥Lines 6–27: Mythological Narrative
    ➥Lines 17–18: Lyric
Lines 28–32: *Gnôma*

Nemean 1

Lines 1–6: *Eukhesthai*
Line 7: Lyric
Lines 8–11: *Gnôma*
Lines 11–12: Lyric
Lines 13–18: *Eukhesthai*
➥Lines 13–18: Mythological Narrative
Line 18: Lyric
Lines 19–22: Lyric
Lines 22–25: *Angelia*
Line 25: *Gnôma*
Lines 26–28: *Gnôma*
Lines 29–30: *Eukhesthai*
Lines 31–32: Lyric
Lines 32–33: *Gnôma*
Lines 33–53: Lyric
➥35–53: Mythological Narrative
Lines 53–54: *Gnôma*
Lines 55–72: Mythological Narrative

Three ring-composition sections pattern this song. The discursive structure (form) and content of lines 18–32 indicate that the *angelia* and *eukhesthai* are corresponding terms of the central ring-composition pattern: the *eukhesthai*, addressed to the song's *laudandus*, whose wisdom and strength the utterance celebrates (so that he possesses the qualities exemplified in the preceding gnomic statement at lines 26–28); an *eukhesthai* utterance in the mode of an *eukhos* 'vaunt' is analogous to the *angelia* of lines 22–25.

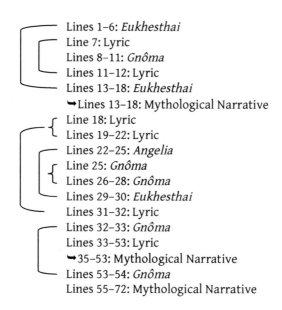

Nemean 2

Lines 1–5: *Angelia*
Lines 6–10: *Angelia*
Lines 10–12: *Gnôma*
Lines 13–14: Mythological Narrative
Lines 14–15: *Eukhesthai*
Lines 16–24: *Angelia*
Lines 24–25: *Eukhesthai*

The utterance at lines 10–12 has gnomic style, but is connected to the preceding *angelia*. Taking lines 1–12 together, there is an interlocking pattern, A-C-B-A-B.

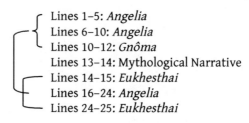

Nemean 3

Lines 1–3: *Eukhesthai*
Lines 3–5: *Eukhesthai*
Lines 6–8: *Gnôma*
Line 9: *Eukhesthai*
Lines 10–11: *Eukhesthai*
Lines 11–12: *Eukhesthai*
Lines 12–17: *Eukhesthai*
➥Lines 13–14: Mythological Narrative
➥Lines 14–17: *Angelia*
Lines 18–19: *Angelia*
Lines 19–26: *Angelia*
➥Lines 22–26: Mythological Narrative
Lines 26–27: *Eukhesthai*
Line 28: *Eukhesthai*
Lines 29–30: *Gnôma*
Line 31: *Eukhesthai*
Lines 31–32: *Eukhesthai*
Lines 32–39: Mythological Narrative
Line 40: *Gnôma*
Lines 41–42: *Gnôma*
Lines 43–52: Mythological Narrative
Lines 52–53: Lyric
Lines 53–63: Mythological Narrative
Line 64: *Angelia*
Lines 65–66: *Eukhesthai*
Lines 67–70: *Angelia*
Lines 70–74: *Gnôma*
Lines 74–75: *Gnôma*
Line 76: *Eukhesthai*
Line 76: *Eukhesthai*
Lines 76–80: *Eukhesthai*
Lines 80–82: *Gnôma*
Lines 83–84: *Eukhesthai*

Lines 1–32 have a ring-composition pattern; lines 70–84, an interlocking pattern. Lines 32–70 are a series of simple ring-composition patterns.

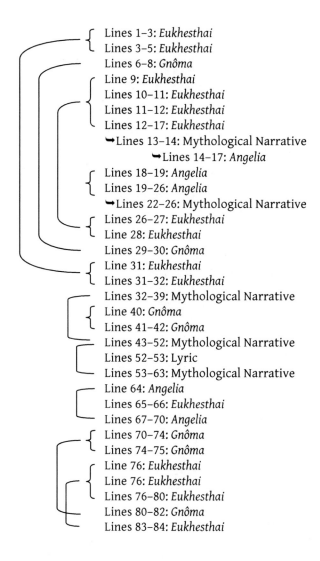

Nemean 4

Lines 1–2: *Gnôma*
Lines 2–3: *Gnôma*
Lines 4–5: Lyric
Lines 6–8: Lyric
Lines 9–11: *Eukhesthai*
Lines 11–13: *Eukhesthai*
Lines 13–22: *Eukhesthai*
Lines 22–30: *Angelia*
➥Lines 25–30: Mythological Narrative
Lines 30–32: *Gnôma*
Lines 33–34: Lyric
Line 35: Lyric
Lines 36–37: *Eukhesthai*
Lines 37–38: *Eukhesthai*
Lines 39–41: *Gnôma*
Lines 41–43: Lyric
Lines 44–47: *Eukhesthai*
➥Lines 46–47: Mythological Narrative
Lines 47–68: Mythological Narrative
Line 69: *Gnôma*
Lines 69–70: *Eukhesthai*
Lines 71–72: Lyric
Lines 73–81: Lyric
➥Lines 76–77: *Angelia*
➥Lines 77–79: *Eukhesthai*
➥Lines 79–81: *Eukhesthai*
Lines 82–85: *Gnôma*
Lines 85–88: *Eukhesthai*
➥Lines 86–88: *Angelia*
➥Lines 89–90: *Eukhesthai*
Line 91: *Gnôma*
Lines 91–92: *Gnôma*
Lines 93–96: *Gnôma*

Features of the lyric speech genre are dominant in lines 4–8, but there are gnomic inflections, which suggest treating 1–8 as a unit that corresponds to the closing lines. I take lines 22–30 as contiguous with preceding lines 13–22, given their *angelia* inflections. The speech object of the *eukhesthai* at lines 13–22 is the same as the grammatical subject (and speech object) of the *angelia* at lines 22–30. The discursive structure of lines 85–90 suggests a parallel *angelia-eukesthai* speech genre blending in its ring-composition antecedent at lines 9–30. The parallel content of lines 9–30 and 85–90 corroborates this suggestion: Timasarkhos' father, Timokritos, is mentioned in line 13, his grandfather Euphanes in line 89; both are represented as singing. Lines 93–96 are gnomic in style, but the passage has content appropriate to *angelia*.

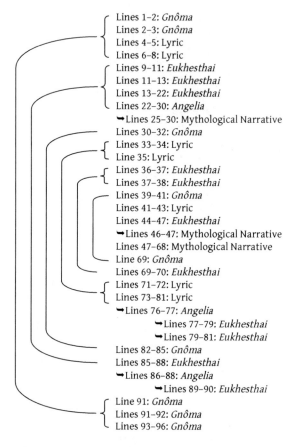

Nemean 5

Lines 1–2: Lyric
Lines 2–8: *Eukhesthai*
➥Lines 4–8: *Angelia*
  ➥Lines 9–13: Mythological Narrative
Lines 14–16: Lyric
➥Lines 15–16: Mythological Narrative
Line 16: *Eukhesthai*
Lines 16–17: *Gnôma*
Line 18: *Gnôma*
Lines 19–20: *Eukhesthai*
Line 20: Lyric
Line 21: *Gnôma*
Lines 22–39: Mythological Narrative (37–39 too?)
Lines 40–41: *Gnôma*
Lines 41–42: *Eukhesthai*
Line 43: *Eukhesthai*
Line 44: *Angelia*
Lines 45–46: *Angelia*
Lines 47–48: Lyric
Lines 48–49: *Eukhesthai*
Line 49: *Gnôma*
Line 50: *Eukhesthai*
Lines 50–53: *Eukhesthai*
Lines 53–54: *Eukhesthai*

Lines 1–16 have an interlocking pattern, A-B-C-A-B, lines 16–21 a ring pattern, A-B-A, taking the *eukhesthai* utterance of lines 19–20 and the lyric utterance of line 20 together, given that the lyric passage sustains the metaphor of the *eukhesthai* passage. After the central mythological narrative (lines 22–39), lines 40–54 have an overall interlocking pattern, A-B-C-D-A-B-C. This interpretation of the discursive structure of lines 40–54 depends upon treating the *angelia* inflections of the *eukhesthai* utterances at lines 50–54 as meaningful and as corresponding to the *angelia* of 44–46.

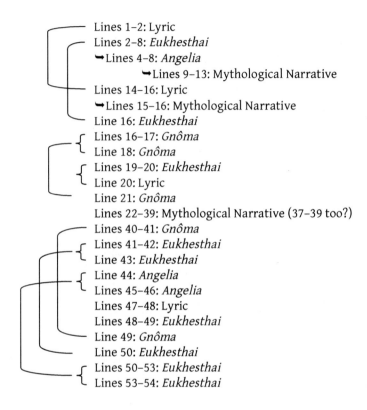

Nemean 6

Lines 1–2: *Gnôma*
Lines 2–4: *Gnôma*
Lines 4–7: *Gnôma*
Lines 8–11: *Angelia*
Lines 11–16: *Angelia*
Lines 17–24: *Angelia*
Lines 24–26: *Angelia*
Lines 26–28: *Eukhesthai*
Lines 28–29: *Eukhesthai*
Lines 29–44: *Gnôma*
➥Line 31: *Angelia*
➥Lines 31–44: *Angelia*
Lines 45–46: Lyric
Lines 46–49: *Angelia*
Lines 49–53: Mythological Narrative
Lines 53–54: Lyric
Lines 55–57: *Gnôma*
Lines 57–61: *Eukhesthai*
Lines 61–63: *Eukhesthai*
Lines 64–66: Lyric

Although it is possible to interpret the discursive structure of this song in other ways, I opt for the interpretation that there is an interlocking pattern, A-B-C-A-D-B-E-C-D.

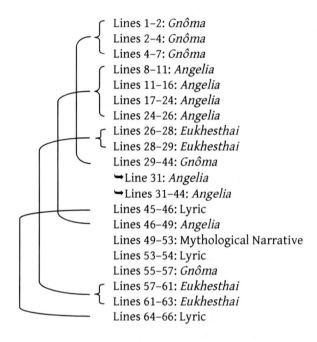

Nemean 7

Lines 1–4: *Eukhesthai*
Lines 5–6: *Gnômai*
Lines 6–8: *Eukhesthai*
Lines 9–10: *Angelia*
Lines 11–12: *Gnôma*
Lines 12–16: Lyric
Lines 17–20: *Gnômai*
Lines 20–23: Lyric
Lines 23–24: *Gnômai*
Lines 24–30: Mythological Narrative
Lines 30–32: *Gnômai*
Lines 33–34: Lyric
Lines 34–48: Mythological Narrative
Lines 49–52: *Eukhesthai*
Lines 52–56: *Gnômai*
Lines 56–58: Lyric
Lines 58–60: *Eukhesthai*
Line 61: Lyric
Lines 61–63: *Eukhesthai*
Lines 63–67: Lyric
Lines 67–68: *Eukhesthai*
Lines 68–69: Lyric
Lines 70–73: *Eukhesthai*
Line 74: *Gnôma*
Line 75: *Eukhesthai*
Lines 75–77: Lyric
Line 77: *Eukhesthai*
Lines 77–79: Lyric
Lines 80–82: *Eukhesthai*
Lines 82–84: *Gnôma*
Lines 84–86: *Eukhesthai*
Lines 86–89: Lyric
Lines 89–92: *Eukhesthai*
Lines 93–94: *Eukhesthai*
Lines 95–96: *Eukhesthai*
Lines 96–97: *Eukhesthai*
Lines 98–101: *Eukhesthai*
Lines 102–104: *Eukhesthai*
Lines 104–105: *Gnôma*

There is a series of interlocking patterns: A-B-A-C-B (lines 1–13), A-B-A-B (lines 12–24), A-B-C-A-D-B-C (lines 24–58), and A-B-A-B (lines 58–67). Ring composition shapes the discursive structure of lines 67–104. There is a gnomic coda. This song exhibits an especially high degree of stylistic hybridization.

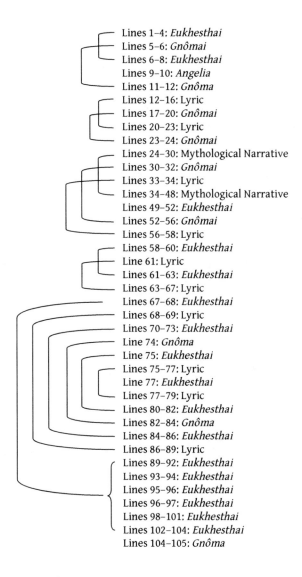

Nemean 8

Lines 1–3: *Eukhesthai*
Lines 4–5: *Gnôma*
Lines 6–12: Mythological Narrative
Lines 13–16: Lyric
Lines 17–18: *Gnôma*
➥Line 18: Mythological Narrative
Line 19: Lyric
Lines 20–21: *Gnôma*
Lines 21–22: *Gnôma*
Line 23: Mythological Narrative
Lines 24–25: *Gnôma*
Line 25: *Gnôma*
Lines 26–32: Mythological Narrative
Lines 32–34: *Gnôma*
Lines 35–37: *Eukhesthai*
Lines 37–39: *Eukhesthai*
Lines 40–42: *Gnôma*
Line 42: *Gnôma*
Lines 42–44: *Gnôma*
Lines 44–45: *Eukhesthai*
Lines 46–48: *Eukhesthai*
Lines 48–49: Lyric
Lines 49–50: *Gnôma*
Lines 50–51: Mythological Narrative

After an opening *eukhesthai* the patterning of lines 4–25 blends ring and interlocking discursive structures: A-B-C-D-C-D-B-A. Lines 26–51 have an overall ring-composition structure from which the lyric passage at lines 48–49 deviates.

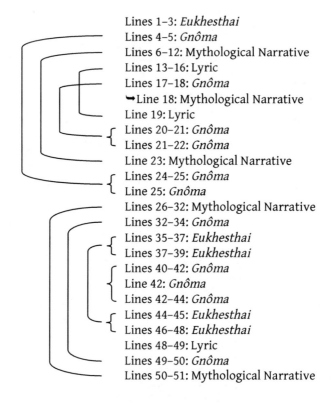

Nemean 9

Lines 1–3: *Eukhesthai*
Line 3: *Eukhesthai*
Lines 4–5: *Angelia*
Lines 6–7: *Gnôma*
Lines 8–27: *Eukhesthai*
→Line 9: Mythological Narrative
→Lines 9–10: *Eukhesthai*
→Lines 11–27: Mythological Narrative
Line 27: *Gnôma*
Lines 28–29: *Eukhesthai*
Lines 29–32: *Eukhesthai*
Lines 32–33: *Angelia*
Line 33: Lyric
Line 33–34: *Gnôma*
Lines 34–37: *Eukhesthai*
Lines 37–39: *Gnôma*
Lines 39–40: Mythological Narrative
Lines 40–42: *Angelia*
Lines 42–43: *Eukhesthai*
Line 44: *Gnôma*
Line 45: *Eukhesthai*
Lines 46–47: *Gnôma*
Lines 48–49: Lyric
Lines 50–53: *Eukhesthai*
→Lines 52–53: *Angelia*
Lines 53–55: *Eukhesthai*

Indicating a structural correspondence between the passages on the basis of content, the lyric utterance at 48–49 asserts the power of song to augment an athletic victory, answering to the *angelia* at lines 4–5, which claims that victory motivates song.

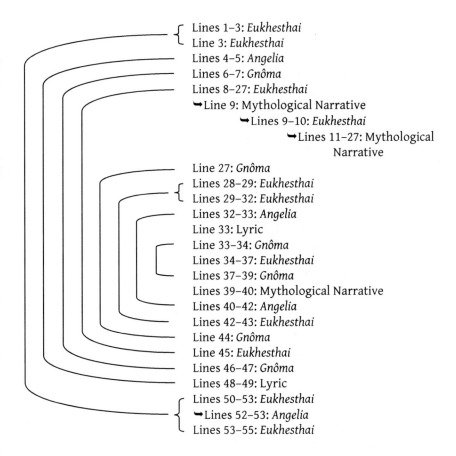

Nemean 10

Lines 1–2: *Eukhesthai*
Lines 2–3: *Angelia*
Lines 4–18: Mythological Narrative
Lines 19–20: Lyric
Line 20: *Gnôma*
Lines 21–22: *Eukhesthai*
Lines 22–28: *Angelia*
Lines 29–30: *Eukhesthai*
Lines 31–32: Lyric
Lines 32–36: *Angelia*
Lines 37–38: *Eukhesthai*
Lines 39–41: Lyric
Lines 41–44: *Angelia*
Lines 45–48: *Angelia*
Lines 49–54: *Angelia*
Line 54: *Gnôma*
Lines 55–72: Mythological Narrative
Line 72: *Gnôma*
Lines 73–90: Mythological Narrative

- ➥Lines 76–79: Direct Discourse
    - ➥Lines 76–77: *Eukhesthai*
    - ➥Line 77: *Eukhesthai*
    - ➥Line 78: *Gnôma*
    - ➥Lines 78–79: *Gnôma*
- ➥Lines 80–88: Direct Discourse
    - ➥Line 80: *Eukhesthai*
    - ➥Lines 80–82: Mythological Narrative
    - ➥Lines 82–83: *Eukhesthai*
    - ➥Lines 83–85: *Eukhesthai*
    - ➥Lines 85–87: *Eukhesthai*

This song's discursive structure includes three sections with interlocking patterns among ways of epinician speaking: A-B-X-Y-Z-A-B (lines 1–28), A-B-C-A-B-C (lines 29–54), and A-B-A-B (lines 55–90).

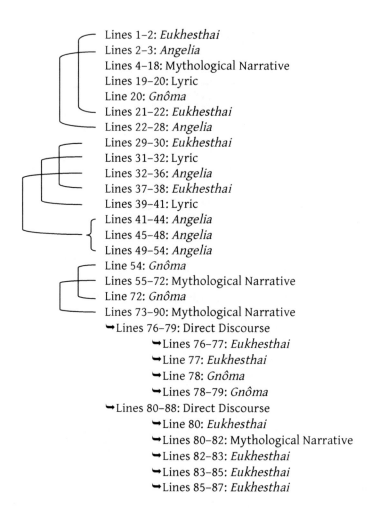

Nemean 11

A Lines 1–7: *Eukhesthai*
↪Lines 5–7: *Angelia*
B { Line 7: Lyric
Lines 8–9: Lyric
A Lines 9–10: *Eukhesthai*
B Lines 11–12: Lyric
Lines 13–16: *Gnôma*
Lines 17–18: Lyric
Lines 19–23: *Angelia*
Lines 24–29: Lyric
Lines 29–32: *Gnôma*
Lines 33–37: Mythological Narrative
Lines 37–38: *Gnôma*
Lines 39–42: *Gnôma*
Lines 42–43: *Gnôma*
Lines 43–44: *Gnôma*
Lines 44–45: *Gnôma*
Lines 45–46: *Gnôma*
Line 46: *Gnôma*
Line 47: *Gnôma*
Line 48: *Gnôma*

Lines 1–12 exhibit an interlocking pattern, A-B-A-B. Lines 29–48 have a simple ring-composition pattern, A-B-A.

Isthmian 1

Lines 1–3: *Eukhesthai*
Lines 3–4: *Eukhesthai*
Line 5: *Gnôma*
Line 6: *Eukhesthai*
Lines 6–10: *Eukhesthai*
Lines 10–13: *Angelia*
➥Lines 12–13: Mythological Narrative
Lines 14–16: *Eukhesthai*
Lines 17–31: Mythological Narrative
Line 32: *Eukhesthai*
Lines 32–40: *Eukhesthai*
➥Lines 36–40: *Angelia*
Line 40: *Gnôma*
Lines 41–46: *Gnôma*
Lines 47–49: *Gnôma*
Lines 50–51: *Gnôma*
Lines 52–57: Lyric
Lines 58–59: *Eukhesthai*
Lines 60–63: Lyric
➥Lines 60–62: *Angelia*
Line 63: *Gnôma*
Lines 64–67: *Eukhesthai*
Lines 67–68: *Gnôma*

The beginning and end of the song form a chiastic pattern, A-B-B-A. Lines 6–16 have a small ring-composition pattern, A-B-A. Lines 32–63 have an interlocking pattern that embraces a third term, the gnomic passage at lines 41–51: A-C-B-A-B. The mythological narrative of lines 17–31 is at the discursive core of *Isthmian* 1. There is a gnomic coda.

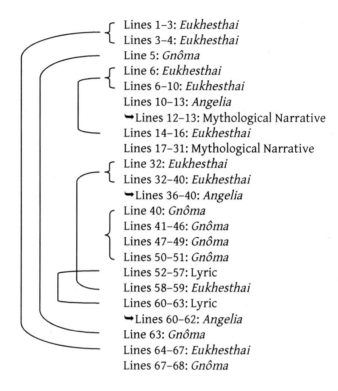

Isthmian 2

Lines 1–12: *Eukhesthai*
Lines 12–13: Lyric
Lines 14–29: *Angelia*
Lines 30–32: *Eukhesthai*
Lines 33–34: *Gnôma*
Lines 35–37: *Eukhesthai*
Lines 37–38: *Angelia*
Lines 39–40: *Angelia*
Lines 41–42: *Angelia*
Lines 43–46: *Eukhesthai*
➥Line 43: *Gnôma*
Lines 47–48: *Eukhesthai*

The second-person address in lines 1 and 12 (the opening and closing of the passage) recommend describing lines 1–12 as an *eukhesthai* passage. Given this, the song has a ring-composition pattern, from which the lyric passage at lines 12–13 deviates. The topic of *Isthmian* 2's opening and closing lines is song, so that there is a thematic, as well as discursive, dimension to the ring-composition pattern of the song.

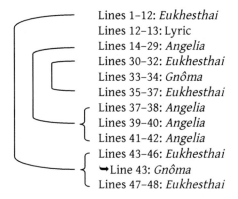

Isthmian 3

Lines 1–3: *Gnôma*
Lines 4–5: *Eukhesthai*
Lines 5–6: *Gnôma*
Lines 7–8: Lyric
Lines 9–14: *Angelia*
Lines 15–16: *Eukhesthai*
Line 17: *Angelia*
Line 18: *Gnôma*
Line 18: *Gnôma*

This short song has two sections (lines 1–6 and 9–17) patterned A-B-A; B in both sections is a form of *eukhesthai*. There is a gnomic coda.

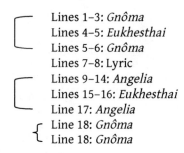

Isthmian 4

Lines 1–5: *Eukhesthai*
➥Lines 4–5: *Angelia*
Lines 5–6: *Gnôma*
Lines 7–13: *Angelia*
Lines 14–19: *Angelia*
Lines 19–23: Lyric
Lines 23–29: *Angelia*
Line 30: *Gnôma*
Lines 31–33: *Gnôma*
Lines 34–35: *Gnôma*
Lines 35–39: *Eukhesthai*
➥Lines 35–39: Mythological Narrative
Lines 40–41: *Gnôma*
Lines 41–42: *Gnôma*
Lines 43–45: *Eukhesthai*
Lines 45–47: *Angelia*
Line 48: *Gnôma*
Lines 49–51: *Angelia*
Lines 52–60: Mythological Narrative
Lines 61–66: *Eukhesthai*
➥Line 64: Mythological Narrative
Lines 69–72: *Angelia*
Line 72: *Eukhesthai*

Lines 1–39 have a ring-composition pattern, A-B-C-D-C-B-A. Lines 40–51 have an interlocking pattern (with an outlier), A-C-B-A-B. Lines 61–72 have a simple ring-composition pattern, A-B-A.

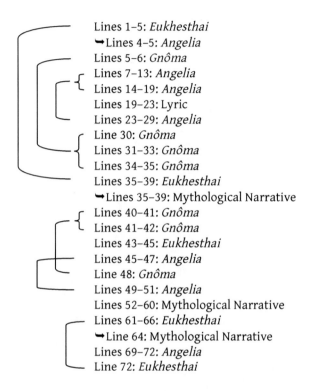

Isthmian 5

Lines 1–3: *Eukhesthai*
Lines 4–6: *Eukhesthai*
Lines 7–10: *Gnôma*
Line 11: *Gnôma*
Lines 12–13: *Gnôma*
Line 14: *Eukhesthai*
Lines 14–15: *Eukhesthai*
Line 16: *Gnôma*
Lines 17–19: *Eukhesthai*
Lines 19–20: Lyric
Lines 21–22: Lyric
Lines 22–25: *Eukhesthai*
Lines 26–27: *Gnôma*
Lines 27–28: *Gnôma*
Lines 28–29: *Gnôma*
Lines 30–38: Mythological Narrative
Line 38: *Eukhesthai*
Lines 39–42: *Eukhesthai*
Lines 43–44: Lyric
Lines 44–45: *Angelia*
Lines 46–48: Lyric
Lines 48–50: *Angelia*
Line 51: *Eukhesthai*
Lines 52–53: *Gnôma*
Lines 53–54: Lyric
Lines 54–56: *Eukhesthai*
Lines 56–58: *Gnôma*
Lines 59–61: Lyric
Lines 62–63: *Eukhesthai*

Lines 1–29 have two ring patterns, one A-B-A (lines 1–15), the other A-B-C-B-A (lines 16–29). On the other "side" of the mythological narrative of lines 30–38, which is the discursive core of this song, there are two sections of interlocking patterns (A-B-A-B, lines 43–50, and A-B-C-A-B-C, lines 51–61) embraced by *eukhesthai* passages at lines 38–42 and 62–63.

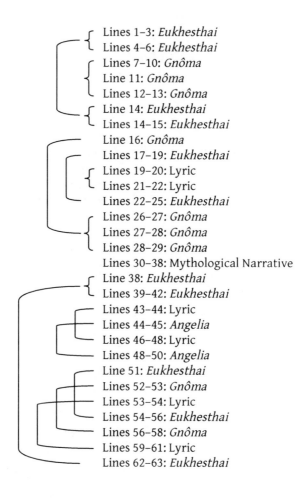

Isthmian 6

Lines 1–7: *Eukhesthai*
Lines 7–9: *Eukhesthai*
Lines 10–13: *Gnôma*
Lines 14–16: *Angelia*
Lines 16–18: *Eukhesthai*
Lines 19–21: *Eukhesthai*
Lines 22–23: *Angelia*
Lines 24–56: Mythological Narrative
↳Lines 42–49: Direct Discourse
  ↳Lines 42–48: *Eukhesthai*
    ↳Line 48: Mythological Narrative
  ↳Line 49: *Eukhesthai*
↳Lines 52–54: Direct Discourse
  ↳Line 52: *Eukhesthai*
  ↳Lines 53–54: *Eukhesthai*
Line 56: Lyric
Lines 57–58: *Eukhesthai*
Lines 58–59: *Angelia*
Lines 60–62: *Angelia*
Line 62: *Angelia*
Lines 63–64: *Angelia*
Lines 65–66: *Angelia*
Lines 66–71: *Angelia*
Line 72: *Angelia*
Lines 72–73: *Eukhesthai*
Lines 74–75: *Eukhesthai*
↳Lines 74–75: Mythological Narrative

Isthmian 6 has two patterned sections located before and after a discursively central mythological narrative. Lines 1–27 have an interlocking pattern among *eukhesthai* (A) and *angelia* (B), utterances that incorporate a gnomic statement (C), with the resulting structure A-C-B-A-B. After the lyric passage at line 56, lines 57–75 have a simple ring-composition pattern, A-B-A.

Isthmian 7

Lines 1–15: *Eukhesthai*
Lines 16–17: *Gnôma*
Lines 17–19: *Gnôma*
Lines 20–21: *Eukhesthai*
Lines 21–25: *Angelia*
Line 26: *Gnôma*
Lines 27–30: *Eukhesthai*
Lines 31–36: *Eukhesthai*
➥Lines 35–36: *Angelia*
Lines 37–39: Lyric
Line 39: *Eukhesthai*
Lines 39–42: *Euhkesthai*
Line 42: *Gnôma*
Line 43: *Gnôma*
Lines 43–44: *Gnôma*
Lines 44–47: Mythological Narrative
Lines 47–48: *Gnôma*
Lines 49–51: *Eukhesthai*

Isthmian 7 generally has a ring-composition pattern, from which lines 20–25 and 44–47 deviate.

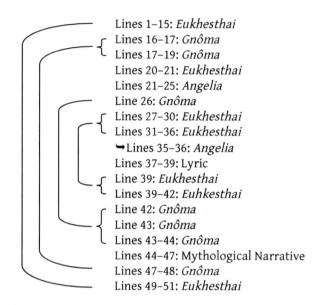

Isthmian 8

A Lines 1–5: *Eukhesthai*
B Lines 5–6: Lyric
A { Lines 6–7: *Eukhesthai*
  Lines 7–11: *Eukhesthai*
B Lines 11–12: Lyric
C { Lines 12–14: *Gnôma*
  Lines 14–15: *Gnôma*
  Line 15: *Gnôma*
  Line 15: *Gnôma*
B Lines 16–20: Lyric
 ➥Lines 17–20: Mythological Narrative
A Lines 21–23: *Eukhesthai*
D Lines 23–60: Mythological Narrative
 ➥Lines 35–45: Direct Discourse
  ➥Lines 35–36: *Eukhesthai*
  ➥Lines 36–37: *Eukhesthai*
  ➥Lines 38–40: Lyric
  ➥Line 41: *Eukhesthai*
  ➥Lines 42–44: *Eukhesthai*
  ➥Lined 44–45: *Eukhesthai*
B Lines 61–62: Lyric
A { Lines 62–66: *Eukhesthai*
  ➥Lines 63–66: *Angelia*
  Lines 66–68: *Eukhesthai*
  ➥Lines 67–68: *Angelia*
E Lines 69–70: *Angelia*

Ring composition organizes the discursive structure among utterances of two speech genres, *eukhesthai* (A) and lyric (B).

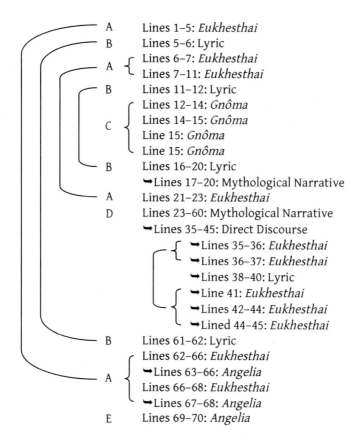

Isthmian 9

Line 1: *Angelia*
Lines 2–4: Mythological Narrative
Lines 4–8: *Angelia*

Bibliography

Aloni, A. 1998. *Cantare glorie di eroi: Comunicazione e performance poetica nella Grecia arcaica*. Turin.

Anzai, M. 1994. "First-Person Forms in Pindar: A Re-Examination." *Bulletin of the Institute of Classical Studies* 39:141–150.

Athanassaki, L. 2004. "Deixis, Performance, and Poetics in Pindar's *First Olympian Ode*." In Felson 2004a:317–341.

Austin, J. L. 1975. *How to Do Things with Words*. 2nd ed. Cambridge, MA.

Babcock, B. A. 1977. "The Story in the Story: Metanarrative in Folk Narrative." In Bauman 1977:61–79.

Bakhtin, M. M. 1981. *The Dialogic Imagination: Four Essays by M. M. Bakhtin*. Trans. C. Emerson and M. Holquist. Austin.

——. 1986. *Speech Genres and Other Late Essays* (eds. C. Emerson and M. Holquist). Trans. V. W. McGee. Austin.

Bakker, E. J. 1997. *Poetry in Speech: Orality and Homeric Discourse*. Ithaca.

——. 2005. *Pointing at the Past: From Formula to Performance in Homeric Poetics*. Hellenic Studies 12. Washington, DC.

Bauman, R. 1977. *Verbal Art as Performance*. Prospect Heights.

——. 1982. "Conceptions of Folklore in the Development of Literary Semiotics." *Semiotica* 39:1–20.

——. 1983. *Let Your Words Be Few: Symbolism of Speaking and Silence among Seventeenth-Century Quakers*. Reprint 1998. London.

——. 1986a. *Story, Performance, and Event*. Cambridge.

——. 1986b. "Performance and Honor in 13th-Century Iceland." *Journal of American Folklore* 99:131–50.

——. 1992. "Contextualization, Tradition, and the Dialogue of Genres: Icelandic Legends of the Kraftaskáld." In Duranti and Goodwin 1992:125–145.

——. 1996. "Transformations of the Word in the Production of Mexican Festival Drama." In Silverstein and Urban 1996:301–327.

Bauman, R. and Briggs, C. L. 1990. "Poetics and Performance as Critical Perspectives on Language and Social Life." *Annual Review of Anthropology* 19:59–88.

Bauman, R. and Sherzer, J., eds. 1989. *Explorations in the Ethnography of Speaking*. 2nd ed. Cambridge.

Benveniste, E. 1971. *Problems in General Linguistics*. Trans. M. E. Meek. Coral Gables.

Berge, L. van den. 2007. "Mythological Chronology in the Odes of Pindar. The Cases of *Pythian* 10 and *Olympian* 3." *The Language of Literature: Linguistic Approaches to Classical Texts* (eds. R. J. Allan and M. Buijs) 29–41. Leiden.

Bergren, A. L. T. 1982. "Sacred Apostrophe: Re-Presentation and Imitation in the Homeric Hymns." *Arethusa* 15:83–108.

Bernardini, P. A. 1983. *Mito e attualità nelle odi di Pindaro. La Nemea 4, l'Olimpica 9, l'Olimpica 7*. Rome.

Bischoff, H. 1938. *Gnomen Pindars*. Würzberg.

Boeckh, A. 1811, 1819, 1821. *Pindari opera quae supersunt* I, II-1, II-2. Leipzig.

Boeke, H. 2007. *The Value of Victory in Pindar's Odes: Gnomai, Cosmology and the Role of the Poet*. Mnemosyne Supplement 285. Leiden.

Bogatyrev, P. 1936. "La chanson populaire du point de vue fonctionnel." *Travaux du Cercle linguistique de Prague* 6:222–234. Reprinted in English as "Folk Song from a Functional Point of View." *Semiotics of Art: Prague School Contributions* (eds. L. Matejka and I. R. Titunik; trans. Y. Lockwood) 1976:20–32. Cambridge, MA.

Bogatyrev, P. and Jakobson, R. 1929. "Die Folklore als eine besondere Form des Schaffens." *Donum natalicium Schrijnen. Verzameling van opstellen door oud-leerlingen en bevriende vakgenooten opgedragen aan* (eds. J. Schrijnen and W. J. St. Teeuwen) 900–913. Reprinted in English as "Folklore as a Special Form of Creativity." *The Prague School: Selected Writings, 1929-1946* (ed. P. Steiner; trans. J. Burbank) 1982:32–46. Austin.

Bonifazi, A. 2000. "Sull'idea di sotterfugio orale negli epinici pindarici." *Quaderni Urbinati di Cultura Classica* 60:69–86.

——. 2001. *Mescolare un cratere di canti: Pragmatica della poesia epinicia in Pindaro.* Alessandria.

——. 2004a. "Communication in Pindar's Deictic Acts." In Felson 2004a:391–414.

——. 2004b. "Relative Pronouns and Memory: Pindar Beyond Syntax." *Harvard Studies in Classical Philology* 102:41–68.

——. 2004c. "ΚΕΙΝΟΣ in Pindar: Between Grammar and Poetic Intention." *Classical Philology* 99:283–299.

Bourdieu, P. 1977. *Outline of the Theory of Practice.* Trans. R. Nice. Cambridge.

Bowra, C. M., ed. 1935. *Pindari carmina cum fragmentis.* Oxford.

——. 1964. *Pindar.* Oxford.

Braswell, B. K. 1988. *A Commentary on the Fourth Pythian Ode of Pindar.* Berlin.

Bremer, J. M. 1990. "Pindar's Paradoxical Ἐγώ and a Recent Controversy about the Performance of his Epinicia." *The Poet's I in Archaic Greek Lyric: Proceedings of a Symposium Held at the Vrije Universiteit Amsterdam* (ed. S. R. Slings) 41–58. Amsterdam.

——. 2008. "Traces of the Hymn in the *Epinikion*." *Mnemosyne* 61:1–17.

Briggs, C. L. and Bauman, R. 1992. "Genre, Intertextuality and Social Power." *Journal of Linguistic Anthropology* 2:131–172.

Brik, O. 1923. "T.n. 'formalnyi metod'." *LEF: Zhurnal Levogo fronta iskusstv* 1:213–215. Reprinted in English as "The So-Called Formal Method." *Formalist Theory.* Vol. 4 of *Russian Poetics in Translation* (eds. and trans. L. M. O'Toole and A. Shukman) 1977:90–91. Oxford.

Bühler, K. 1934. *Sprachtheorie: Die Darstellungsfunktion der Sprache.* Jena. Reprinted in English as *The Theory of Language: The Representational Function of Language.* Trans. D. F. Goodwin. 1990. Philadelphia.

Bulman, P. 1992. *Phthonos in Pindar.* Berkeley.

Bundy, E. L. 1962. *Studia Pindarica* I, II. Reprint 1986. Berkeley.

Burke, K. 1941. *The Philosophy of Literary Form: Studies in Symbolic Action.* Baton Rouge.

——. 1962. "What are the Signs of What?: A Theory of 'Entitlement.'" *Anthropological Linguistics* 4:1–23.

Burnett, A. P. 1989. "Performing Pindar's Odes." *Classical Philology* 84:283–293.

——. 2005. *Pindar's Songs for Young Athletes of Aigina*. Oxford.

Burton, R. W. B. 1962. *Pindar's Pythian Odes, Essays in Interpretation*. Oxford.

Cairns, F. 1977. "Ἔρως in Pindar's First Olympian Ode." *Hermes* 105:129–132.

Calame, C. 1995. *The Craft of Poetic Speech in Ancient Greece*. Trans. J. Orion. Ithaca.

——. 2001. *Choruses of Young Women in Ancient Greece: Their Morphology, Religious Role, and Social Functions*. New and revised ed. Trans. D. Collins and J. Orion. Lanham.

——. 2004. "Deictic Ambiguity and Auto-Referentiality: Some Examples from Greek Poetics." Trans. J. S. Clay. In Felson 2004a:415–443.

Carey, C. 1981. *A Commentary on Five Odes of Pindar: Pythian 2, Pythian 9, Nemean 1, Nemean 7, Isthmian 8*. Salem, NH.

——. 1989. "The Performance of the Victory Ode." *American Journal of Philology* 110:545–565.

——. 1991. "The Victory Ode in Performance: The Case for the Chorus." *Classical Philology* 86:192–200.

——. 1995. "Pindar and the Victory Ode." *The Passionate Intellect: Essays on the Transformation of Classical Traditions* (ed. L. Ayers) 85–103. New Brunswick.

——. 2007. "Pindar, Place, and Performance." In Hornblower and Morgan 2007:199–210.

Carne-Ross, D. S. 1985. *Pindar*. New Haven.

Clay, J. S. 1992. "Pindar's Twelfth Pythian: Reed and Bronze." *The American Journal of Philology* 113:519–525.

——. 1999. "Pindar's Sympotic Epinicia." *Quaderni Urbinati di Cultura Classica* 62:25–34.

Cole, T. 1992. *Pindar's Feasts or The Music of Power*. Rome.

Crotty, K. 1982. *Song and Action: The Victory Odes of Pindar*. Baltimore.

Currie, B. 2004. "Reperformance Scenarios for Pindar's Odes." *Oral Performance and its Context* (ed. C. J. Mackie) 2004:49–69. Mnemosyne Supplement 248. Leiden.

——. 2005. *Pindar and the Cult of Heroes*. Oxford.

D'Alessio, G. B. 1994. "First-Person Problems in Pindar." *Bulletin of the Institute of Classical Studies* 39:117–139.

——. 2004. "Past Future and Present Past: Temporal Deixis in Greek Archaic Lyric." In Felson 2004a:267–294.

Danielewicz, J. 1990. "Deixis in Greek Choral Lyric." *Quaderni Urbinati di Cultura Classica* 34:7–17.

Davies, M. 1988. "Monody, Choral Lyric, and the Tyranny of the Handbook." *The Classical Quarterly* 38:52–64.

Descat, R. 1985. "Autour d'une fonction social de l'oralité: Travail, échange, et parole chez Pindare." *Oralità: Cultura, letteratura, discorso: Atti del convegno internazionale* (ed. B. Gentili and G. Paioni) 69–76. Rome.

Des Places, E. 1947. *Le pronom chez Pindare.* Études et Commentaires 3. Paris.

Dickie, M.W. 1984. "*Hêsychia* and *Hybris* in Pindar." In Gerber 1984:85–109.

Dissen, L. G. 1830. *Pindari carmina quae supersunt cum deperditorum fragmentis selectis ex recensione Boeckhii commentario perpetuo illustravit* I, II. Gotha.

Dornseiff, F. 1921. *Pindars Stil.* Berlin.

Dougherty, C. 1993. *The Poetics of Colonization: From City to Text in Archaic Greece.* New York.

Dougherty, C. and Kurke, L., eds. 1993. *Cultural Poetics in Archaic Greece: Cult, Performance, Politics.* Cambridge.

Dover, K. J. 1989. *Greek Homosexuality.* Revised ed. Cambridge, MA.

Drachmann, A. B. 1903, 1910, 1927. *Scholia vetera in Pindari carmina* I, II, III. Leipzig.

Duranti, A. and Goodwin, C., eds. 1992. *Rethinking Context: Language as an Interactive Phenomenon.* Cambridge.

Èjxenbaum, B. 1927. "Teorija 'formalnogo metoda'." *Literatura: Teorija, Kritika, Polemika,* 116–148. Leningrad. Reprinted in English as "The Theory of the Formal Method." *Readings in Russian Poetics: Formalist and Structuralist Views* (eds. L. Matejka and K. Pomorska) 1978:3–37. Cambridge, MA.

Ervin-Tripp, S. 1972. "On Sociolinguistic Rules: Alternation and Co-Occurrence." In Gumperz and Hymes 1972:213–250. Oxford.

Farnell, L. R. 1930, 1932. *The Works of Pindar* I, II. London.

Fearn, D. 2007. *Bacchylides: Politics, Performance, Poetic Tradition.* Oxford.

Feldman, B. and Richardson, R. D. 1972. *The Rise of Modern Mythology, 1680–1860.* Bloomington.

Felson, N. 1984. "The Epinician Speaker in Pindar's First Olympian: Toward a Model for Analyzing Character in Ancient Choral Lyric." *Poetics Today* 5:377–397.

——. 1999. "Vicarious Transport: Fictive Deixis in Pindar's *Pythian Four*." *Harvard Studies in Classical Philology* 99:1–31.

——, ed. 2004a. *The Poetics of Deixis in Alcman, Pindar, and Other Lyric*. Special issue, *Arethusa* 37.3.

——. 2004b. "Introduction." In Felson 2004a:253–266.

——. 2004c. "The Poetic Effects of Deixis in Pindar's *Ninth Pythian Ode*." In Felson 2004a:365–389.

Fennell, C. A. M. 1893. *Pindar: The Olympian and Pythian Odes*. 2nd ed. Cambridge.

——. 1899. *Pindar: The Nemean and Isthmian Odes*. 2nd ed. Cambridge.

Fisker, D. 1990. *Pindars erste olympische Ode*. Odense University Classical Studies 15. Odense.

Floyd, E. D. 1965. "The Performance of Pindar, *Pythian* 8.55–70." *Greek Roman and Byzantine Studies* 6:187–200.

Foley, J. M. 1986. "Tradition and the Collective Talent: Oral Epic, Textual Meaning, and Receptionalist Theory." *Cultural Anthropology* 1:203–222.

——. 1990. *Traditional Oral Epic: The Odyssey, Beowulf, and the Serbo-Croatian Return Song*. Berkeley.

——. 1991. *Immanent Art: From Structure to Meaning in Traditional Oral Epic*. Bloomington.

——. 1992. "Word-Power, Performance, and Tradition." *Journal of American Folklore* 105:275–301.

——. 1995. *The Singer of Tales in Performance*. Bloomington.

——. 1998. "Individual Poet and Epic Tradition: The Legendary Singer." *Arethusa* 31:149–178.

——. 1999. *Homer's Traditional Art*. University Park.

——. 2002. *How to Read an Oral Poem*. Urbana.

Ford, A. 2002. *The Origins of Criticism: Literary Culture and Poetic Theory in Classical Greece*. Princeton.

Forssman, B. 1966. *Untersuchungen zur Sprache Pindars*. Klassisch-philologische Studien 33. Wiesbaden.

Fränkel, H. F. 1975. *Early Greek Poetry and Philosophy*. Trans. M. Hadas and J. Willis. New York.

García, J. F. 2002. "Ritual Speech in Early Greek Song." *Epea and Grammata: Oral and Written Communication in Ancient Greece* (eds. I. Worthington and J. M. Foley) 29–53. Leiden.

Gentili, B. 1988. *Poetry and its Public in Ancient Greece: from Homer to the Fifth Century*. Trans. A. T. Cole. Baltimore.

——, ed. 1995. *Pindaro. Le Pitiche*. With commentary by P. A. Bernardini, E. Cingano, and P. Giannini. Scrittori greci e latini. Rome.

Gerber, D. E. 1982. *Pindar's Olympian One: A Commentary*. Toronto.

——, ed. 1984. *Greek Poetry and Philosophy: Studies in Honour of Leonard Woodbury*. Chico.

Gildersleeve, B. L. 1890. *Pindar: The Olympian and Pythian Odes*. Reprint 1965. Amsterdam.

Goffman, E. 1974. *Frame Analysis: An Essay on the Organization of Experience*. Reprint 1986. Boston.

——. 1981. *Forms of Talk*. Philadelphia.

Goldhill, S. 1991. *The Poet's Voice: Essays on Poetics and Greek Literature*. Cambridge.

Grant, M. A. 1967. *Folktale and Hero-Tale Motifs in the Odes of Pindar*. Lawrence.

Greengard, C. 1980. *The Structure of Pindar's Epinician Odes*. Amsterdam.

Griffith, R. D. 1991. "Person and Presence in Pindar (Olympian 1.24–53)." *Arethusa* 24:31–42.

Gumperz, J. J. and Hymes, D. H., eds. 1972. *Directions in Sociolinguistics: The Ethnography of Communication*. Reprint 1986. Oxford.

Hamilton, J. T. 2003. *Soliciting Darkness: Pindar, Obscurity, and the Classical Tradition*. Cambridge, MA.

Hamilton, R. 1974. *Epinikion: General Form in the Odes of Pindar*. The Hague.

Hanks, W. F. 1987. "Discourse Genres in a Theory of Practice." *American Ethnologist* 14:668–692.

——. 1989. "Text and Textuality." *Annual Review of Anthropology* 18:95–127.

——. 1990. *Referential Practice: Language and Lived Space Among the Maya*. Chicago.

——. 1992. "The Indexical Ground of the Deictic Reference." In Duranti and Goodwin 1992:46–76.

———. 1993. "Metalanguage and Pragmatics of Deixis." *Reflexive Language: Reported Speech and Metapragmatics* (ed. J. A. Lucy) 127–157. Cambridge.

———. 1996a. *Language and Communicative Practices.* Boulder.

———. 1996b. "Exorcism and the Description of Participant Roles." In Silverstein and Urban 1993:160–200.

Hansen, W. 1982. "The Applied Message in Storytelling." *Folklorica: Festschrift for Felix J. Oinas* (eds. P. Voorheis and E. V. Zygas) 99–109. Bloomington.

———. 1990. "Odysseus and the Oar: A Folkloric Approach." *Approaches to Greek Myth* (ed. L. Edmunds) 241–272. Baltimore.

———. 2000. "The Winning of Hippodameia." *Transactions of the American Philological Association* 130:19–40.

———. 2002. *Ariadne's Thread: A Guide to International Tales Found in Classical Literature.* Ithaca.

———. 2003. "Strategies of Authentication in Ancient Popular Literature." *The Ancient Novel and Beyond* (eds. S. Panayotakis, M. Zimmerman, and W. Keulen) 301–314. Leiden.

Havránek, B. 1932. "Úkoly spisovného jazyka a jeho kultura." *Spisovná Čeština a Jazyková Kultura* (eds. B. Havránek and M. Weingart) 32–84. Prague. Reprinted in English as "The Functional Differentiation of the Standard Language." *A Prague School Reader on Esthetics, Literary Structure, and Style* (ed. and trans. P. L. Garvin) 1964:3–16. Washington, DC.

Heath, M. 1986. "The Origins of Modern Pindaric Criticism." *The Journal of Hellenic Studies* 106:85–98.

———. 1988. "Receiving the Κῶμος: The Context and Performance of Epinician." *American Journal of Philology* 109:180–195.

Heath, M. and Lefkowitz, M. 1991. "Epinician Performance." *Classical Philology* 86:173–191.

Herington, J. 1985. *Poetry into Drama: Early Tragedy and the Greek Poetic Tradition.* Berkeley.

Heyne, C. G. 1798. *Pindari carmina* I, II, III. Revised ed. 1824. London.

Hornblower, S. 2004. *Thucydides and Pindar: Historical Narrative and the World of Epinikian Poetry.* Oxford.

Hornblower, S. and Morgan, C., eds. 2007. *Pindar's Poetry, Patrons, and Festivals: From Archaic Greece to the Roman Empire.* Oxford.

Horrocks, G. 1997. *Greek: A History of the Language and its Speakers*. London.

Horváth, J. 1976. "The Language of Pindar." *Annales Universitatis Scientiarum Budapestinensis de Rolando Eötvös Nominatae, Sectio Classica* 4:3–11.

Hubbard, T. K. 1985. *The Pindaric Mind: A Study of Logical Structure in Early Greek Poetry*. Mnemosyne Supplement 85. Leiden.

——. 1987. "The 'Cooking' of Pelops: Pindar and the Process of Mythological Revisionism." *Helios* 14:3–21.

——. 1995. "On Implied Wishes for Olympic Victory in Pindar." *Illinois Classical Studies* 20:35–56.

——. 2002. "Pindar, Theoxenus, and the Homoerotic Eye." *Arethusa* 35:255–296.

——. 2004. "The Dissemination of Epinician Lyric: Pan-Hellenism, Reperformance, Written Texts." *Oral Performance and its Context* (ed. C. J. Mackie) 71–93. Mnemosyne Supplement 248. Leiden.

Hummel, P. 1993. *La syntaxe de Pindare*. Bibliothèque de l'Information grammaticale 24. Paris.

——. 2001. "Polysyntaxe et polysémie dans la poésie de Pindare." *Quaderni Urbinati di Cultura Classica* 68:43–48.

Hymes, D. 1972. "Models of the Interaction of Language and Social Life." In Gumperz and Hymes 1972:38–71.

——. 1974. *Foundations in Sociolinguistics: An Ethnographic Approach*. Philadelphia.

——. 1989. "Ways of Speaking." In Bauman and Sherzer 1989:433–451, 473–474.

Illig, L. 1932. *Zur Form der pindarischen Erzählung*. Berlin.

Irigoin, J. 1952. *Histoire du texte de Pindare*. Paris.

Jakobson, R. 1935. Unpublished Lecture from a Course on Russian Formalism, Masaryk University, Brno. Reprinted in English as "The Dominant." *Readings in Russian Poetics: Formalist and Structuralist Views* (eds. L. Matejka and K. Pomorska) 1978:82–87. Cambridge, MA.

——. 1956. Presidential Address, Linguistic Society of America, December 27, 1956. Reprinted as "Metalanguage as a Linguistic Problem." *The Framework of Language* 1980:81–92. Ann Arbor.

——. 1957. Contribution to the Project "Description and Analysis of Contemporary Standard Russian," Department of Slavic Languages and Literatures, Harvard University, 1957. Reprinted as "Shifters, Verbal Categories, and the Russian Verb." *Roman Jakobson: Russian and Slavic Grammar: Studies 1931-1981* (eds. L. R. Waugh and M. Halle) 1984:41–58. Berlin.

——. 1960. “Linguistics and Poetics.” *Style in Language* (ed. T. A. Sebeok) 350–377. Cambridge, MA.

——. 1966. “Grammatical Parallelism and its Russian Facet.” *Language* 42:399–429.

——. 1968. “Poetry of Grammar and Grammar of Poetry.” *Lingua* 21:597–609.

Jurenka, H. 1986. “Humor bei Pindar.” *Wiener Studien* 18:91–98.

Kirkwood, G. 1982. *Selections from Pindar*. Chico.

——. 1984. “Blame and Envy in Pindaric Epinician.” In Gerber 1984:169–183.

Koehl, R. B. 1986. “The Chieftan Cup and a Minoan Rite of Passage.” *Journal of Hellenic Studies* 106:99–110.

Köhnken, A. 1971. *Die Funktion des Mythos bei Pindar: Interpretationen zu sechs Pindargedichten*. Untersuchungen zur antiken Literatur und Geschichte 12. Berlin.

——. 1974. “Pindar as Innovator: Poseidon Hippios and the Relevance of the Pelops Story in *Olympian* 1.” *The Classical Quarterly* 24:199–206.

——. 1983. “Time and Event in Pindar *O*. 1.25–53.” *Studies in Classical Lyric: A Homage to Elroy Bundy* (eds. T. D’Evelyn, P. N. Psoinos, and T. R. Walsh). *Classical Antiquity* 2:66–76.

——. 2005. “Obscurity and Obscurantism: How to Read Pindar.” *International Journal of the Classical Tradition* 12:602–606.

Kollmann, O. 1989. *Das Prooimion der ersten Pythischen Ode Pindars: ein sprachlich-poetischer Kommentar*. Vienna.

Kopff, E. C. 1981. “American Pindaric Criticism After Bundy.” *Aischylos und Pindar: Studien zu Werk und Nachwirkung* (ed. E. G. Schmidt) 49–53. Berlin.

Krummen, E. 1990. *Pyrsos Hymnon: Festliche Gegenwart und mythisch-rituelle Tradition als Voraussetzung einer Pindarinterpretation (Isthmie 4, Pythie 5, Olympie 1 und 3)*. Untersuchungen zur antiken Literatur und Geschicte, 35. Berlin.

Kurke, L. 1988. “The Poet’s Pentathlon: Genre in Pindar’s *First Isthmian*.” *Greek, Roman, and Byzantine Studies* 29:97–113.

——. 1990. “Pindar’s Sixth Pythian and the Tradition of Advice Poetry.” *Transactions of the American Philological Association* 120:85–107.

——. 1991. *The Traffic in Praise: Pindar and the Poetics of Social Economy*. Ithaca.

——. 1993. "The Economy of *Kudos*." In Dougherty and Kurke 1993:131–163.

——. 2000. "The Strangeness of 'Song Culture': Archaic Greek Poetry." *Literature in the Greek World* (ed. O. Taplin) 40–69. Oxford.

——. 2005. "Choral Lyric as 'Ritualization': Poetic Sacrifice and Poetic *Ego* in Pindar's *Sixth Paian*." *Classical Antiquity* 24:81–130.

——. 2007. "Archaic Greek Poetry." *The Cambridge Companion to Archaic Greece* (ed. H. A. Shapiro) 141–168. Cambridge.

Kyriakou, P. 1996. "A Variation of the Pindaric Break-off in *Nemean 4*." *American Journal of Philology* 117:17–35.

Lefkowitz, M. R. 1963. "ΤΩ ΚΑΙ ΕΓΩ: The First Person in Pindar." *Harvard Studies in Classical Philology* 67:177–253.

——. 1988. "Who Sang Pindar's Victory Odes?" *American Journal of Philology* 109:1–11.

——. 1991. *First-Person Fictions: Pindar's Poetic 'I'*. Oxford.

——. 1995. "The First Person in Pindar Reconsidered—Again." *Bulletin of the Institute of Classical Studies* 40:139–150.

Levinson, S. C. 1983. *Pragmatics*. Cambridge.

Lloyd-Jones, H. 1973. "Modern Interpretation of Pindar: The Second Pythian and Seventh Nemean Odes." *Journal of Hellenic Studies* 93:109–137.

Lord, A. B. 1960. *The Singer of Tales*. Cambridge, MA.

Loscalzo, D. 2003. *La parola inestinguibile: Studi sull'epinicio pindarico*. Rome.

Lowe, N. J. 2007. "Epinikian Eidography." In Hornblower and Morgan 2007:167–176.

Mackie, H. 2003. *Graceful Errors: Pindar and the Performance of Praise*. Ann Arbor.

Maehler, H., ed. 1989. *Pindari carmina cum fragmentis. Pars II: Fragmenta, indices*. Bibliotheca Scriptorum Graecorum et Romanorum Teubneriana. Leipzig.

Malinowski, B. 1923. "The Problem of Meaning in Primitive Languages." *The Meaning of Meaning: A Study of the Influence of Language Upon Thought and of the Science of Symbolism* (eds. C. K. Ogden and I. A. Richards) 296–336. New York.

Martin, R. P. 1984. "Hesiod, Odysseus, and the Instruction of Princes." *Transactions of the American Philological Association* 114:29–48.

——. 1989. *The Language of Heroes: Speech and Performance in the Iliad*. Ithaca.

——. 1992. "Hesiod's Metanastic Poetics." *Ramus* 21:11–33.

——. 1993. "The Seven Sages as Performers of Wisdom." In Dougherty and Kurke 1993:108–128.

——. 1997. "Similes and Performance." *Written Voices, Spoken Signs* (eds. E. Bakker and A. Kahane) 138–166, 249–253. Cambridge.

——. 2000. "Wrapping Homer Up: Cohesion, Discourse, and Deviation in the *Iliad*." *Intratextuality: Greek and Roman Textual Relations* (eds. A. Sharrock and H. Morales) 43–65. Oxford.

——. 2003. "The Pipes are Brawling: Conceptualizing Musical Performance in Athens." *The Cultures within Ancient Greek Culture: Contact, Conflict, Collaboration* (eds. C. Dougherty and L. Kurke) 153–180. Cambridge.

——. 2004. "Home is the Hero: Deixis and Semantics in Pindar *Pythian* 8." In Felson 2004a:343–363.

Miller, A. M. 1993a. "Inventa Componere: Rhetorical Process and Poetic Composition in Pindar's *Ninth Olympian Ode*." *Transactions of the American Philological Association* 123:109–147.

——. 1993b. "Pindaric Mimesis: The Associative Mode." *Classical Journal* 89:21–53.

Morgan, K. A. 1993. "Pindar the Professional and the Rhetoric of the ΚΩΜΟΣ." *Classical Philology* 88:1–15.

Morris, C. 1938. *Foundations of the Theory of Signs*. Chicago.

Morrison, A. D. 2007. *Performances and Audiences in Pindar's Sicilian Victory Odes*. Bulletin of the Institute of Classical Studies Supplement 95. London.

Most, G. W. 1985. *The Measures of Praise: Structure and Function in Pindar's Second Pythian and Seventh Nemean Odes*. Hypomnemata 83. Göttingen.

Mukařovský, J. 1940. "Estetika jazyka." *Slovo a slovesnost* 6:1–27. Reprinted in English as "The Esthetics of Language." *A Prague School Reader on Esthetics, Literary Structure, and Style* (ed. and trans. P. L. Garvin) 1964:31–69. Washington, DC.

Mullen, W. 1982. *Choreia: Pindar and Dance*. Princeton.

Nagy, G. 1979. *The Best of the Achaians: Concepts of the Hero in Archaic Greek Poetry*. Revised ed. 1999. Baltimore.

——. 1983. "*Sêma* and *Noêsis*: Some Illustrations." *Arethusa* 16:35–55.

——. 1990. *Pindar's Homer: The Lyric Possession of an Epic Past*. Baltimore.

——. 1994/1995. "Genre and Occasion." *Mêtis* 9/10:11–25.

——. 1996. *Poetry as Performance: Homer and Beyond*. Cambridge.

Nash, L. L. 1990. *The Aggelia in Pindar*. New York.

Newman, J. K. and Newman, F. S. 1984. *Pindar's Art: Its Tradition and Aims*. Hildesheim.

Nicholson, N. J. 2000. "Polysemy and Ideology in Pindar 'Pythian' 4.229–230." *Phoenix* 54:191–202.

——. 2001. "Victory without Defeat? Carnival Laughter and its Appropriation in Pindar's Victory Odes." *Carnivalizing Difference: Bakhtin and the Other* (eds. P. I. Barta, P. A. Miller, C. Platter, and D. Shepherd) 79-98. London.

——. 2005. *Aristocracy and Athletics in Archaic and Classical Greece*. Cambridge.

——. 2007. "Pindar, History, and Historicism." *Classical Philology* 102:208–227.

Nisetich, F. J. 1977. "The Leaves of Triumph and Mortality: Transformation of a Traditional Image in Pindar's *Olympian* 12." *Transactions of the American Philological Association* 107:235–264.

——. 1988. "Immortality in Acragas: Poetry and Religion in Pindar's Second Olympian Ode." *Classical Philology* 83:1–19.

——. 1989. *Pindar and Homer*. Baltimore.

Norwood, G. 1945. *Pindar*. Reprint 1974. Berkeley.

Palmer, L. R. 1980. *Greek Language*. Atlantic Highlands.

Parker, H. 1997. "The Teratogenic Grid." *Roman Sexualities* (eds. J. P. Hallet and M. B. Skinner) 47–65. Princeton.

Pavese, C. O. 1993. "Il coro nel sesto Peana di Pindaro." *Tradizione e innovazione nella cultura greca da Omero all'età ellenistica: Scritti in onore di Bruno Gentili* (ed. R. Pretagostini) 469–479. Rome.

Pelliccia, H. 1995. *Mind, Body, and Speech in Homer and Pindar*. Göttingen.

Peponi, A.-E. 2004. "Initiating the Viewer: Deixis and Visual Perception in Alcman's Lyric Drama." In Felson 2004a:295–316.

Pfeijffer, I. L. 1999a. *Three Aeginetan Odes of Pindar: A Commentary on Nemean V, Nemean III, & Pythian VIII*. Leiden.

——. 1999b. *First Person Futures in Pindar*. Hermes Einzelschriften 81. Stuttgart.

Race, W. H. 1980. "Some Digressions and Returns in Greek Authors." *Classical Journal* 76:1–8.

——. 1986. *Pindar*. Boston.

——. 1990. *Style and Rhetoric in Pindar's Odes*. Atlanta.

——, ed. and trans. 1997a. *Pindar. Vol. 1: Olympian Odes. Pythian Odes*. The Loeb Classical Library. Cambridge, MA.

——, ed. and trans. 1997b. *Pindar. Vol. 2: Nemean Odes. Isthmian Odes. Fragments*. The Loeb Classical Library. Cambridge, MA.

——. 2004. "Pindar's *Olympian* 11 Revisited Post Bundy." *Harvard Studies in Classical Philology* 102:69–96.

Radt, S. L. 1958. *Pindars zweiter und sechster Paian: Text, Scholien und Kommentar*. Amsterdam.

Robbins, E. 1990. "The Gifts of the Gods: Pindar's Third *Pythian*." *The Classical Quarterly* 40:307–318.

Rose, P. W. 1982. "Towards a Dialectical Hermeneutic of Pindar's *Pythian* X." *Helios* 9:47–73.

Rothwell, Jr., K. S. 2007. *Nature, Culture, and the Origins of Greek Comedy: A Study of Animal Choruses*. Cambridge.

Saussure, F. de. 1983. *Course in General Linguistics*. Trans. R. Harris. Chicago.

Scanlon, T. F. 2002. *Eros and Greek Athletics*. New York.

Schadewaldt, W. 1928. *Der Aufbau des pindarischen Epinikion*. Halle.

Schroeder, O. 1922. *Pindars Pythien*. Leipzig.

Schürch, P. 1971. *Zur Wortresponsion bei Pindar*. Bern.

Scodel, R. 2001. "Poetic Authority and Oral Tradition in Hesiod and Pindar." *Speaking Volumes: Orality and Literacy in the Greek and Roman World* (ed. J. Watson) 109–137. Leiden.

Segal, C. 1986. *Pindar's Mythmaking: The Fourth Pythian Ode*. Princeton.

Silk, M. 2007. "Pindar's Poetry as Poetry: A Literary Commentary on *Olympian* 12." In Hornblower and Morgan 2007:177–197.

Silverstein, M. 1993. "Metapragmatic Discourse and Metapragmatic Function." *Reflexive Language: Reported Speech and Metapragmatics* (ed. J. A. Lucy) 33–58. Cambridge.

——. 1996. "The Secret Life of Texts." In Silverstein and Urban 1996:81–105. Chicago.

Silverstein, M. and Urban, G. 1996. "The Natural History of Discourse." In Silverstein and Urban 1996:1–17.

——, eds. 1996. *Natural Histories of Discourse*. Chicago.

Skinner, M. B. 2005. *Sexuality in Greek and Roman Culture*. Malden, MA.

Slater, W. J. 1969a. "Futures in Pindar." *The Classical Quarterly* 19:86–94.

——. 1969b. *Lexicon to Pindar*. Berlin.

——. 1979. "Pindar's Myths: Two Pragmatic Explanations." *Arktouros: Hellenic Studies Presented to Bernard M.W. Knox on the Occasion of His 65th Birthday* (eds. G. W. Bowersock, W. Burkert, and M. C. J. Putnam) 63–70. Berlin.

——. 1983. "Lyric Narrative: Structure and Principle." *Studies in Classical Lyric: A Homage to Elroy Bundy* (eds. T. D'Evelyn, P. N. Psoinos, and T. R. Walsh). *Classical Antiquity* 2:117–132.

——. 1984. "*Nemean One*: The Victor's Return in Poetry and Politics." In Gerber 1984:241–264.

Smith, R. R. R. 2007. "Pindar, Athletes, and the Early Greek Statue Habit." In Hornblower and Morgan 2007:83–139.

Snell, B. and Maehler, H., eds. 1997. *Pindari carmina cum fragmentis. Pars I: Epinicia*. Bibliotheca Scriptorum Graecorum et Romanorum Teubneriana. 8th ed. Leipzig.

Stehle, E. 1997. *Performance and Gender in Ancient Greece: Nondramatic Poetry in its Setting*. Princeton.

Steiner, D. 1986. *The Crown of Song: Metaphor in Pindar*. New York.

——. 1998. "Moving Images: Fifth-Century Victory Monuments and the Athlete's Allure." *Classical Antiquity* 17:123–149.

——. 2002. "Indecorous Dining, Indecorous Speech: Pindar's First *Olympian* and the Poetics of Consumption." *Arethusa* 35:297–314.

Stockert, W. 1969. *Klangfiguren und Wortresponsionen bei Pindar*. Vienna.

Tarkka, L. 1993. "Intertextuality, Rhetorics and the Interpretation of Oral Poetry: The Case of Archived Orality." *Nordic Frontiers: Recent Issues in the Study of Modern Traditional Culture in the Nordic Countries* (eds. P. J. Anttonen and R. Kvideland) 165–193. Torku.

Thiersch, F. W. von. 1820. *Pindarus Werke*. Leipzig.

Thomas, R. 2007. "Fame, Memorial, and Choral Poetry: The Origins of Epinikian Poetry—An Historical Study." In Hornblower and Morgan 2007:141–166.

Todorov, T. 1981. *Introduction to Poetics*. Trans. R. Howard. Minneapolis.

——. 1984. *Mikhail Bakhtin: The Dialogical Principle*. Trans. W. Godzich. Minneapolis.

Tynjanov, J. 1927. "O literaturnoi èvolutsii." *Na literaturnom postu* 4. Reprinted in English as "On Literary Evolution." *Readings in Russian Poetics: Formalist and Structuralist Views* (eds. L. Matejka and K. Pomorska) 1978:66–78. Cambridge, MA.

Urban, G. 1989. "The 'I' of Discourse." *Semiotics, Self, and Society* (eds. B. Lee and G. Urban) 27–51. Berlin.

——. 1991. *A Discourse-Centered Approach to Culture: Native South American Myths and Rituals*. Austin.

Vološinov, V. N. 1986. *Marxism and the Philosophy of Language*. Trans. L. Matejka and I. R. Titunik. Cambridge, MA.

Waugh, L. R. 1980. "The Poetic Function in the Theory of Roman Jakobson." *Poetics Today* 2:57–82.

——. 1982. "Marked and Unmarked: A Choice Between Unequals in Semiotic Structure." *Semiotica* 38:299–318.

West, M. L. 1982. *Greek Metre*. Oxford.

West, S. 1988. "Archilochus' Message-Stick." *The Classical Quarterly* 38:42–48.

Wilamowitz-Moellendorff, U. von. 1922. *Pindaros*. Reprint 1966. Berlin.

Young, D. C. 1968. *Three Odes of Pindar: A Literary Study of Pythian 11, Pythian 3, and Olympian 7*. Mnemosyne Supplement 9. Leiden.

——. 1970. "Pindaric Criticism." *Pindaros und Bakchylides* (eds. W. M. Calder III and J. Stern) 1–95. Wege der Forschung 134. Darmstadt.

——. 1971. *Pindar Isthmian 7, Myth and Exempla*. Mnemosyne Supplement 15. Leiden.

——. 1982. "Pindar." *Ancient Writers: Greece and Rome* (ed. T. J. Luce) 157–77. New York.

Index Locorum

Subject Index

CPSIA information can be obtained at www.ICGtesting.com
260434BV00006B/20/P

9 780674 036277